WOMEN AND RELIGION IN INDIA

WOMEN AND RELIGION IN INDIA

AN ANNOTATED BIBLIOGRAPHY OF SOURCES IN ENGLISH 1975–92

NANCY AUER FALK

ॐ

NEW ISSUES PRESS
College of Arts and Sciences

WESTERN MICHIGAN UNIVERSITY
Kalamazoo, Michigan

1994

Women and religion – India – bibliography

ISBN 0-932826-36-9
ISBN 0-932826-37-7 (pbk)

Cover design by Linda K. Judy

Printed in the United States of America

To all my Indian friends and colleagues,

in thanks for your ever-generous hospitality

Contents

Preface

A friend had warned me, when I told her that I was working on a bibliographic project on women and religion in India: "Nancy, it will eat you alive. Bibliographies expand all over the place; it's hard to control them, and harder still to end them. A bibliography means guaranteed frustration."

Her predictions came true. The following bibliography, product of that project, has doubled several times over in complexity and scope. It has grown from what I thought would be a simple listing of Indian English-language sources planned for informal distribution, to a published annotated volume listing works by authors around the globe. It has stretched my understanding of boundaries and of the perils inherent in trying to draw them, and has forced me to draw several in places where I would rather avoid the subject. It has made me far more sensitive to the impact of context upon academic work—the context of struggle upon the work of fellow women's studies scholars in India, and the context of outsider status upon the work of foreign South Asian religionists like myself.

It has also made me appreciate far more acutely the tolerance and good will that I receive from Indian colleagues whose framing of their own studies' central issues is often at wide variance with my own. My bibliography is not finished, only ended; my time and patience have run out, but not my range of potential sources. It is full of warts and glitches that I would handle differently if I could go back and start again. Assembling it was indeed frustrating, and I would not want to repeat the effort; yet, I do not regret the time and work I have invested. The discoveries that it has brought me have left me wiser and better-informed; I only hope it will yield as much benefit for the colleagues and friends with whom I now share it.

Preface

Rude Awakenings: The Undertaking and its Problems

The time period extending from 1975 through the early 1990s proved to be both a turbulent and an exciting time for Indian women. It had begun with the shock of a depressing report from the 1975 International Women's Year Commission; entitled *Towards Equality*, this report had all too clearly shown that Indian women were still a long distance from any egalitarian goal. Yet this same year had also seen the founding of the first research program in Women's Studies, at SNDT Women's University in Bombay (1975), and the founding of the first all-India Women's Studies Association was to come just a few years later (1980). In subsequent years research centers on women funded by the Indian government were sown throughout the country's system of higher education, and conferences were held where women from all walks of life met to assess their common problems. It seemed at last as though women's worlds were changing, as though the push towards equality was at last truly underway.

I was aware of these changes when I offered to collect, while in India, a bibliography of new Indian works on the relationship between Indian women and religion. I had planned to be in New Delhi working on a related field project; while thus resident, I could update my command over Indian resources by checking catalogues in bookstores and libraries. I knew it was sometimes hard for American scholars like myself to find information about work newly published in India; hence I would generously plan to share my findings with them.

But I did not expect to find very much. A previous contact with Indian Women's Studies scholars in India had convinced me that they were much like their counterparts in the United States— largely trained in the social sciences and concerned almost exclusively with the political, social, and economic factors shaping women. Nor did the two grounds exist that had jointly given root

x

to the growth of feminist scholarship on religion in the U.S. Women of India's varied religious communities had not challenged their own traditions' latent androcentrism as Christian, Jewish, and Buddhist feminist theologians had done in the U.S. Moreover, my own discipline, the academic study of religion, had as yet little parallel in Indian scholarship; I knew of only two longstanding programs in comparative religious studies, one at Punjab University, and one at Vishvabharati in Bengal. Without a discipline of religion to take up women's studies, or a tradition of feminist theological protest, how could there be much writing on women in religion?

I was wrong, of course, as the large number of Indian-authored works in the following bibliography attests. I should have known better. Religion had played too large a role in Indian women's history to be ignored. In ancient times, it had given women their few moments of public prominence, as nuns of various *shramana* communities such as Buddhism and Jainism had gained access to education and won occasional eminence as teachers and models. During medieval times, it had sent great saints into flights of soaring poetry that had left the revolutionary *bhakti* movements with an enduring touch of women's experience.

Conversely, the grip of religious precept and custom on Hindu women's destiny had been a focal target of the long campaign for women's liberation that had so dramatically reshaped women's lives during the nineteenth and early twentieth centuries. That struggle had begun with Bengali reformer Rammohan Roy's impassioned plea to the British colonial government to ban the religiously sanctioned upper-caste Hindu custom of encouraging widows to immolate themselves on their husbands' funeral pyres (*sati*). Its issues had been framed as orthodox leaders, seeking to protect ancient traditions from change, discovered that they had potential allies in secularized nationalists who were eager to limit the spread of British political and cultural interference. Women would thenceforth be pawns in the long battle to set India's direction. Reformers embracing Anglicization damned *sati*, child-hood marriage, and lifelong strictures on widows, while forcing wives and daughters into conflict with joint family elders by demanding that the women learn to read and write. The orthodox, who feared the loss of prerogatives they had acquired through the older traditions, fought for customs they might otherwise not have sanctioned—defending the seclusion of women, charging that women's education would destroy family discipline, and citing scrip-tural passages that required the marriage of girls before first men-struation, that permitted *sati*, and that forbade widows from marrying again. The nationalists, attempting to build Indian pride and a sense of cultural identity, dug into India's more ancient heritage, seeking models that would let them have both change and continuity with the past. Such battles were waged within religious communities as well as between those communities and secularists, as leaders combined calls for change in custom with calls for change in the underlying worldviews of which such custom had been the product.

The women and men who produced India's scholarship on women were still intimately linked to this struggle of the past century; some had attended schools and colleges founded by reform movements, and many were direct descendants of the movements' leading families. No recollection of their recent past could ignore the struggle's ramifications or the impact of religion on its under-takings. Moreover, they were still fighting several of the struggle's old battles. As recently as 1987, a young Rajasthani widow, Roop Kanwar, was burned on her husband's pyre while local police looked on and failed to prevent the illegal action. The old dispute about the relationship between the state and religion was also still alive and, in the form of disputes about the continuing legitimacy of sectarian "personal laws" (i.e., domestic codes), cut a destructive swath through a nation that otherwise eschewed any establishment of religion. Even the prevailing views of India's overall story—its links to the distant past, its cultural heritage—were ideological products of that nineteenth-century struggle and intimately linked to its intentions for women's future. By now that link was being recognized and its resulting constructions called into question.

I had furthermore misestimated the potential range of contributions to my list from religious communities. It is true that few Indian religious groups have an internal tradition of feminist critique resembling that of their Western counterparts: noteworthy exceptions are a group of Christian women writing women-centered Bible studies (see entries 156–57 and 527) and the controversial Muslim reformist Asghar Ali Engineer (see especially entries 255–60). But the awareness of all movements, like that of feminist scholars, has been shaped by past struggles over the "women question." Virtually every important movement has, therefore, at least one tract by its founder or another distinguished leader that states its understanding of women's roles and possibilities. In Islam, where the problem of women's place remains an active source of controversy, dozens of such tracts exist, with more emerging at all times. Virtually every movement also can cite model women to emulate, often described in laudatory books or articles. Some have known great women teachers, whose lives are described and whose words are recorded in exhausting and often repetitious detail; many have known dedicated women disciples who have recorded their own conversations with and perceptions of teachers who were male. All of these were potential grist for my bibliographic mill.

Finally, by the time I found myself actually in Delhi, both the study of religion and the study of women had begun to evolve more rapidly. A fledgling Ph.D. program in the history of religion was in place in the History Department at the University of Delhi; its first dissertations were nearing completion. Dissertations relating to religion had already been written in the same univer-

sity's Department of Sociology. Feminist scholars who had shown
an interest in religion were finding their work less scorned by the
established disciplines. Meanwhile the promised women's research
centers were by now in existence, and the word "Religion" was
appearing in titles of conferences and publications sponsored by
these centers.

In sum, there was a literature, and that literature was exploding, much as literature on women and religion was exploding
on the opposite side of the planet. Yet the very wide variety of its
sources made it difficult to locate. It was not gathered at one
central location. The library visits I had planned could yield me
older academic sources, but to catch the brand new issues, I had to
add visits to booksellers and academic publishers. Books issued by
religious communities required still more visits, to booksellers
handling religious works and sometimes to publishers' outlets at
the communities' central *ashrams*.

Moreover, the fact that scholarly attention both to women
and to religion was scattered throughout many disciplines meant
that I could not search just the one subdivision called "religion" on
sellers' lists or bookshelves; I would find titles under categories
ranging from history and sociology to literature and folklore.
Because women's experience and dilemmas with religion were often
background issues for inquiry rather than foreground concerns, I
often found, as well, that important work lay buried in books with
titles that bore no clues to potentialities within them. Chapters on
contributions by the Brahmo Samaj and Arya Samaj movements lay
within books that discussed the struggle for women's rights in
general, or even the rise of women's education. Critiques of systems
of religious laws lay within more general works on women's legal
dilemmas. Materials on women's domestic religious practice were
buried in works on *purdah*, on family life, or on women's customs
during past centuries. Collections of essays on contemporary issues
affecting women—a common genre of publication during the

seventies and eighties—tossed in a chapter or two on the status of women in Indian Islam and in Hinduism. Writings on women saints appeared in studies of Indian women's literature, or in more general anthologies and histories of medieval devotional movements. Sociological studies of changing attitudes in India added a few—but invaluable—questions about the importance of belief in God, the frequency of visits to temples, or the maintenance of daily worship at the shrines traditionally kept in Hindu homes.

Journal articles were comparably scattered. India has no periodical comparable to the U.S. *Journal of Feminist Studies in Religion*. Instead, consultation of periodical indexes brought me references to works of interest in fifty-three different journals, representing thirteen disciplinary and twelve sectarian persuasions. (I would later add thirty-six more journal titles in the United States.) The richest source for serious articles on the intersection between women and religion turned out to be *The Economic and Political Weekly*, a work I would never have thought to consult had I been searching by title alone. Some important work was not even published at all; it lay in the form of bound manuscripts and typescripts of conference collections in small women's studies collections housed in the new centers and in independent research institutes.

Decisions

Such discoveries about the disparate and disguised nature of my subject matter led to a pair of decisions that more than doubled initial estimates of the time and energy required for my search. The first was that I could not simply pull appropriate-seeming titles out of catalogues and publishers listings. I had to conduct a hands-on search, going to shelves in libraries and bookstores, pulling down volumes that I suspected might include materials for me, examining their contents, asking librarians to show me what they had of manuscripts and conference materials. Where I found leads in existing bibliographies, I had to locate the works cited and look through them. Eventually this decision would result in my handling well over one thousand journals, books, and papers.

The second decision was that I had to offer users of my bibliography more aid than a simple listing of the titles I had found. I had to annotate, to tell what I had found useful within the volumes and articles cited. This in turn led to further problems, for there was no way that I could read through all the works passing through my hands in the few months I had available. Often a book's Table of Contents alone, or its introduction, or an article's first paragraphs, would offer a clear picture of the author's project; often not. I was to become very grateful for long years of experience in skimming.

Yet another level of decision-making was imposed by the amorphous nature of my subject matter itself; I would have to do much defining and circumscribing. The term "women" itself was already a problem, as previous bibliographies and texts in my discipline had shown. What is a woman, anyway, in the context of religious studies? Is she simply the flesh-and-blood female of the human species that most non-religionists picture when they hear the term "woman"? Or might she also be a goddess—a crystallization of sacred power imaged in female form? I had long since decided for myself that women and goddesses were separate problems, that many goddesses, though invigorating for Western women to contemplate, tell us far more about male needs and nightmares than they do about female humans. So I drew one boundary line for my listing and left most works on goddesses on their shelves. They are present in this bibliography only if they illuminate some aspect of human women's relationship to the divine females studied.

The various rules and pronouncements that tell women our

"place" in religious worlds likewise tend to tell us more about men's requirements than about the needs of women. But eliminating these from my list would pose more difficulties. My studies of women's experience in religion had evidenced again and again, sometimes with devastating clarity, that men's rules and pronouncements do affect women, especially when robed in religious authority. They define the parameters of women's lives, raise obstacles to their aspirations, permeate and enchain their very consciousness, and sometimes—wildly, crazily—rip off previous chains and set potentialities free. Like it or not—and I myself do not like it—no story of women's religion can be written without taking into account the intentions that men have had for us. Men's rules for women in religion therefore remain in my listing—sometimes in very depressing abundance.

For the same reason, I have included studies of model women; although in India, the fine line between such women and goddesses often dissolves. What is Sita, anyway—that long-suffering wife of the epic hero-divinity Rama, born from a furrow and received back into the earth's womb when rejected by her husband? She is at least an image of feminine perfection still aspired to by countless Hindu women. That is enough for me; Sita's titles remained in my listing.

Further decisions initially seemed less tricky: anything emanating from women that could be called "religious"—women's norms, experiences, teachings, practices, movements, communities, predicaments—was definitely in. But that held a pitfall too. What was I calling "religious," given the Indian context of my list? As Indian scholars now and then delight in pointing out to Western religionists, the term "religion" has no true counterpart in the conceptual schema of pre-colonial India. That is to say, nothing in the Indian heritage corresponds to the sum total of characteristics of the model of religion evoked in Western minds when the word "religion" is uttered. The word "religion" for Westerners hooks up images of deity, scripture, congregations, specialists, spiritual discipline, moral norms, and ritual into integrated spheres of human endeavor; furthermore, it separates those spheres from others, such as law, politics, family, or play. Since ancient times, India has had institutions that match the components of Western religion—rituals and specialists, teachings, norms, disciplines, and communities of people who follow these. If these had not been found in India, colonial powers would not have been able to speak of "Indian religion" at all. Nonetheless, these aspects of Indian life are not joined to one another in the same way as things are in Western "religion," nor are they separated in the same way from other aspects of life.

For example, *dharma*, the term that Hindus have most often chosen to translate "religion," entails a code of prescriptions for human behavior that appeals to scripture for authority and is interpreted by brahmins, the hereditary caste of Hindu "priests." *Dharma* even established a sort of religious community, if one can look at the whole buzzing complexity of caste as a single system instead of the group of loosely linked parts that it often seems more concretely to be. But deity plays a very ambiguous role within the literature on *dharma*, while definitions of family, social system, and polity are well within its reach. Meanwhile the phenomenon called *bhakti* (devotion) has its deities, saints, hymns, and *sampradyay*s (communities of the faithful). However, scriptures and specialists may be mistrusted in *bhakti* traditions, while *lila* (play) is often a central component of *bhakti* practice and ideology. Another word that comes close to matching the Western complex of meanings associated with religion is the term *yoga,* especially as interpreted by the *Bhagavad-Gita*: it includes the path of *karma-yoga* (observance of one's *dharma*) along with *bhakti-yoga* (devotion) and *jnana-yoga* (pursuit of the knowledge of God). But the *Gita* has narrowed the reach of the term, which evokes any method or discipline, such as the "yoking" of animals from which *yuj*, the verbal root of the

Preface

term *yoga,* is drawn. The concept of *marga* (path), used by Buddhists of ancient India, entails disciplines, specialists, and a community of the faithful. Yet the "scriptures" that guide human life appeal to human insight and reason, not to divine legitimation. Even Islam, that close cousin to Judaism and Christianity, to some extent stretches Western conceptions of "religion," for the ideal Muslim community would be also a Muslim state, with all precepts for human behavior acquiring the force of law.

What then should I call "religion," if Indian religion was to be my focus? Like my favorite trick on objective quizzes, the answer was, for the most part, "all of the above." My discipline had come to include under the common rubric "religion" not only *dharma, bhakti, yoga*, and the Buddhist—and Jain—*marga*s, but also Parseeism, Indian Judaism and Christianity, plus *tantra* and many customs of the "little" village and tribal traditions. I did likewise; I was trying, after all, to provide a service to my discipline, not to challenge its admittedly challengeable consensus on its subject matter.

But could I call anything "not religion," given the tendency in India to include in the category "religion" more than the Western model? Again I followed my discipline's lead, which is to recognize all of the problems entailed but to confine inquiry largely to dimensions of the materials that even non-expert members of my own culture might recognize as religious. Rituals, festivals, vows, spiritual disciplines, world renouncers, *yogini*s, *guru*s, and women's *sampradhyay*s, missions, *math*s (monasteries), and *ashram*s were in. So were women's roles in various mixed celebrations and communities. So were the so-called "sacred norms" of *dharmasastra*, Islamic *shari'a*, and Buddhist and Jaina *dharma*, where these were demonstrably pertinent to the lives of women. So were, with some hesitation, the modern codes of Hindu, Muslim, Christian, and Parsee domestic law codified from these older prescriptions under the aegis of the British colonial administration. Finely-honed argu-

xix

ments about cases written for lawyers by lawyers were out, having crossed my own Western divide between religious and legal scholarship. So were sociological analyses of the finer points of marital exchanges, even though the basic rules for these were enshrined in *dharmasastra*. Also out, by and large, were studies of women of particular religious groups that singled them out to examine a specific economic activity—for example, fish marketing among Bombay Muslims. But sometimes in were materials on political leaders and movements if these had drawn on religious symbols and disciplines; Gandhi and his *satyagrahi*s are the most noteworthy example.

Sometimes as I drew my tremulous lines of inclusion/exclusion, I found that boundaries between the religious and the non-religious were hotly contested. Here, instead of making a judgment of my own, I attempted to draw in all available records of the contest. The argument over *sati* is such a boundary conflict: some call *sati* a time-honored religious custom that transforms a woman into a goddess; others call it a swindle set up in the name of religion to deprive widows of their claims on a departed husband's property. Some say the law should not touch *sati*, following the principle of separation between religion and state; others say the laws that ban it should be more strictly enforced, given a women's right to full protection of her physical safety. Is *sati* religious? It has at least provoked significant controversy about religion and therefore belongs in this bibliography. Yet another recent boundary dispute was the so-called Shah Bano case: Here an outcry had been prompted by the so-called "interference" by a secular law court into a Muslim court's authority over a divorced Muslim's woman's appeal for maintenance from her husband. Modern secularist Hindus claim that the right to maintenance should be extended equally to women of all communities, because the Indian constitution guarantees equal protection under law to all of its citizens. Conservative Muslims point out that divorce is a

Preface

classic category of the "personal" law codes left under Muslim authority; "equal protection" must protect the rights of Muslims as a whole to live according to sacred *shari'a*. An older argument among Hindus over prohibition of *devadasi* dedication—marrying a young girl to a god—was a third boundary dispute requiring full coverage. Those favoring prohibition claimed that a custom cannot claim the protected status of "religion" if it entails potential abuse, for the young girls thus dedicated often fell into concubinage and/or prostitution. Those arguing against—most notably *devadasi*s themselves—cried that the state was depriving women of their access to priestly roles, property, and independence. The latter dispute has brought in several entries that may look very strange in a religion bibliography, such as volumes on the history of prostitution that may include one or more chapters on the role of *devadasi*s.

Just when I finally thought I had all my definitions covered, I met another fuzzy boundary. What on earth did I mean when I claimed to be searching for works on India? I know India's modern geographic borders, of course, as well as her border disputes. I also know that before her partition in 1947 she was more than these boundaries, that in fact these boundaries had split in half two important regions with considerable internal cultural integrity. Had Pakistan and Bangladesh been "Indian" before 1947 and after that date something else? Politically, yes, but surely not culturally and religiously. What about Sri Lanka, also a part of the Raj until Independence and still containing a very large community of immigrant Tamils? What about Nepal, never politically a part of India, but possessed of a thoroughly India-derived religious culture? Last but certainly not least, what about the Tibetans who had settled in India after fleeing the Chinese invasion of their homeland during the fifties? Was their heritage now "Indian?" In the end, I decided to include materials from greater South Asia when they might shed light on groups with current Indian residence. Bangladeshi Muslim birth rites are in, as are the life-cycle rites of Tamil Brahmin women of Sri Lanka and the Hinduized festivals of Nepal. Most post-partition Pakistani materials are out, save only those that compare new developments to those of the Indian Muslim past. Tibetan Buddhist materials are in so long as they trace the heritage of refugee communities, but new teachings mined from the Tibetan lode by contemporary practitioners in such distant lands as America are out.

Western Authors Added: Resulting Discoveries

A chance conversation provoked the last and most illuminating expansion of my task. I had initially planned to limit my list only to works by Indian authors; Western titles, after all, were available here through fine libraries and computer data bases. Western scholars did not need them nearly so badly as we needed to know about the work done in India itself. Then one day I handed an early version of my bibliography to an Indian colleague who had agreed to scan it for errors. She sighed and said to me, "You know, Nancy, I am very glad that you are gathering our titles for your American colleagues. But I wish you were also gathering their work for us." She had a real and distressing point; because of the lack of mechanical aids and adequate funds for libraries, it is far harder for Indian scholars to keep up with research done in the West than it is for Westerners to keep tabs on research in India.

She was not aware—and I did not tell her at the time—that I already had the nucleus for such a Western listing in my computer files. I could never resist the temptation while doing bibliographic research to pick up titles extraneous to my focus that I thought I might nonetheless find useful. As I had come across Western work new to me during my search of Indian libraries, I had kept a separate file to be added to lists that I kept at home. Now I thought I had found an excellent way to return the help given to me by Indian friends. I would annotate this file also, combine it with my files at home, and send it back after I had gone. Soon I was as much obsessed with this Western list as I was with the list of works by Indian authors. After a search of nearby U.S. libraries helped me to update this, I decided all users might be best aided if I made the two lists one.

By this time, however, I had kept the two lists side by side for a full ten months and was well aware of an intrinsic mismatch between them. The Western list consisted mostly of academic papers and monographs by secular scholars. Indian genres ranged from polemics to hagiography, and Indian authors ranged from political activists to scholars to saints. Fewer than half the Indian sources were of academic provenance. The discrepancy was in part a result of my own search methods: in India, I had made a deliberate attempt to gather the full sampling of materials available, while in the U.S. I had had time and resources principally for searches in academic libraries. In part the mismatch was also a simple result of the universal human tendency to be more interested in one's own traditions than those of others; one would expect most religious presses in the United States to produce works about Christian or Jewish heroines and dilemmas for women, not about women of Hinduism or Islam. The result was nonetheless the same: I had one basket consisting of apples and another of apples, mangos, and bananas and was proposing to combine them, with a lopsided outcome.

Moreover, even my apples seemed to be of strikingly different variety. If one compared only works by academics on the two lists, the sense of discrepancy persisted. The Westerners' approach, by and large, was interpretive and explanatory; they strove to "make sense" of phenomena studied by locating them within their greater cultural and social context. They were polite and cautious where critical—clearly the work of guests in others' territory who did not wish to give offense. Works produced by Indian scholars on their own home turf were far more likely to be agonistic. They argued, contested, assessed; they attacked and defended positions. Where they examined motives for the present, it was often to expose these so that existing practice could change. Sometimes they showed little patience with those who did strive to understand before judging, charging them with covert collaboration with the enemy. (See, for example, the criticism of Ashis Nandy's article on *sati* in entry 719.) In sum, they were the works of people still caught up in the battle for women's future, having little time, energy, or patience for disinterested contemplation.

In part because the Indian literature *was* a product of struggle, the focus and tone of our two scholarships differed also. For the Indian scholars, women and women's predicaments were the main substance of the study, while religion remained an accident. That is to say, the Indian studies were interested in religion only insofar as it had defined and delimited women; they were far less concerned with the converse. They talked of the impact *on* women of religious laws and customs such as *sati* and *devadasi* dedication; they asked how religious reform movements had shaped women's options and experience. Western scholars were concerned with such subjects also, but they were just as likely to make religion their substance and to ask what women had done to define their own religious worlds. They asked about women's festivals, women's rituals, women ascetics and *guru*s, women's movements. In an extraordinary twist of irony this meant that the Western works had granted to Indian women a dimension of agency that indigenous works were denying; they had shown that women were creators of religion and not forever its victims.

But this distinction is no longer true across the board. Where religion has been an agent of change and not of oppressing stasis, women whom it brings to prominence are receiving new and searching attention in India. This has been turned already to women poets of the medieval *bhakti* tradition; note especially listed

Preface

entries 225, 668–69, 786, and 1002. Lately it has been reaching also to women of the period of nineteenth-century reform; see, for example, entries 450, 456, and 501. But even here, the difference between Eastern and Western approaches remains. The Western scholars tend to be more optimistic and perhaps more naive, to see the religious experience in these movements itself as a source of transformation and empowerment. Indian feminist researchers are far more skeptical and hardnosed, more probingly critical; they closely examine social factors that shape their subjects' experience and tone, and may show how a saint's message confirms traditional values for women, even while her actions seem an overt challenge.

This same critical bent is carrying Indian scholars into one arena that Western feminist religionists have not yet entered. A few—the very best—are questioning the whole ground beneath our feet, the central paradigms that inform our view of Indian religious development and our received lore about the respective roles of women in various periods. Their work is perhaps the most important discovery of my Indian search. All users of this bibliography, whatever their special interests, should consult at least this body of methodological critique and reconstruction; see especially entries 144, 146, 559, 790, and 953.

At the end, I have finally decided that the different flavors and levels of tartness of Indians and Westerners are potential sources of strength; we challenge one another and offset one another's shortfalls. Western scholars still have a great deal to learn about the dynamics of South Asia's relationship to religion and the role of women within this—both as victims and as critics. South Asian scholars can learn more both from us and from their own religious communities about women's potential and religion's ability to unlock this. We complement one another both in style and substance. Indians can teach Westerners much about the intricacies of religious custom and law and their relationship to realities of community and politics. Westerners observing the life of Indian villages, sacred cities, and *ashram*s have been creating quite a rich record of the range of women's religiosity; it is there for whatever purpose our embattled South Asian counterparts may need to use it. So what if I have found apples, mangoes, and bananas; so what if the apples are a mixture of Granny Smith, Paula Red, and Macintosh? Fruit salad is delicious.

The Product

The result of all these labors is a list of 1015 entries, of which approximately 650 have been produced by authors who are or have been long-term residents of India. Topics range from legal provisions of Hindu law codes, to ritual, to the transformative experiences that have driven some women to renounce all ties with family and world; subjects range from wealthy women to the poorest poor, from women considered living goddesses to house-wives to young girls caught up in prostitution. Authors are devotees, journalists, activists, scholars, and the professional religious; their tone extends from protest to celebration. Sources include scholarly monographs, tracts bent on persuasion, seminar volumes and conference collections, and articles from scholarly journals, religious periodicals, and India's respected feminist magazine *Manushi*.

I have not screened my entries for levels of sophistication. Some are deeply penetrating analyses by scholars of international standing; others are impressionistic and uncritical works by academic amateurs. Nor have I selected for a particular political stance. Views that I myself would call reactionary are represented here, as well as those of feminists for whom I feel a much stronger sympathy. I did try to give some indication in my annotation if I found a work exceptionally penetrating, confusing, or superficial; when works addressed controversial topics, I did attempt to locate their authors' positions. But my notes should not be considered reviews; I could not read most works closely enough to give a fair picture of quality or possible hidden agendas. I have stressed the type of helpful information that can be extracted from a swift survey—the topics covered by a work, the angle of approach and/or method, and the thesis, where this was readily determinable. For some works, my comments have been more thorough than for others; the level of care expended reflects less the quality of the volume than the degree of exhaustion and writer's cramp in the collector as she took notes at white heat in Indian libraries that were often stuffy and uncomfortable.

I did presuppose that at least some who use my work will have a chance to use some of those same libraries. I have deliberately included such hard-to-access esoterica as collections of papers from Indian conferences because the knowledge of their existence may help promising scholars to frame more detailed and viable research proposals. For the same reason, I have listed locations for Indian materials not widely available. Nonetheless, access was a factor in my selections. I had searched seven libraries in Delhi, another in Bombay, and four more in the U.S. In addition, I had canvassed nineteen booksellers and/or publishing houses (see appended list). If I had a lead for some work, but did not find it either in India *or* through Interlibrary Loan in the United States, then I gave it up as a lost cause, too difficult to locate to be useful. Similarly I gave up on attempting to list such hard to locate ephemera as articles in newspapers or the unbound newsletters that many religious groups put out. Serious scholars can find files of back newspaper clippings relating to religion at either New Delhi's Centre for Women's Development Studies or Bombay's Centre for Women's Studies at SNDT Women's University; the Centre for Women's Development Studies even keeps a catalogue of its clippings. Religious publications are usually best accessed by contacting national headquarters for their respective groups. Some groups, however, print journals that are substantial enough to be collected, bound, and catalogued by major libraries—both in India and the U.S.; I have included selections from these where appropriate.

I regret one exclusion that had to be made simply because of limitations on my time. I have by and large not listed reviews of the books included, unless these include important new materials or arguments introduced by the reviewer. I know that reviews are important aids in evaluating new works, especially for young and inexperienced researchers. But there were too many for me to manage, given the limited time I had available. Some of the best and most responsible reviews by Indian scholars are published in *Economic and Political Weekly*, while good reviews by Western scholars are found in many American and British journals of Asian studies. Researchers wishing to secure reviews are referred to these sources.

Indian libraries strictly regulate the materials and equipment that can enter a library with a researcher; a pen and tablet will get past the door guard, but not a computer. Because all Indian entries and notes therefore had to be written initially in longhand, I followed the principle that "less is more." I have recorded the bare minimum of information about individual titles that would (a) allow researchers to size up contents and (b) yield enough basics so that materials can be ordered via Interlibrary Loan. All entries will have basics: author, title, place of publication, publisher, and date for books; author, title, source, volume, date, and pages for periodicals. Information on series of which volumes are a part has been excluded unless it would be an important factor in finding the work. Editors of collections of course are included; translators are usually listed also. Multiple editors or authors of volumes are cited rather than the standard *et al.* abbreviation, but writers of forewords and prefaces are out in the cold. In general, I have not cited pages for articles listed in published volumes, on the premise that researchers wishing to consult such segments should be able to secure the entire work. Nor have I listed total numbers of pages in listed volumes; this was an oversight, pure and simple, recognized too late for easy correction.

Where two or more articles on disparate topics are collected in a single volume, the volume is generally cited as a whole, with full names of authors and relevant titles cited in the annotation. Where titles give adequate clues to contents, annotations generally do not comment on individual essays in such collective volumes. If, however, the volume includes just a single article appropriate for this listing, then the article is treated as separate. In the case of single authors who have multiple works, one or more of which are in collections, cross-references to the latter are included along with the author's prime list.

Finding Your Way Around

Unlike many bibliographies, this one has not been arranged according to topic. Although I initially planned to follow the topical model, I have found too many cross-currents to make such a breakdown feasible. Instead the main text consists of a simple numbered list that is alphabetized by author. The magic key designed to unlock this is the index that follows the numbered list of entries. This index incorporates three different sorts of reference, the first two aimed at facilitating quick access to specific titles, and the third aimed at helping the reader to pull out related blocks of material.

The first variety of material incorporated in the index is the sort found in indexes of most scholarly books. It consists mostly of names—names of people, of mythical heroines, of deities, doctrines, rituals, works of literature, movements, groups, and places. If you know that you wish to find materials on the Rajasthani saint Mirabai, on the concept of *shakti*, on references to women in *dharmashastra*, or on Bengali Durga Puja, look first for the topic that you have specifically in mind. The chances are very good that you will find a reference that will speed you directly toward your goal. By the way, numbers listed with each index entry refer to individual items, *not* to the pages on which they are found.

The second variety of quick-access entry is designed to help persons already somewhat familiar with titles to speed towards works they may wish to consult. If a title contains any unique word, phrase, or image that can distinguish it readily from others of its ilk, that word, phrase, or image is also listed in the index. If you know, for example, that someone named Wendy wrote a book with androgynes in its title, you can straightaway find Wendy O'Flaherty's *Women, Androgynes, and Other Mythical Beasts* by checking the index for *Androgynes. Coloured Rice* will lead you to Suzanne Hanchett's work on Hindu family festivals; *Battle* will take you to Kamala Chattopadhayay's *Indian Women's Battle for Freedom*. Similar key word and phrase coding has also been used to identify articles. To help you identify which index references refer to specific titles, I have cited book title fragments in italics and article titles with their initial capitalizations.

Not all researchers know enough to pursue specific names or titles; nor do all titles lend themselves to the type of unique word coding described above. (I have found dozens of books titled *Women in India, Indian Women*, or *Status of Women in India*.) To help in isolating general categories of books, or to find familiar works known only by their subjects, I have also inserted into the index subject listings that group works (usually) into larger clusters; these are somewhat like the old subject listings that one used to find in non-computerized library catalogues. For example, Mirabai—cited above—not only has a listing of her own, she is also clustered with Lal Ded, Andal, Mahadeviyakka, and several others in the general category titled "Saints." Durga Puja also finds itself in "Festival"; Sister Nivedita's Girls' School in Calcutta has second listings under both "Schools" and "Education." At times where a category is important in its own right, such as the category of ritual known as *Vrata*, its numerals have not been duplicated in the appropriate subject listing (in this case, "Ritual"). Instead it is cross-listed, with a *See also* indicator.

To help people who are really unfamiliar with Indian religions, or who want a quick overview of available subject listings, I have appended to this introduction a Guide to Index Categories that will help you discover quickly what subject groupings are available. The Guide is divided into ten major categories. The first, "Introductory Works," lists all subject designations that will lead to overviews of women's status, roles, and problems of women in India, or in specific Indian religions. The second, "Women as Objects of Religion," identifies subject listings that explore aspects of Indian religion determining women's lives. The third, "Women as Subjects of Religion," points to subject listings that give an entrée to women's own experiences, practices, teachings, roles, and movements. The fourth, "Areas of Controversy," offers subject listings for the "hot spots" of Indian women's interaction with religion, where religion's conservators and challengers often lock horns with one another. The fifth, "Trends and Predicaments," is the inevitable catch-all for subjects not readily categorized elsewhere, such as "Change," for example, and "Dilemmas."

All of the above categories group by topics of a type often found in more conventional bibliographies. The remaining five offer alternative types of groupings. Category six, "Location in Space," singles out works that focus on women and religion in particular places. If the focus of such works is narrow enough, they are grouped by state; if it is somewhat broader, they are located by region. This special attention to spatial clustering is intended to aid researchers who are enriching our knowledge of regional diversity in India. Category seven, "Location in Time," is intended as an aid to those who wish to study the religious history of women. Like spatial location, location in time is handled in two complementary ways. A special subject heading labeled "Chronology" in the index lists all time spans cited in an entry's title or description, in the order of centuries in which such time spans begin. Thus someone interested explicitly in the fourteenth through sixteenth centuries—or in the turbulent nineteenth—can find under "Chronology" all works specifically addressed to these eras. Once again, these very specific listings are supplemented with others that offer more generalized timespans—"Ancient Period," "Medieval Period," "Modern," and so on.

Category eight, "Social Divisions," classifies in yet another way. It sorts its works by religious or social communities. You can find all works referring to Parsees here, or to Buddhists, Christians, Jains, and Muslims. Similarly, using this category, you can find all references to all works that study specifically low-caste women, or the middle classes, or middle-aged.

Category nine, entitled "Genres," is a methodological category, clustering works by particular approaches they may take. Using this category, you can quickly locate, for example, all of the bibliography's autobiographies, or works that feature analysis of works of literature, or questionnaire-based surveys.

Finally, category ten, entitled "Research Resources," offers resources that can help you to go beyond this listing—to other biliographies, libraries, and archives, or to India's various Women's Studies centers or Women's organizations.

Users of the index are hereby warned that it is unrepentantly gynocentric. The qualifiers "women's" or "female" are assumed for all subject listings unless the qualifiers "men's" or "male" is added. Thus the listing "guru" refers to female gurus, and the listing "experience" refers to women's experience. The index is also, more regrettably, somewhat Hinducentric. If a group being studied is not specifically labelled as "Muslim," "Christian," "Jain," "tribal," etc., it can usually be assumed to be part of the family of traditions commonly known as Hinduism. Finally, the index is contemporary-centric; although the "Location in Time" category does have subject listings labelled "Twentieth century," "Modern," and "Contemporary," these include only works that incorporate such labels in their titles. The vast majority of works cited refer to twentieth-century phenomena; as has so often been the case in the religious history of women, much of Indian women's past is lost.

Postscript

My bibliography is offered with hopes that it will continue a trend that has already begun. My most encouraging finding while searching through these 1015 sources has been the rich evidence of expanding interest and competence in explorations of the complex relationship between women and religion. An arena of human experience so little explored twenty years ago that students wishing to approach it had virtually no available texts is blossoming now, with a double benefit. Improved understanding of religion's power over and within women's lives must of necessity yield improved understanding of women. Improved understanding of women's experience of and contributions to religion must of necessity yield improved understanding of religion.

Acknowledgments

Contributions from many institutions and people have made this bibliography possible. I must first thank Western Michigan University and the American Institute of Indian Studies—the former for granting the sabbatical leave that made my research in India possible, and the latter for funding the research itself. Nehru Memorial Library in New Delhi, my "search headquarters," was the next largest contributor; its staff taught me Indian reference tools, helped me to locate books and articles, and copied huge heaps of periodical articles for me. Special thanks go to the nameless shelver of books who took it upon himself to teach me how the Nehru Library numbering system worked. Staff members at the Institute for Social Studies Research spent several days pulling out unpublished conference materials for me. At the Women's Studies and Development Centre of the University of Delhi, yet another busy staffer spent her day searching my list and her shelves for materials that I had not yet found. At the Centre for Women's Development Studies, I found the entire collection of books packed up in boxes and waiting for a long-delayed move; yet staffers there patiently hunted down for me copies of hard-to-get papers and reference aids produced by the Centre. The librarian at Jamia Millia University was likewise unfailingly helpful during my several days' work there. Among the Delhi/New Delhi booksellers, I must single out the staff at Manohar, who surrounded me with stacks of recent books in Women's Studies, even though they knew I was there to make notes rather than to buy.

Multiple thanks are required for persons at SNDT Women's University: to Vice-Chancellor Suma Chitnis and Women's Research Centre Director Meera Kosambi for inviting me to visit and speak; to Ramala Baxamusa and Veena Poonacha for giving hours of time

Acknowledgments

in advice and conversation; and to the librarians for making my needs their own and locating many items that I would not have known to look for had I been searching on my own. I am grateful, too, to my colleague Subhash Sonnad's sister Hemlata, just for offering her friendship and introducing me to the university's extension program. Multiple thanks likewise go to the Home Economics program for housing and feeding me so well for a week, and especially to the student who painted the landing in front of my door each morning with auspicious rice-flour designs.

Professors J. P. S. Uberoi of the University of Delhi Sociology Department and K. M. Srimali of History are owed thanks for their willingness to serve as faculty supervisors to a stranger during this visit and my previous sabbatical in India. Professors Veena Das and D. N. Jha, department chairs at the time, also have my gratitude for their willingness to host me. Uma Chakravarti, Ramala Baxamusa, and Kumkum Sangari took time from very busy schedules to read early versions of my list and suggest additions or corrections. I feel privileged just to know these super people, let alone to have had their aid. Janet Chawla and Rajni Palriwala were also important as routing agents during early stages of my work, helping me to identify people I needed to know. Janet, especially, was a repeatedly important source of introductions for me.

On the American side, I owe very special thanks to the staff of the Western Michigan University Interlibrary Loan program, who countless times helped me follow often tenuous or garbled leads. Over this past two years, they have processed more than one hundred requests from me, going as far as England in their searches, and producing most in record time. Friends Rita Gross and Kay Jordan have read my list and supplemented it with titles from their own specializations: Rita is responsible for most entries on Tibetan Buddhism, while Kay has given me many of the titles on *devadasi*s. Leslie Orr of Concordia University in Canada was kind enough to send me her own two substantial bibliographies on

Acknowledgments

Hinduism and Buddhism, which enabled me to fill in a number of holes in my own. I am especially pleased with the leads they gave me to materials published by Leslie's fellow Canadians.

Thanks go likewise to Thomas H. Seiler of New Issues Press and his colleague Juleen Eichinger for agreeing to publish a book that might have a limited market. The chance to publish locally has eliminated much hassle for me, and the chance to work with former student Juleen has been an especial treat.

Finally, last but never least, I must celebrate this volume's secret hero, my husband Arthur Falk, who came to the rescue again and again when computer glitches threatened to undo me. The demands of such a large and complicated work have severely taxed my very limited computing skills; I could not have even attempted it without such a handy and patient computer consultant. Arthur has moreover endured without complaint my nine months' disappearance to India, half a dozen more overnight absences for Michigan library visits, and many months of a less than well-kept household and a very distracted wife. Both he and I are very glad to see this project finally ended.

Guide to Index Categories

Category 1: Introductory Works

See: Impact of religion; Introductory and General Works; Position of Women; Role; Status

Category 2: Women as Objects of Religion

A: *Thoughts that Shape Women's Lives*

See: *Ahimsa*, woman incarnates; Auspicious; *Dharma*; Female body, constructions of the; Femaleness; Femininity; Field, wife as husband's; Gandhi, on women; Gender; *Karma*; Leaders, male religious, on women; Liberation; Manliness, ideal of; Men: their conceptions of women; Nature of women; Oppositions; *Pativrata*; Pollution; Power; *Prakriti*; Prejudices, rankings of; Purity; Sacrament; Sex; Sexual; Sexuality; *Shakti*; Sinfulness natural to women; Womanhood; Womanliness

B: *Feminine Models and Their Sources*

See: Epic; Evil, wives; Fiction, in; Goddess; *Gopi*; Great Women; Heroic women; Iconography; Ideal woman; Images of women; Models; Myth; Mythology; *Sati*; Sita; Symbol; Symbolism; Wife, ideal

C: *Norms and Precepts for Women*

See: Astrology; Authority; *Dharmashastra*; Duties; Guidebooks; *Streedharma*

D: *Institutions that Affect Women*

See: Ashram; Caste; Church; Class; Community; Constitution; Education; Family; Law (*note cross-references also*); Marriage (*note cross-references also*); Matriliny; Matrilocal marriage; Media; *Niyoga*; Patriarchy; Patriliny; Politics; Press; Property; Prostitution; Scripture; Slaves; State; *Stridhan*; Supreme Court

E: *Practices that Women Share*

See: Astrology; Drama, sacred; Exorcism; Festival; Healing; Marriage rites and customs; Pilgrimage; Sacrifice

F: *Historical Movements and Groups that Changed Women's Roles*

See: <u>Movements:</u> *Bhakti*; Education; Emancipation; Freedom Movement; Missionaries; Modernization; Reform; Reform movements; Secularization; Westernization

   <u>Groups:</u> Arya Samaj; Brahmo Samaj; Prarthana Samaj; Ramakrishna Movement; Rashtriya Svayamsevak Sangh; Sarvodaya Movement; Satyagraha Movement; Schools; Theosophical Society

Category 3: Women as Subjects of Religion

A: *Women's Experiences*

See: Autobiography; Childhood, memories; Ecstasy, religious; Everyday life; Female body, constructions of the; Folklore; Partition; Political: realities for Muslim women; Possession; Riots; Self-perception; Sex; Sexual; Sexuality

B: *Women's Values*

See: Attraction to religion; Attitudes; Auspicious; Auspiciousness; Freedom, spiritual; *Pativrata*; Perceptions; Purity; *Shakti*; Values

C: *Women's Practice*

See: Astrology; *Bhakti*; *Burqa*; Calendrical ritual; Charms; Childbirth rites; Childhood, rites; Children, pilgrimage to secure; Dance; Death; Divination; Domestic rites; Dress; Evil, warding off; Exorcism; Fast; Fertility, cult; Festival; Folk rituals; Folk songs; Food; Goddess, cult of; Henna; Household rites; Husband, worship of; *Kirtan*; Kitchen, purity in; Life-cycle, rites of the; Marriage rites and customs; Marriage songs; Menstruation; Pilgrimage; Pollution restrictions; Possession; Pre-puberty rites; Pregnancy, rites of; Protest; Puberty, rites; *Puja*; Rites; Ritual; Songs; Stories that women tell; Struggle; Symbolism; *Tilak*; Temple; *Vrata*; Widow, ascetic disciplines of; Yoga

D: *Women's Roles*

See: <u>Ordinary:</u> Child; Courtesan; Daughter; Daughter-in-Law; Educators; Freedom fighters; Girlfriend; Grandmother; Heroic women; Housewife; Intellectual; Life-cycle; Mother; Mother-in-Law; Political leaders; Prostitute; Prostitution; Reformers (female); Sister; Teachers; Unmarried women; Widow; Widowhood; Wife; Wives

Special Religious: Ascetics (*note cross references also*); *devadasi*; Devotee; Donor; Guru; Holy women; *Kumari*; Laywomen; Midwife; Missionaries; Mystic; Nun; Priestess; *Rishi*; Saint; *Sannyasini*; Singer; Sufi; Theologically trained women; Witch

E: *Women Leaders' Publications*

See: Bible study; Devotional poetry, in translation; Prayers and meditations; Teachings; Theology; Writings

F: *Women's Movements and Groups*

See: Movements: Birth Control; Feminism; Feminist; Women's Liberation; Women's Movement

Groups: All India Women's Conference; Ashrama; Brahma Kumari; Brahma Vidya Mandir; Kanya Kumari Sthan; Nunneries; Sakyadhita; Sarada Math and Mission; School; Sri Sri Saradeshwari; Women's Organizations

Category 4: Areas of Controversy

See: Communalism; *Devadasi*; Divorce; Dowry; Equality for women; Fundamentalism; Inequality; Inheritance; *Jogin*; Maintenance; Polygamy; Property rights; *Purdah*; Rights of women; Roop Kanwar; *Sati*; Shah Bano; Uniform Civil Code; Women's Question

Category 5: Trends and Predicaments

See: Abuse; Change; Changing; Dilemmas; Discrimination; Exploitation; Mobility; Modernization; Oppression; Subjection; Submissiveness; Subordination; Subservience; Violence; Westernization

Guide to Index Categories

Category 6 : Location in Space

A: *By State or Major City*

See: Andhra Pradesh; Arunachal Pradesh; Assam; Bengal; Bihar; Bombay; Calcutta; Delhi; Goa; Gujarat; Haryana; Himachal Pradesh; Karnataka; Kashmir/Kashmiri; Kerala; Madhya Pradesh; Maharashtra; Megalaya; Orissa; Punjab; Rajasthan; Tamil/Tamilnadu; Uttar Pradesh

B. *By Region*

See: Central India; Eastern India; North Central India; North India; Northeast India; Northwest India; South India

C: *Neighboring Nations*

See: Afghanistan; Bangladesh; Malaysia; Nepal; Pakistan; Sri Lanka; Tibet

Category 7: Location in Time

A: *By Century*

See: Chronology

B: *By Historical Period*

See: Chola Period; Colonial Period; Colonialism; Contemporary; Early India; Medieval Period; Modern Period; Mughal India; Veda; Vedic Period

Category 8: Social Divisions

A: *Religious Communities*

See: Buddhism/Buddhist; Christian/Christianity; Conservative; Hindu/Hinduism; Islam; Jewish; Muslim; Orthodox; Parsee; Radha Soami; Shaiva/Shaivism; Shaktism; Shia Islam; Siddha Yoga; Sikh/Sikhism; Sunni Islam; Swaminarayan Religion; Syrian Christians; Vaishnava/Vaishnivism; Virashaivism; Yoga Siddhas. *See also* 2.F and 3.F (Groups) *above*

B: *Caste/class Divisions*

See: Brahman; British women; Caste; Class; Dalit; Harijan; Low-caste women and girls; Middle class women; Oppressed; Poor women; Rajput; Scheduled caste; *Shudra*; Untouchables; Upper-caste; Upper-class

C: *Age Sets*

See: Child; Childhood; Middle-aged women; Young women

D: *Residential Unit*

See: Rural; Tribal; Urban; Village

Category 9: Genres

Search for: Anthology; Autobiography; Biography; Case study; Comparison; Devotional poetry, in translation; Fiction; Folklore; Generational studies; Historiography; Inscriptions; Interviews; Letters; Life History; Literary Criticism; Magazines; Methodological reflection; Psychological approaches; Survey, sociological. *See also* village, for village studies

Guide to Index Categories

Category 10: Research Resources

See: Bibliography; Biographical dictionary; Directory;
Research resources; Unpublished conferences,
seminars, and consultations; Women's Studies in
India; Libraries and archives

Special Notes

On Transliterations. The variety of transliteration methods used
in both India and the U.S. have proved to be the biggest headache
of this project. In general, I have followed the following principles:

1) Where terms from Sanskrit or modern Indian languages appear
in titles, I have left them untouched insofar as possible. The lone
departure from this rule was elimination of diacritical marks. The
computer that I carried to India had no Sanskrit diacritical
capacities, and it has proved too daunting to reconstruct the
diacriticals retrospectively.

2) Where terms have been used in my own text or the index, I
have followed the principle of "most common occurrence" in
rendering them, even though this sometimes results in inconsistencies. Thus, for example, I have used "purdah" rather than "parda"
and "swami" rather than "svami," but, nonetheless, "sati" rather
than "suttee." The sibilant "ś" has been rendered as "sh" throughout; thus I have "Shaiva" rather than "Saiva," "ashram" rather than
"asram," and "shakti" rather than "sakti"; an exception is made for
"official" transliterations (such as Swami *S*ivananda. Similarly, the
semivowel "r" has been rendered as "ri"; thus I have "Krishna"
rather than "Krsna." Wherever transliteration discrepancies have
created potential problems in locating words within the index, I
have cross-listed alternative spellings.

3) At times, I have found discrepancies between transliterations in Indian author's names used in title pages of books and transliterations utilized in the OCLC list—which, in turn, is a key aid for locating books through computer networks within the United States. When this has been the case—and when I could verify the discrepancy—I have utilized the title-page version of the name for my own alphabetical listing and have inserted in brackets the Library of Congress version. Such entries will read as follows: Last name of author, first name [OCLC lists as _____].

On Abbreviations:

OCLC = OCLC Online Computer Library Center, Inc.
DAI = Dissertation Abstracts International

On Sources after 1992:

Bibliographies *are* unending. Although the "official" search that gave rise to this one ended with the year 1992, I did, from time to time, come across still more recent sources while the final editing and checking of sources was in process. When this happened, I tucked them in. The list is, however, not complete after 1992.

On Problems:

Persons using this list who have questions or difficulty in finding specific materials are welcome to direct questions to me through the internet email system. My email address is nancy.falk@wmich. edu.

Bibliography

1. "Abusing Religion to Oppress Women: A Challenge to Muslim Personal Law by a Muslim Woman." *Manushi* 4, No. 4 (=No. 22; May–June, 1984), 9–13.
    [Summarizes contents of a petition filed by a divorced Muslim woman; this petition charges that the government of India's policy of accepting personal laws of religious communities violates Muslim women's constitutional rights to equal protection.]

2. Adhav, Shamsundar Mohan. *Pandita Ramabai*. Madras: Christian Literacy Society, 1979.
    [Briefly describes the life and teachings of India's first woman to work in behalf of reform for women, citing extensive selections from her writings, including poems and letters. Pandita Ramabai began her life as a reciter of Sanskrit Puranas and ended it a Christian convert and foundress of a school for widows.]

3. Agarwal, Meera. *Women and the Law: Matrimonial Rights of Women*. New Delhi: Delhi Legal and Advice Board, n.d.
    [This twelve-page pamphlet describing laws on marriage and divorce in lay language is available at Nehru Memorial Library, New Delhi.]

4. Agarwala, B. R. *The Shah Bano Case: Plight of a Muslim Woman*. New Delhi: Arnold-Heinemann, 1986.
    [Includes a text of the judgment and a compilation of responses to this notorious case of a seventy-five year old Muslim woman denied the right to maintenance from her husband; responses include both articles and interviews.]

5. Agnes, Flavia. "Maintenance for Women: Rhetoric of Equality." *Economic and Political Weekly* 27, No. 41 (October 10, 1992), 2233–35.

[Asserts that judges in India charged to make decisions on maintenance under the revised Hindu code are still guided by the model of the ideal Hindu wife: humiliation is ennobling, servitude appropriate, and divorce is distasteful enough so that women who undertake it should have to suffer economically for it. Meanwhile "liberal" provisions of the code are twisted: the requirement of monogamy is used by illicit bigamists to deny maintenance to a second wife. A wife who works may nonetheless have to pay maintenance to her husband. Includes also a brief description of women's problems under other communal codes.]

6.   Agrawala, S. K. *Directory of Women's Studies in India*. New Delhi: Association of Indian Universities, 1991.
      [A survey of women's studies centers and programs; includes curricula.]

7.   Ahangar, Mohd Altaf Hussain. *Customary Succession among Muslims: A Critical Appraisal of Judicial Interpretation in Kashmir*. New Delhi: Uppal Publishing House, 1986.
      [Includes a discussion of inheritance by widows and daughters.]

8.   Ahluwalia, B. K. "Mother Teresa 'The Spirit of Mercy'." *Indian and Foreign Review* 21, No. 11 (March 31, 1984), 12–13, 26.
      [Reviews the calling, work, ideals, and honors of India's most famous Catholic nun.]

9.   Ahluwalia, B. K., and Shashi Ahluwalia. *Mother Teresa and Missionaries of Charity*. New Delhi: Harnam Publications, 1984.
      [This collection of brief testimonial essays is principally anecdotal.]

10.   Ahmad, Imtiaz, ed. *Family, Kinship, and Marriage among Muslims in India*. New Delhi: Vikas Publishing House, 1976; Columbia, Mo.: South Asia Books, 1976.

[Kinship is the principal subject of this edited collection, but essays include some materials on marriage customs. See especially Victor S. D'Souza, "Kinship Organization and Marriage Customs among the Moplahs on the Southwest Coast of India"; Doranne Jacobson, "The Veil of Virtue: *Purdah* and the Muslim Family in the Bhopal Region of Central India"; and A. R. Saiyed, assisted by Pathan Mirkhan, "*Purdah*, Family Structure and the Status of Women: A Note on a Deviant Case." The "deviant case" of the latter chapter is a lack of *purdah* in a Muslim community whose men must leave to do absentee work.]

For Ahmad, Imtiaz, see also entry 287; and see also Ahmed, Imtiaz.

11.   Ahmad, Karuna. "Women's Life Cycle and Identity." *Economic and Political Weekly* 17, Nos. 1–2 (January 2–9, 1982), 15–17.
[Reports on a seminar focused on change in women's lives and "components of selfhood" over three generations, drawing on autobiographical accounts by participants and by women of the past century. Includes some discussion of the role of ritual in shaping female identity.]

12.   Ahmad, Karuna Chanana. "Gandhi, Women's Roles and the Freedom Movement." Occasional Papers on History and Society 19. New Delhi: Nehru Memorial Library and Museum, 1984.
[This mimeographed paper housed at the Nehru Library explores the connection between Gandhi's conception of women's roles and women's participation in the freedom movement. Gandhi's ideas are treated more extensively than women's responses to them; the latter are drawn solely from documents.]

See also Chanana, Karuna.

13.   Ahmad, Shadbano. "Education and *Purdah* Nuances: A

Note on Muslim Women in Aligarh." *Social Action* 27 (January–March 1977), 45–52.
[Reports the findings of a study of the relationship between education and variations in the observance of *purdah* (seclusion) among middle-class Muslim women in Aligarh city. Finds that "the observance of *purdah* tends to vary inversely with the degree of education received." But this is true only in the case of modern, secular education—and even educated women tend to observe *purdah* either "partially or intermittently."]

For Ahmad, Shadbano, see also entry 38.

14.   Ahmed, Imtiaz, ed. *Modernization and Social Change among Muslims in India*. New Delhi: Manohar, 1983.
[Includes several articles on women, most with self-descriptive titles: Shahida Lateef, "Modernization in India and the Status of Muslim Women"; Niesha Z. Haniff, "Muslim Women and the Minority Mentality"; and Gail Minault, "Shaikh Abdallah, Begum Abdallah, and Sharif Education for Girls at Aligarh." An article by Suma Chitnis, "Tenacity and Luck: The Story of Bilquis," describes the struggles of a girl from the Bombay slums to take advantage of an opportunity for schooling.]

15.   Ahmed, Rahnuma. "Religious Ideology and the Women's Movement in Bangladesh." Bombay: Research Centre for Women's Studies, SNDT Women's University, 1986.
[This duplicated typescript of a paper presented at the New Delhi World Congress of the International Sociological Association is housed at the library of the SNDT Women's University Research Centre for Women's Studies. Highly critical of Islamic subordination of women and the classic defenses thereof, it challenges Muslim claims that Islam historically liberated women from degradation in preceding ages; it also questions the conservative Muslim tenet that Islam should be exempt from legal intervention because re-

ligion is "personal." Reprinted in Swarup and Bisaria, *Women, Politics, and Religion*; entry 920 below.]

16.   Ahmed, Zainab. *The Entitlement of Women under Section 14 of the (Indian) Hindu Succession Act, 1956.* Ph.D. diss., University of London, 1984.
[No further information is available.]

17.   Ali, Firasat, and Furqan Ahmed. *Divorce in Mohammedan Law: The Law of "Triple Divorce."* New Delhi: Deep and Deep, 1983.
[Includes a discussion of religious aspects of divorce laws; cites laws and ordinances.]

18.   Ali, Tahira Mazhar. "Mujahidin Atrocities on Women." *Mainstream* 4, No. 32 (June 17, 1989), 4, 32.
[Protests the Muslim fundamentalist backlash against women, charging that Mujahidin groups of Afghanistan have kidnapped and raped women and have sold some into slavery.]

19.   Ali Baig, Tara [OCLC lists as Baig, Tara Ali]. *India's Woman Power.* New Delhi: S. Chand, 1976.
[In a chapter titled "The Meaning of Existence," the author discusses women's attraction to religious practice and its sources.]

20.   ———. "A Divorcee's Right to Maintenance." *Mainstream* (May 18, 1985), 15–16.
[This article is the first in a 1985 *Mainstream* series that debated the Supreme Court decision in the Shah Bano case (on the right to maintenance of Muslim women divorcees). For others of the series, see Asghar Ali Engineer (May 25 and August 3), Syed Shahabuddin (June 1 and July 13), Vasudha Dhagamwar (July 6), Nusrat Bano Ruhi (July 20), and Sakina Hyder (August 24). Note also Rumki Basu's two-part article "Divorce in India" published on March 2 and 9 of the same year; entry 90 below.]

21.   Allen, Michael. *The Cult of* Kumari: *Virgin Worship in Nepal*. Kirtipur: Institute of Nepal and Asian Studies, Tribhuvan University, 1975.
[In Nepal, young Newar girls are consecrated and worshipped as living incarnations of the goddess. This volume discusses the social and cultural context, beliefs about the *kumaris*, the practice surrounding individual examples, and pre-puberty rites performed for all Newar girls. Includes many photographs.]

22.   ————. *"Kumari* or 'Virgin' Worship in Kathmandu Valley." *Contributions to Indian Sociology (NS)* 10, No. 1 (1976).
[Describes varieties of a Newar rite in which a young living virgin is worshipped to invoke the spirit of the (non-virginal) goddess Sakti, Durga, or Kali. Argues that the ambiguity inherent in the rite is mirrored by similar ambiguity in Hindu conceptions of women's role. Includes some description of menstrual beliefs and taboos.]

23.   Allen, Michael, and S. N. Mukherjee, eds. *Women in India and Nepal*. New Delhi: Sterling Publishers, 1990.
[Chapters of special interest to religionists are S. N. Mukherjee, "Raja Rammohun Roy and the Debate on the Status of Women in Bengal"; Elizabeth Leigh Stutchbury, "Blood, Fire and Mediation: Human Sacrifice and Widow Burning in Nineteenth-Century India"; Michael Allen, "The Hindu View of Women" and "Girls' Pre-Puberty Rites amongst the Newars in Kathmandu Valley"; and John Gray, "Chatri Women in Domestic Groups and Rituals."]

24.   Allione, Tsultrim. *Women of Wisdom*. London: Routledge and Kegan Paul, 1984.
[Allione tells the stories of six distinguished women of the Tibetan Buddhist past. The author herself spent three and one half years as a Tibetan Buddhist nun and studied Tibetan; hence she has received "inside" aid in assembling the volume.]

25. Allison, Charlene Jones. *Belief and Symbolic Action: A Cultural Analysis of a Non-Brahmin Marriage Ritual Cycle.* Ph.D. diss., University of Washington, 1980.
[A detailed emic analysis of the marriage ritual cycle of the Tamil Vellampillai caste; the main intent is to uncover the underlying world view. Described *DAI* 41, No. 5 (November 1980), A-2187.]

26. Alston, A. J., ed. and trans. *The Devotional Poems of Mirabai.* Delhi: Motilal Banarsidass, 1980.
[Two hundred and two devotional poems by India's most famous woman saint, the sixteenth-century Mirabai of Rajasthan. Includes a thirty-two page introduction by the translator on Mirabai's life, her place in the *bhakti* movement, and "the literary and spiritual content of her *Padavali*."]

27. Altekar, Anant Sadashiv. *The Position of Women in Hindu Civilisation, from Prehistoric Times to the Present Day.* 3rd ed. Delhi: Motilal Banarsidass, 1987; from 1956 original.
[A classic, comprehensive history of women's status and roles from Vedic times until the Raj. Features separate treatments of childhood, education, marriage, widowhood, and *sati*. A special chapter titled "Women and Religion" covers women's roles in sacrifices, early eligibility for Vedic study, later prohibition of Vedic study, and Puranic, Buddhist, and Jain roles.]

28. Amalaprana, Pravrajika. "Role of Women in Spreading Spiritual Ideals in India." Parts I–VII in *Bulletin of the Ramakrishna Mission Institute of Culture* 35: No. 4 (April 1984), 75–78; No. 5 (May 1984), 113–14; No. 6 (June 1984), 128–32; No. 7 (July 1984), 155–61; No. 8 (August 1984), 179–85; No. 9 (September 1984), 15–16, 24; No. 10 (October 1984), 232–34.
[From the Vedas through the epics, Buddhism, Jainism, and the great regional saints of devotionalism to women who helped to nurture and shape the Ramakrishna movement,

7

this series summarizes women's contributions to Indian religion.]

29. ———. "Akka Mahadevi." *Samvit* 14 (September 1986), 24–28.
[A brief biographical sketch of a famous twelfth-century woman Shaiva saint of Karnataka. According to hagiographies, Akka Mahadevi married a king, but left him when he tried to violate her relationship to her Lord.]

30. ———. "Sara Bull, the Steady Mother." *Samvit* 20 (September 1989), 13–25.
[Describes the life and contributions to Vivekananda's work of "Granny" Sara Bull, American widow of the violinist Ole Bull. Mrs. Bull was friend, disciple, confidante, and generous donor to the swami, who once cited her as his own model of a saint. Sara Bull was one of a small group of Westerners who accompanied Vivekananda during his final pilgrimage in India.]

31. ———. "Yogin-Ma." *Samvit* 24 (September 1991), 34–38.
[Describes the life, accomplishments, and relationship to Shri Ramakrishna of a distinguished woman disciple and close friend of Sarada Devi.]

32. Amore, Roy C., and Larry D. Shinn. *Lustful Maidens and Ascetic Kings: Buddhist and Hindu Stories of Life*. New York: Oxford University Press, 1981.
[In this collection of stories from classical Buddhist and Hindu texts, a monk is cured of desire for a beautiful courtesan ("The Prostitute Who Lost Her Charm"), two wives demonstrate the power of their wit and faithful virtue ("Savitri and the God of Death"; "The Radiant Sambula"), a princess seduces a drought-bringing ascetic ("How a Youth Lost His Virtue"), Sita demonstrates her faithfulness to Rama ("A Test of Fire"), a servant-girl becomes an "angel" ("A Mansion in Heaven"), a good girl finds her true

husband ("An Act of Truth"), an evil woman achieves an appropriate fate ("The Woman Who Cursed Herself"), and monks overcome their need for women ("Asceticism Now, Nymphs Later" and "The Man Who Didn't Notice Women").]

33. Amritasvarupananda, Swami. *Mata Amritanandamayi: Her Life and the Experiences of Her Devotees*. San Ramon, Calif.: Mata Amritanandamayi Centers, 1988.
[Recounts the life story of a contemporary woman *guru* of Kerala. Mata Amritanandamayi was born into a fisher caste and reared as a virtual servant because of her dark color and eccentric behavior. She is one of the few well-publicized living women *guru*s who has achieved recognition and disciples on her own, rather than inheriting her following from an established male teacher. A short section describes the *bhava*s, or divine manifestations, that Mata Amritananadamayi undergoes while in a state of trance. Another, somewhat longer, contains thirty-eight brief anecdotal accounts of disciples' experiences of her.]

34. Anand, C. L. *Equality, Justice, and Reverse Discrimination in India*. Delhi: Mittal Publications, 1987.
[Women are especially stressed in this critical analysis of laws intended to benefit scheduled castes and women.]

35. Anand, Mulk Raj. *Sati: A Writeup of Raja Ram Mohan Roy about Burning of Widows Alive*. Delhi: B.R. Publishing Corporation, 1989.
[Reproduces Ram Mohan Roy's two famous mock-dialogues on *sati*, along with his summary of his own position, the texts of two petitions, his address to Lord William Bentinck, and selections from the reactions to his dialogues. Appended are fifteen selections from periodical articles responding to the Roop Kanwar *sati*, including articles from the February 1988 special issue of *Mainstream* by Romila Thapar, Sudesh Vaid, Kumkum Sangari, and Vasudha Dhagamwar, as well as others by Namita Sinha, Mod-

humita Mojumdar, Inderjit Badhwar, Ashis Nandy, Vidya
Subramaniam, V. R. Krishna Iyer, and Anuradha Dutt.]

36.   Anandakrishnan, Martha Elizabeth. *Ashes to Fruit: Empow-
      erment through Death among Women Devotees of Vira-
      bhadra*. Ph.D. diss., University of Wisconsin at Madison,
      1990.
      [Explores rituals of low-caste women in a cult of coastal
      Andhra Pradesh. Performed after a child's violent or pre-
      mature death, these rites may include episodes of posses-
      sion and self-mutilation. The dissertation asks how rites af-
      fect a woman's community status and sense of personal
      identity; it takes a psychological, case-history approach.
      Described *DAI* 51, No. 12 (June 1991), A-4170.]

37.   Andal. *The Poems of Andal: Tiruppavai and Nacchiyar
      Tirumozhi*. Trans. P. S. Sundaram. Bombay: Anantha-
      charya Indological Research Institute, 1987.
      [This entire volume consists of Tamil text and translations
      except for a four-page introduction; the work is that of the
      woman Alvar (poet-saint) Andal (also written Antal). Some
      use is made of archaic language and sentences are some-
      times contorted for meter, but these are nonetheless mostly
      readable and usable translations.]

38.   Anjum, Mohini, ed. *Muslim Women in India*. New Delhi:
      Radiant Publishers, 1992.
      [The volume's fifteen brief articles on the plight of Muslim
      women are products of a 1986 workshop held at New
      Delhi's Jamia Millia Islamia University; coverage extends
      from methodology to repercussions of the Gulf oil boom for
      poor women of Hyderabad. Most relevant for this bibliogra-
      phy are A. R. Saiyed, "Muslim Women in India: An Over-
      view"; H. Y. Siddiqui, "The Studies of Muslim Women in
      India: Approaches and Methodology"; Shadbano Ahmad,
      "Methodological Problems in the Study of Muslim Women";
      Indu Prakash Singh, "Indian Muslim Women: Prisoners of

the Capitalist Patriarchate"; P. K. Mathur, "Inequality in the Status of Women and Minority Identity in India"; Jahanzeb Akhtarm, "Muslim Women's Education in India"; Leela Dube, "Women in a Matrilineal Muslim Community"; and Puma Iftikhar, "Indian Muslim Women: Plight and Remedy."]

39.   Ansari, Iqbal A. "Muslim Women's Rights: Goals and Strategies of Reform." *Economic and Political Weekly* 26, No. 17 (April 27, 1991), 1095–97.
[Pleads with readers to resolve the problems of Muslim women "within the Islamic framework of value direction."]

40.   "Anti-Women Law." *Economic and Political Weekly* 21, No. 19 (May 10, 1986), 801–02.
[An editorial responds to the Muslim Women (Protection of Rights on Divorce) Bill arguing that this law denies to Muslim women their rights to non-discrimination on grounds of religion, race, caste, and sex.]

41.   Appadurai, Arjun, Frank J. Korom, and Margaret A. Mills. *Gender, Genre, and Power in South Asian Expressive Traditions.* Philadelphia: University of Pennsylvania Press, 1991.
[Three articles of the first section of this fifteen-essay volume include materials related to religion: A. K. Ramanujan, "Toward a Counter-System: Women's Tales"; Ann Grodzins Gold, "Gender and Illusion in a Rajasthani Yogic Tradition"; and Peter J. Claus, "Kin Songs."]

42.   Apte, Usha M. *The Sacrament of Marriage in Hindu Society, from Vedic Period to Dharmasastras.* Delhi: Ajanta Publications, 1978.
[This textual survey is principally concerned with the rites themselves but also includes other information, such as age of bride, choice of partners, types of marriage, and status of wives.]

43.　　———. *Vedic, Hindu, and Tribal Marriage: A Study in Culture Change*. Hyderabad: AWARE, 1982.
[A comprehensive survey of marriage customs, negotiations, and rites, this volume covers fifty-one Indian groups.]

44.　　Aravamudan, Gita. *Voices in My Blood*. New Delhi: Sterling Publishers, 1990.
[A journalist's collection of women's accounts of their own everyday life experiences includes a brief chapter titled "Religion: Whose Solace?" Women interviewed were from Kerala, Karnataka, and Tamil Nadu.]

45.　　Archer, William G. *Songs for the Bride: Wedding Rites of Rural India*. New York: Columbia University Press, 1985.
[Features songs sung and composed mostly by women, set within their ritual context; the marriages described are those of Hindu Kayasths from northern Bihar. Published posthumously; the songs in question are translations from materials published in Hindi during the 1940s.]

46.　　Arunchalam, M. "The *Sati* Cult in Tamilnadu." *Bulletin of the Institute of Traditional Cultures (Madras)* (July–December 1978), 59–104.
[Examines evidence of *sati* cults in Tamilnadu prior to *sati* abolition in 1929, assessing the prevalence of *sati*, conditions under which it was performed, and the status of widows who burned themselves.]

47.　　Arya, Sadhna. "Women, Religion and State in India." *Teaching Politics* 15, No. 1 (1989), 13–24.
[Published by University of Delhi Political Science Department. Shows how the State's penchant for playing communalist politics has undermined the drive for women's rights. Argues that women must work for true separation between religion and state.]

48.　　Asaf Ali, Aruna. *Resurgence of Indian Women*. New Delhi: Radiant Publishers, 1991.

[Incorporates chapters on women's status in various traditions, and on religious reformers (saints, Islamic, and modern). Includes materials relevant to women's responses to communalism: e.g., the role of women in the anti-partition movement.]

49. *Asian Conference on Women, Religion, and Family Laws.* Bombay, 1987.
[Available at the Institute for Social Studies Trust, New Delhi. This conference drew principally on presenters in the Bombay area. Conference proceedings include not only papers but also a summary of the conference intent, day-to-day proceedings, and the discussion. Papers cover Bangladesh, Korea, Indonesia, Sri Lanka, India, Singapore, China, and Malaysia; although these are mostly surveys of legal precepts, one paper on Bangladesh examines broader social practice. See especially Anberiya Hanifa, "Contemporary Family Laws Applicable to Muslims of Sri Lanka"; Ammu Abraham, "Personal Laws in India"; Vimochana, "The Quest for a Uniform Code: Some Dilemmas, Some Issues"; Ubining, "Women, Religion, and Family Laws: The Situation in Bangladesh"; and Sultana Kamal, "Impact of Colonialism on the Family Laws of Bangladesh."]

50. Assayag, Jackie. "Women-Goddess, Women-Distress: Yellamma Goddess' Devotees in South India (Karnataka)." *Man in India* 69, No. 4 (December 1989), 359–73.
[Treats the process of dedication and the practice of *yogammas*, women dedicated to the goddess; contests the belief that *yogammas* are mere prostitutes, but concedes that many are presently "in distress."]

51. Athavale, Parvati. *Hindu Widow: An Autobiography, Written in the Marathi Language.* Trans. Justin E. Abbot. New Delhi: Reliance Publishing House, 1986; original version New York and London: G.P. Putnam's Sons, 1930.
[Parvati Athavale was the sister-in-law of Maharashtrian

13

educator D. K. Karve and an important fund-raiser for his widows' school. She describes her early life, her marriage and widowhood, her widowed sister's marriage to Karve and the public outrage it inspired, Karve's successful efforts to coax her out of her own strict widow's discipline and into his school, her subsequent work for the school, and her later journey to America to gain fluency in English. This autobiography is one of several that are invaluable for showing the change in values and perceptions that occurred as women were affected by various reform efforts. The translation is the original.]

52. Athyal, Sakhi Mariyamma. *Women's Roles in Ministries in Select Churches in India after Independence.* Diss., Fuller Theological Seminary School of World Mission, 1991.
[Asks how new attention to women's rights has affected the Indian Christian church, studying especially the development of women's roles in ministry; primary attention is paid to the Church of South India, the Church of North India, and the Mar Thoma Church. Includes a description of trends in theological reflection on women's status. Finds increasing numbers of women in ministry and significant movement towards male/female partnership in all areas. Described *DAI* 52, No. 3 (September 1991), A-958.]

53. Atkinson, Clarissa W., Constance H. Buchanan, and Margaret R. Miles, eds. *Immaculate and Powerful: The Female in Sacred Image and Social Reality.* Boston: Beacon Press, 1985.
[Two essays from this collection of twelve pertain to India. Frederique Apffel Marglin's "Female Sexuality in the Hindu World" examines meanings associated with sexuality, particularly the dichotomy between auspicious and inauspicious. Anne C. Klein's "Primordial Purity and Everyday Life: Exalted Female Symbols and the Women of Tibet" shows that positive female imagery of the Tibetan Buddhist tradition has not necessarily translated into social egalitarianism.]

54.   Atmaprana, Pravrajika. "Saraswati—Sarada, a Revelation."
        Samvit 8 (September 1983), 14–19.
        [A *sannyasini* from the Sarada Mission reflects on the
        significance of a goddess and the once-living woman said to
        be an incarnation of her.]

55.   ———. "Sister Nivedita's Discipleship." *Samvit* 16
        (September 1987), 9–16.
        [Examines the relationship between Swami Vivekananda
        and Sister Nivedita (Margaret Noble), who gave up her life
        in England to become a *sannyasini* and girls' school found-
        ress in India.]

56.   ———. *The Story of Sister Nivedita*. Calcutta: Rama-
        krishna Sarada Mission Sister Nivedita Girls' School, 1988.
        [This small book of seventy-three pages is clearly intended
        as an introduction to the famous Irish educator and Indian
        nationalist Sister Nivedita. It summarizes materials from
        the author's much more extensive biography of Nivedita,
        published in 1961.]

57.   Augustine, John S., ed. The *Indian Family in Transition*.
        New Delhi: Vikas Publishing House, 1982.
        [This slim but ambitious volume tends to take Hindu
        families as normative and treat others as special cases. Ar-
        ticles included are K. Ishwaran, "Interdependence of the
        Elementary and Extended Family"; George Kurian, "A Re-
        view of Marriage and Adjustment in Indian Families"; H. D.
        Lakshminarayana, "The Rural Family in Transition"; T. K.
        Oommen, "The Urban Family in Transition"; John S. Au-
        gustine, "The Christian Family in Transition: Patterns of
        Westernization"; A. R. Saiyed and V. V. Saiyed, "The Mus-
        lim Family in Transition: Orthodoxy and Change in a Min-
        ority Group Family"; A. Ramanamma and Usha Bamba-
        wale, "Family Mobility and the Position of Women in the

Indian Family"; and D. Murmu, "The Tribal Family in Transition."]

58.   *Authority of the Religions and the Status of Women.* Joint Women's Programme, Bangalore, India, May 29–31, 1985. [Available at Institute for Social Studies Trust, New Delhi; selected papers from this "consultation" of the Joint Women's Programme have been published in entries 160 and 750. Papers cover Hinduism, Islam, Christianity, Sikhism, Buddhism, Jainism, and Zoroastrianism; most are at an exploratory, descriptive level. Contributors were K. V. K. Thampuran and Ranjana Kumari on Hinduism; Asghar Ali Engineer, Zeenat Ali, Shehnaz Sheikh, Mumtaz Ali Khan, Ramala Baxamusa, and Muzammil Siddiqui on Islam; Doris Franklin, Joseph Velancherry, Marian Chachox, Sheila Varghese, and Padmalaya Das on Christianity; P. S. Luthra and Surinda Suri on Sikhism; N. D. Kamalde and S. Rangaswamy on Buddhism; Chandra Keerthy and A. K. Nagaraj on Jainism; and Dastoor N. D. Minochehr-Homji and Deenaz Damania on Zoroastrianism (see also entries 159 and 750.]

59.   Ayyar, Chandrika. *Education and Intellectual Pursuits: with Special Reference to Bengal: 1817–57.* Kanpur: Prajna Publications, 1987.
[Includes a chapter on "New Education and Women," the role of missionary schools, and resistance of upper-class Hindu families to women's education.]

60.   Babb, Lawrence A. *The Divine Hierarchy: Popular Hinduism in Central India.* New York: Columbia University Press, 1975.
[A chapter entitled "The Foods of the Gods: *Puja*" includes women's fasts; another entitled "Rituals of the Life Cycle" includes childbirth and marriage rites.]

61. ————. "Amnesia and Resemblance in a Hindu Theory of History." *Asian Folklore Studies* 41/1 (1982), 49–66.
[Discusses the catastrophic theory of history motivating the contemporary Brahma Kumaris, a contemporary group headed and taught by women.]

62. ————. "Indigenous Feminism in a Modern Hindu Sect." *Signs* 9, No. 3 (Spring 1984), 399–416.
[Positing that the contemporary Brahma Kumaris (Daughters of Brahma) are feminists of a distinctively Indian variety, author Babb examines central themes of their teaching and reveals their implicit critique of their cultural context.]

63. ————. *Redemptive Encounters: Three Modern Styles in the Hindu Tradition*. Berkeley: University of California Press, 1986; Delhi: Oxford University Press, 1987.
[One third of the volume is devoted to the Brahma Kumari movement, describing its history, social context, eschatological teachings, organizational structure, central practices and ceremonies, its "otherworldly feminism," and its views concerning gender.]

For Babb, Lawrence A., see also entries 83 and 301.

64. Badhwar, Inderjit. "*Sati*: A Pagan Sacrifice." *India Today* (October 15, 1987), 58–61.
[Covers the Roop Kanwar *sati* in Rajasthan and events immediately following.]

65. ————. "Kalyan Singh Kalvi: Beliefs Cannot Be Repressed." *India Today* (October 31, 1987), 20.
[Cites excerpts from an interview with the Rajasthan Janata party leader, who supported Roop Kanwar's *sati*.]

66. ————. "Rajasthan: Militant Defiance." *India Today* (October 31, 1987), 18–20.
[Describes an illegal rally of 70,000 Rajasthanis to consecrate the *sati* Roop Kanwar as a deity.]

Bibliography

For Badhwar, Inderjit, see also entry 35.

67. Bagchi, Jasodhara. "Positivism and Nationalism; Womanhood and Crisis in Nationalist Fiction: Bankimchandra's *Anandmath.*" *Economic and Political Weekly* 20, No. 43 (October 26, 1985), WS58–WS62.
[Bengali author Bankimchandra Chatterjee inverted India's classic contrast between the feared independent temptress and the faithful, dependent, *sahadharmini* spouse in his nationalistic novel *Anandmath*. His faithful one is the ascetic Shanti, devoted to the nation, while the "domestic wife" Kalyani is the fearsome temptress.]

For Bagchi, Jasodhara, see also entry 611.

For Baig, Tara Ali, see entry 19.

68. Baird, Robert, ed. *Religion and Law in Independent India.* New Delhi: Manohar, 1993.
[Eighteen articles cover topics from the constitutional status of religion and secularism to studies of specific problems and/or groups. For topics related to this bibliography, see especially Gregory C. Kozlowski, "Muslim Personal Law and Political Identity in Independent India"; Tahir Mahmood, "Interaction of Islam and Public Law in Independent India"; Kavita R. Khory, "The Shah Bano Case: Some Political Implications"; John H. Mansfield, "The Personal Laws or a Uniform Civil Code"; Vasudha Dhagamwar, "Women, Children and the Constitution: Hostages to Religion, Outcaste by Law"; and Kay K. Jordan, *"Devadasi* Reform: Driving the Priestess or the Prostitutes Out of Hindu Temples."]

69. Bakshi, Rajni. "Shame!" *Illustrated Weekly of India* (October 4, 1987), 20–23.
[A photographic essay covers the aftermath of the Roop Kanwar *sati*—includes interviews with both *sati* supporters and protesters.]

18

70. Bakshi, S. R. *Gandhi and Status of Women*. New Delhi: Criterion, 1987.
[Consisting mostly of extracts and reprints from Gandhi's speeches, this volume classifies its contents thematically; headings are "Social Problems," "Equality," and "Roles in the Satyagraha Movement."]

71. Bal, Sharayu. "Muktabai." *Samvit* 1 (March 1980), 26–35.
[Describes the life and teachings of a distinguished thirteenth-century Marathi woman saint and member of a family of celebrated devotees. Muktabai became a guru while a teen-ager and died before she was twenty, leaving songs and sayings that are still repeated.]

72. Balambai, V. "The Role of Women in the Festivals of India." *Bulletin of the Institute of Traditional Cultures (Madras)* (July–December 1977), 109–18.
[Lists important festivals of India and women's practices in them.]

73. Balasubramaniam, C. *The Status of Women in Tamilnadu during the Sangam Age*. Madras: University of Madras, 1976.
[Analyzes Tamil *sangam* poetry to extract social information; includes citations on worship, marriage, "sports," and education.]

74. Balasubrahmanyam, Vimal. "Women, Personal Laws, and the Struggle for Secularism." *Economic and Political Weekly* 20, No. 30 (July 27, 1985), 1260–61.
[A response to the Shah Bano case calls for action by women's groups in defence of a fully secular state.]

75. Bambawale, Usha. *Inter-Religious Marriages*. Pune: Dastane Ramchandra, 1982.
[This sociological study surveys patterns of mate selection, natal family reactions and reconciliations, and marital ad-

justment among one hundred intermarried couples of Pune. One chapter, titled "Religiosity and Secularization," examines conversion patterns among respondents, religious socialization of their children, and evidence of secularization among respondents.]

For Bambawale, Usha, see also entry 57.

76.   Bandopadhyay, Sibaji, et al. *Femininity Redefined: Politics of Home and the World in Colonial Bengal*. New Delhi: Kali for Women, forthcoming.
["This edited selection of textual constructions of Bengali women in the colonial era is arranged around three recurrent patterns: the 'good' woman, the 'other' and the 'heroic' woman. . . . The compilation is designed to give an overview as well as provide a critical assessment of the multiple discourses of the patriarchal social order that have claimed to speak on behalf of women. . . . It also aims to show how power produces certain normative ideals and how those same ideals are continually questioned, subverted, and put to the test" (cited from the publisher's announcement).]

77.   Banerjee, Anindita. "'No Ordinary Girl Would Dare . . .': Challenge to the Hindu Succession Act." *Manushi* 5, No. 6 (=No. 30; September–October 1985), 37–38.
[Interviews Lata Mittal, who has challenged the Hindu succession act in India's Supreme Court. This girl was sent at adolescence to a Brahma Kumari *ashram* in Calcutta; when she returned, the family would not arrange her marriage and her brothers have refused her a share in inheritance.]

78.   Banerjee, Himadri. "Maharani Jindan in Bengali Writings." *Sikh Review* 36 (July 1988), 32–37.
[Reviews works in Bengali on the life of the most famous wife of Raja Ranjit Singh.]

79.   Barnes, Ruth, and Joanne B. Eicher, eds. *Dress and Gender:*

Making and Meaning in Cultural Contexts. Worcester: Billing and Sons, Ltd., 1992; also New York: Berg and St. Martin's Press, 1992.
[The dress of Hindu women is discussed in two essays of this collection. O. P. Joshi's "Change and Continuity in Hindu Women's Dress" surveys the dress of Hindu women historically, with discussion of the implication of purity/pollution concepts for women's clothing. Julia Leslie's "The Significance of Dress for the Orthodox Hindu Women" recounts dicta on what women should and should not wear, as stipulated by the eighteenth-century South Indian manual *Stridharmappaddhati* by Tryambaka. The latter article includes a section on the *tilak* (forehead mark).]

80.   Bartholomeusz, Tessa J. *Women under the Bo Tree.* Ph.D. diss., University of Virginia, 1991.
[Studies Buddhist nuns in Sri Lanka, including both *bhikkuni*s of the past and the present lay renunciants. Reviews the transmission of the nuns' order from India to Sri Lanka. Described *DAI* 52, No. 12 (June 1992), 4358–59.]

81.   ———. *Women under the Bo Tree: Buddhist Nuns in Sri Lanka.* New York: Cambridge University Press, 1994.
[A published version of the author's dissertation. See above, entry 80.]

For Bartholomeusz, Tessa J., see also entry 128.

82.   Barton, Rachel. *The Scarlet Thread: An Indian Woman Speaks.* London: Virago Press, 1987.
[An English teacher and mentor records the life-story of a poor woman sent from India to England to marry. After years of abuse from her husband, she was rescued by her mother. Includes materials on a sister's marriage, a Radha Soami initiation, and the subject's overall experience of religion.]

83.   Basu, Amrita. "Studies in Power and Powerlessness: Women in Contemporary India." *Recent Work in Women's History: East and West.* Ed. Esther Katz. New York: Haworth Press, 1986.
[Describes two antithetical trends in historical studies on Indian women—which are unfortunately mostly Western: the first attempts to locate "positive sources of women's emancipation within the existing social context"—such as concepts of power like *shakti*; the second attacks all existing hierarchical rationales. Includes a brief discussion on Babb's theory of "indigenous feminism" in the Brahma Kumaris as an example under the first category.]

84.   Basu, Aparna, ed. *The Path Finder: Dr. Muthulakshmi Reddy.* New Delhi: All India Women's Conference, 1987.
[No further information available at time of publication.]

85.   ———. "The Reformed Family, Women Reformers: A Case Study of Vidyagauri Nilkanth." *Samya Shakti: A Journal of Women's Studies* 4–5 (1989–90), 62–82.
[Studies four generations of women in a liberated and liberating Gujarati Prarthana Samaj family. Shows how education and public activity of women introduced changes both into the home and the greater society.]

86.   ———. "Women's History in India: A Historiographical Survey." *Writing Women's History: International Perspectives.* Bloomington: Indiana University Press, 1991.
[Surveys work on women's history by both Indian and foreign scholars; included here for its comments concerning the impact of Hindu nationalism on portrayals of women's ancient history, for descriptions of Uma Chakravarti's work on Buddhism and on mythological models, for its summary of the reform movements and their histories, and for reports on studies concerning Pandita Ramabai and concerning Muslim women.]

For Basu, Aparna, see also entry 149.

87.   Basu, Aparna, and Bharati Ray. *Women's Struggle: A History of the All India Women's Conference, 1927–90.* New Delhi: Manohar, 1990.
[The Women's Conference, not itself "religious" in intent, is important to this listing nonetheless for its work to impose legal curbs on abusive practices supported by conservative communities.]

88.   Basu, Krishna. "Movement for Emancipation of Women in the Nineteenth Century." *Role and Status of Women in Indian Society.* Calcutta: Firma KLM, 1978.
[This convenient overview of the reform movements' leadership and social context covers both secular and religious aspects.]

89.   Basu, Rajshekar. "By the Grace of Shasthi." *Manushi* No. 58 (May–June 1990), 39–42.
[A short story translated from Bengali recounts how an overbearing husband is undone with the help of a Hindu goddess.]

90.   Basu, Rumki. "Divorce in India: Position in Law." *Mainstream* 23, No. 27 (2 March 1985), 33–34.
[This article and its sequel (see entry 91 below) preceded a 1985 *Mainstream* series that debated the Supreme Court decision in the Shah Bano case (on the right to maintenance of Muslim women divorcees). The full series includes articles by Tara Ali Baig (May 18), Asghar Ali Engineer (May 25 and August 3), Syed Shahabuddin (June 1 and July 13), Vasudha Dhagamwar (July 6), Nusrat Bano Ruhi (July 20), and Sakina Hyder (August 24).]

91.   ———. "Divorce in India: Reforms and Remedies." *Mainstream* 23, Nos. 28–29 (9 March 1985), 52–53.
[See comment in entry 90 above.]

92.   Baxamusa, Ramala M. "A Historic Perspective on Muslim

Personal Law in India." Bombay: Research Centre for Women's Studies, SNDT Women's University, 1984.
[Duplicated typescript: copies available through the SNDT Women's University Research Centre for Women's Studies. Describes differences in approach to personal law among schools of Muslim law in India; also documents changes in governmental approaches to personal law, especially under the British.]

93. ————. "Muslim Women of Bombay." Bombay: Research Centre for Women's Studies, SNDT Women's University, 1984.
[Duplicated typescript; copies available through the SNDT Women's University Research Centre for Women's Studies. Documents differences in the status of women among five Muslim subgroups and shows how status varies according to the group's socio-economic position.]

94. ————. "Need for Change in Muslim Divorce Personal Law in India." Bombay: Research Centre for Women's Studies, SNDT Women's University, n.d.
[Duplicated typescript; copies available through the SNDT Women's University Research Centre for Women's Studies. Charges that Muslim law governing divorce in India today was corrupted during the British regime and is now both anti-Islamic and anti-female. Discusses various divorce procedures, their Indian variations, and alternative interpretations in other Muslim countries.]

For Baxamusa, Ramala, see also entries 58, 159, 811.

95. Bean, Susan S. "Referential and Indexical Meanings of *amma* in Kannada: Mother, Woman, Goddess, Pox, and Help!" *Journal of Anthropological Research* 31, No. 4 (Winter 1975), 313–30.
[This semantic study draws upon cultural beliefs about women and goddesses to explain how *amma* acquires all the meanings cited.]

96. Bedi, Kultaran Singh, and Rajinder Singh Bedi. *Hindu Marriage and Divorce*. Ambala Cantonment: Lawyers' Publications, 1983.
[Scrutinizes the Hindu Marriage Act of 1955 and its test cases. Includes as topics guardianship in marriage, ceremonies, bigamy, divorce, remarriage, and legitimacy of children.]

97. Behal, Monisha. "Within and Outside the Courtyard: Glimpses into Women's Perceptions." *Economic and Political Weekly* 19, No. 41 (October 13, 1984), 1775–77.
[Reports on *purdah* observance in Karimpur village, Uttar Pradesh; also includes some reference to ritual practice.]

98. Bennett, Lynn. *Mother's Milk and Mother's Blood: The Social and Symbolic Roles of Women among the Brahmans and Chetris of Nepal*. Ph.D. diss., Columbia University, 1977.
[Attempts to show "how women's *social* roles in Hindu kinship and family structure are related to their *symbolic* roles in the ritual and mythic structure of Hinduism." Cited from author's description, *DAI* 38, No. 5 (November 1977), A-2879.]

99. ————. *Dangerous Wives and Sacred Sisters: Social and Symbolic Roles of High-Caste Women in Nepal*. New York: Columbia University Press, 1983.
["Deals with the familiar paradoxical phenomenon of women who are revered as goddess, but powerless as mortals"; incorporates extensive treatment of symbolism, myth, and ritual. The women are Nepali Brahmins and Chetris; rituals described are life-cycle rites and *vratas* (Nepali *barta*); the goddess celebrated is the ubiquitous Devi, in several of her terrible and benign forms. Sexuality and purity are central issues. Unique features are the description of precautions for maintaining kitchen purity, and differences in the form of the goddess honored by women and by men.]

100.   Bhaduri, Chira Kisore. "Widow Marriage in Vedic India."
        Proceedings of the Indian History Congress. Annamalain-
        agar: Annamalai University, 1984, pp. 229–36.
        [Critically reexamines Vedic texts often cited as evidence
        that widows remarried in ancient times; the author con-
        cludes that such interpretations are false.]

101.   Bhai, Nirmala. *Harijan Women in Independent India.* Delhi:
        B. R. Publishing Corporation, 1986.
        [This report from a sociological survey of untouchable
        women of Kerala includes data about pollution restrictions
        observed and performance of religious rituals; however,
        these are quite peripheral to the whole.]

102.   Bhaiji. *Mother as Revealed to Me.* Trans. G. Das Gupta.
        Calcutta: Shree Shree Anandamayee Charitable Society,
        1983.
        [This disciple's tale of the wonders of Anandamayi Ma and
        his own reverence for her brought fame to a modern woman
        saint and guru.]

103.   Bhalla, D. S. "Bhai Takhat Singh: A Pioneer of Women's
        Education." *Sikh Review* 31 (December 1983), 51–56.
        [Describes the life and work of an important Sikh reformer
        who launched a girls' school in Ferozepur with the aid of
        his first and second wives.]

104.   Bharany, Chhote. *Salvation Prison: A Novel.* New Delhi:
        Sterling Publishers, 1992.
        [A rejected wife becomes a guru preaching the virtues of fe-
        male celibacy to take revenge on all the husbands of the
        world. The new guru's neighbor, once a classically devoted
        wife, takes the bait, and her eager pursuit of salvation "im-
        prisons" her once-loving husband. The sad result is a spiral
        of tragedy for both partners, with much condemnation of
        gurus, *ashram*s, and the ideal of renunciation along the
        way.]

105. Bhat, G. K. "'Mother' in Vedic Literature (*Brahmanas* and *Aranyakas*)," *Annals of the Bhandarkar Oriental Research Institute* 68 (1987), 471–89.
[Surveys images of "the mother"—including metaphors—in India's ancient priestly literature.]

106. Bhatnagar, J. P. *Commentaries on the Muslim Women (Protection of Rights on Divorce) Act, 1986 (Act No. 25 of 1986)*. Allahabad: Ashoka Law House, 1987.
[Includes the text of the act itself—a response to the Shah Bano uproar—and explores questions raised by the act. Very technical; not for beginners.]

107. Bhatnagar, Manju. "The Fun and Frolic of Holi Songs: A Note of the Festival in Areas Associated with Lord Krishna." *Folklore* 28 (June 1987), 139–41.
[The "areas" in question are the Braj region of Uttar Pradesh; the author cites themes of Holi songs sung by women.]

108. Bhattacarya, Aparna. "Glimpses of the Views of Bengali Women on the Women's Problem in the 19th century." *Proceedings of the Indian History Congress*. Bambolin: Goa University, 1988, pp. 372–76.
[Covers periodicals and other sources to which women contributed; interesting quotations from women's letters to editors address *stridhan*, widow marriage, and *kulin* marriages.]

109. Bhattacarya, Bholanath. "An Assessment of the *Kumari Brata* of Bengal: A Field of Apprenticeship for Domestic Art." *Folklore* 24, No. 1 (January 1983), 1–6.
[Rites performed by young girls that entail extensive ritual drawing and modeling develop a high level of artistic skill. Includes a description of works created for the cycle of rituals.]

110. Bhattacharjee, K. S. "Thoughts of a Nineteenth-Century Radical of Bengal: Iswarachandra Vidyasagar (1820–1891)," *The Indian Political Science Review* 18, No. 2 (July 1984), 204–22.
[Describes the life and thoughts of a brilliant Brahmin and Sanskrit scholar who became a forceful opponent of child marriage and proponent of widow remarriage; ends with a detailed rebuttal of Vidyasagar's critics.]

111. Bhattacharya, France. "Food Rituals in the *Chandi Mangala*." *Indian International Centre Quarterly* 12 (1985), 169–92.
[Concentrates more on the preparation and signification of foods than on ritual, but note its discussion of the longings of a pregnant woman, and of the meal prepared to welcome a newly returned husband.]

112. Bhattacharya, Vivek. *Famous Indian Sages, Their Immortal Messages*. New Delhi: Sagar Publications, 1982.
[Includes just one woman, the Kashmiri Lalleshwari. This volume was intended to be the first of three on the subject, but the second and third are as yet unavailable.]

113. Bhattacharyya, Minoti. "Hindu Religion and Women's Rights." *Religion and Society* 35, No. 1 (March 1988), 52–61.
[Tracks the legal status of women from the *Rg Veda* through *dharmashastra*, arguing that women's status degenerated during the timespan covered. Includes a section on the origins of child marriage.]

For Bhattacharyya, Minoti, see also entry 920.

114. Bhattacharyya, Narendra Nath. *The Indian Mother Goddess*. 2nd rev. ed. Columbia, Mo.: South Asia Books, 1977; 1st ed. 1970.
[Included for its discussion on women's kingdoms in India,

matrilineal descent, matrilocal marriage practice, and the female principle in rituals, especially Tantric rites.]

115. ———. *Indian Puberty Rites*. 2nd ed. New Delhi: Munshiram Manorharlal Publishers, 1980.
[Includes chapters on the significance of menstrual blood, menstrual rites, ceremonial defloration, and tribal rites.]

116. Bhatty, Zarina. "Muslim Women in Uttar Pradesh: Social Mobility and Directions of Change." *Social Action* 25 (October–December 1975), 365–74.
[Compares the lifestyles and patterns of marriage, education, and work among upper-class and lower-class Muslim women; from a study done in a village near Lucknow.]

For Bhatty, Zarina, see also entries 149, 227, 258, 354, 635, and 920.

117. Bhave, Sumitra. *Pan on Fire: Eight Dalit Women Tell Their Story*. New Delhi: Indian Social Institute, 1988.
[The informants are Maharashtrian women, and several are Buddhists; their accounts include scattered but valuable information on practice in informants' families, on visits to temples, and on observance of festivals.]

118. Bilgrami, Rafat. "Property Rights of Muslim Women in Mughal India." *Proceedings of the Indian History Congress*. Bambolin: Goa University, 1988, pp. 261–70.
[Investigates middle class women's right to land in sixteenth- to nineteenth-century Awadh. Women did have some land rights through inheritance, but only rarely purchased land. Moreover, women could manage and dispose of properties, but not when those properties were held in common with males.]

119. Blanchet, Thérèse. *Meanings and Rituals of Birth in Rural Bangladesh: Women, Pollution, and Marginality*. Dhaka: University Press Limited, 1984.

[Based in a Muslim village of northern Bangladesh, this study covers concepts of pollution, rites of purification, rites of first menstruation, beliefs in *bhut*, practices at birth, rites following birth, beliefs about placentas and mother's milk, the role and status of the midwife, and much more. Occasionally compares Muslim and Hindu practice.]

120. Boonsue, Kornvipa. *Buddhism and Gender Bias: An Analysis of a Jataka Tale*. Bangkok: WIDCIT, 1989.
[The tale analyzed is the long and influential *Vessantara Jataka*. Recognizing that the story serves as a significant Buddhist model, this work analyzes its significations for women, via the character of Maddi, the king-hero's long-suffering wife. Discusses woman as matter, as a being with cravings, as an object possessed, and as a faithful follower of authoritative males.]

121. Borthwick, Meredith Ann. *Shadow or Substance: The Changing Role of Women in Bengal 1849–1905*. Ph.D. diss., Australian National University, 1980.
[Could not examine; assumed to be prototype for *The Changing Role of Women in Bengal* (entry 122 below).]

122. ————. *The Changing Role of Women in Bengal, 1849–1905*. Princeton: Princeton University Press, 1984.
[Examines the new ideal of womanhood that emerged among women of the Bengali English-educated professional classes during the late nineteenth century; materials are gathered from Bengali journals written "by women or about them." Shows the impact of Brahmo Samaj teachings.]

123. Bradford, Nicholas J. "Transgenderism and the Cult of Yellama: Heat, Sex, and Sickness in South Indian Ritual." *Journal of Anthropological Research* 39, No. 3 (Fall 1983), 307–22.
[This study of Yellama devotees distinguishes itself by taking up roles of both men and women, and among the latter,

both "hot" women—*devadasis*—and "cool" women, the *yogammas*, or ascetics.]

124. Braxton, Bernard. *Sex and Religion in Oppression: A View on the Sexual Exploitation of Women under Paganism, Hinduism, Mohammedianism* [sic] *and Christianity*. Washington: Verta Press, 1978.
[Mostly concerns women in Western traditions; eight superficial and scattershot pages address Hindu beliefs and practice, under the general heading "Religious Oppressors of Women."]

125. Brijbhushan, Jamila [OCLC lists as Brij Bhushan]. *Kamaladevi Chattopadhyay: A Portrait of a Rebel*. New Delhi: Abhinav Publications, 1976.
[The biography of a famed Gandhian freedom fighter, by a writer who knew her for twenty years; with extensive quotes from her writings.]

126. ———. *Muslim Women, in* Purdah *and* Out of It. New Delhi: Vikas Publishing House, 1980.
[Descriptive; based on interviews of women in the Delhi area. Includes materials on everyday activities of women in *purdah*, as well as perceptions of marriage, polygamy, divorce, inheritance, adoption, and education.]

127. Bynum, Carolyn Walker, ed. *Gender and Religion: On the Complexity of Symbols*. Boston: Beacon Press, 1986.
[Two of the eleven essays assembled in this volume are based on Indian materials. Paula Sue Richman's "The Portrayal of a Renouncer in a Tamil Buddhist text" examines representations of the nun-heroine of the epic *Manimekalai*. John Stratton Hawley's "Images of Gender in the Poetry of Krishna" analyzes constructions of the *gopi* image and of *yoga* in poems of Mirabai and Sur Das, attempting to discover how the poets' genders have affected their imagery.]

128. Cabezon, Jose Ignacio, ed. *Buddhism, Sexuality, and Gender*. Albany: State University of New York Press, 1992. [Four of ten articles in this volume address roles or portrayals of women in South Asian contexts: Alan Sponberg, "Attitudes toward Women and the Feminine in Early Buddhism"; Tessa Bartholomeusz, "The Female Mendicant in Buddhist Sri Lanka"; Eleanor Zelliot, "Buddhist Women of the Contemporary Maharashtrian Conversion Movement"; and Paula Richman, "Gender and Persuasion: The Portrayal of Beauty, Anguish, and Nurturance in an Account of a Tamil Nun." A fifth, based largely on Tibetan materials, is more concerned with symbolic uses of gender: Jose Cabezon's "Mother Wisdom, Father Love: Gender-Based Imagery in Mahayana Buddhist Thought."]

129. Cabral e Sa, Mario. "The Evolution of a Community—*Devadasis* of Goa." *Manushi* No. 56 (January–February 1990), 25–27. [A community of former "slaves to God" has produced a number of illustrious offspring.]

130. Carmody, Denise Lardner. *Women and World Religions*. 2nd ed. Englewood Cliffs, N.J.: Prentice Hall, 1989. [This text designed for beginning college students contains chapters on Hindu and Buddhist women; a segment of the chapter on Islamic women treats women of Morocco and India.]

131. Carroll, Lucy. "*Talaq-i-Tafwid* and Stipulations in a Muslim Marriage Contract: Important Means of Protecting the Position of the South Asian Muslim Wife." *Modern Asian Studies* 16, No. 2 (April 1982), 277–309. [Describes how the power of the marriage contract can be used to strengthen marital options of Muslim women; includes a discussion of cases.]

132. ————. "Law, Custom and Statutory Social Reform: The

Hindu Widow's Remarriage Act of 1856." *Indian Economic and Social History Review* 20, No. 4 (October–December 1983), 363–88.
[Includes a good description of test cases following the 1856 Act; points out, however, that this act has been superceded by the Hindu Code. This article appears to be identical with one published in J. Krishnamurty's *Women in Colonial Society*; see entry 506.]

133.   ————. "Daughter's Right of Inheritance in India: A Perspective on the Problem of Dowry." *Modern Asian Studies* 25 (October 1991), 791–809.
["The problem of dowry should be seen in the context of other property rights of the daughter, and criticism and condemnation of the dowry system should be coupled with an advocacy of reform of the daughter's rights as an heir to the property of her natal family." Analyzes the immensely complex system of claims to joint property under both the Mitakshara and Dayabhaga systems of Hindu law and proposes reforms that would ameliorate a daughter's position.]

For Carroll, Theodora Foster, see Foster, Theodora Carroll.

134.   Carstairs, G. Morris. *Death of a Witch: A Village in North India 1950–1981.* London: Hutchinson, 1983.
[In 1951, in a Rajasthani village, an old widow accused of being a witch was brutally beaten to death. Anthropologist Carstairs, investigating this incident, discovered at its root a dispute over inheritance and many village fears and resentments readily transformed into witchcraft beliefs. His study also includes some materials on female ghosts, women's worship of Sitala-Mata, their peripheral role in men's *kirtan*s, and the *dharma-bai* ceremony by which two village women became his honorary sisters.]

135.   Chaki-Sircar, Manjusri. *Lai Harouba: The Social Position*

and Ritual Status of Meitei Women of Manipur, India.
Ph.D. diss., Columbia University, 1980.
["Analyzes women's roles in the ritual and non-ritual
spheres of Meitei society. . . . *Lai Harouba*, a principal ritual of the indigenous pre-Hindu faith . . . serves as a major
ethnographic focus." Cited from author's description, *DAI*
41, No. 4 (October 1980), A-1668. Could not examine; assumed to be prototype for *Feminism in a Traditional Society* (entry 136 below).]

136.   ————. *Feminism in a Traditional Society: Women of the
Manipur Valley.* New Delhi: Shakti Books, 1984.
[Meitei women are the subjects of this monograph, which
includes a chapter on the religious context and a long and
rich description of women's roles in the focal ritual called
Lai Harouba.]

For Chaki-Sircar, Manjusri, see also entry 766.

137.   Chakrabarty, Ramakanta. *Vaishnivism in Bengal 1486–
1900.* Calcutta: Sanskrit Pustak Bhandar, 1985.
[This abridgement of the author's Calcutta University dissertation principally describes male leaders and Vaishnava
sects, but includes material on the woman leader Janhava
Devi.]

138.   Chakraborty, Jyotirmoy. "Some Traditional Folk-Art of
Rajasthan." *Folklore* 21 (June 1980), 145–46.
[Surveys types of folk art; some are drawings and paintings
created by women for ritual purposes.]

139.   Chakravarti, Uma. "The Rise of Buddhism as Experienced
by Women." *Manushi* No. 8 (1981), 6–10.
[Describes the experience of housewives, courtesans, and
nuns within Buddhism's patriarchal context.]

140.   ————. "The Myth of the Golden Age of Equality—Women

Slaves in Ancient India." *Manushi* 3, No. 6 (=No. 18; October–November 1983), 8–12, 15.
[Counters the tendency of Indian history-writing to examine only the household roles of upper-class women by tracking references to women slaves. Significant here is the author's discovery of brahmin priests' association with large numbers of women slaves.]

141. ———. "Women in Myth and Literature; A Case Study of the Development of the Sita Myth." *Women's Status and Development in India*. Ed. K. Murali Manohar. Warangal: Society for Women's Studies and Development, 1984.
[By tracking ancient versions of the Rama legend, author Chakravarti shows how the concept of Sita as model of wifely chastity and devotion was grafted onto an originally much simpler story.]

142. ———. "Of *Dasas* and *Karmakaras*: Servile Labour in Ancient India." *Chains of Servitude: Bondage and Slavery in India*. Ed. Utsa Patnaik and Manjari Dingwaney. London: Sangam Books, 1985.
[Very similar to "The Myth of the Golden Age of Equality" (entry 140 above), but treats both male and female slaves.]

143. ———. *"Pativrata."* *Seminar* 318 (February 1986), 17–21.
[Argues that a *"purdah* culture" has existed in India for a very long time; *purdah* is defined as separation between the domains of men and women. Deconstructs popular views of Indian women's glorious past: from the Vedas through Gargi, the Buddhists, and the Sita ideal.]

144. ———. "Beyond the Altekarian Paradigm: Towards a New Understanding of Gender Relations in Early Indian History." *Social Scientist* 16, No. 8 (August 1988), 44–52.
[The political and social preoccupations of nineteenth-century reformers have shaped present Indians' view of their past—especially their view of the history of women. Points

to the work of A. S. Altekar, which still dominates historical writing about women today.]

For Chakravarti, Uma, see also entries 86, 727, 789, 790, and 1002.

145.   Chakravarti, Uma, and Nandita Haksar. *The Delhi Riots: Three Days in the Life of a Nation*. New Delhi: Lander International, 1987.
[Records thirty-one interviews conducted among victims, observers, and relief workers concerning the anti-Sikh riots in Delhi that followed Indira Gandhi's assassination. Ten of those interviewed were Sikh women; seven other interviewees were from various communities, including the Arya Samaj. One interview recounts the fruitless efforts of a Shaiva *sannyasini* to intercede for Sikh victims.]

146.   Chakravarti, Uma, and Kumkum Roy. "In Search of Our Past: A Review of the Limitations and Possibilities of the Historiography of Women in Early India." *Economic and Political Weekly* 23, No. 18 (April 30, 1988), WS2–WS10.
[A critique of the "Altekarian paradigm" and demonstration of its continuing impact on writings about women in Indian history. Calls for a new kind of analysis "which takes into account sexuality, social reproduction and production and their relationship." Included here largely because of the methodological cautions entailed for all students of women's roles in the Indian past.]

147.   Chakravartty, Gargi. "State of Muslim Female Education." *Mainstream* 23, No. 20 (12 January 1985), 26.
[Argues that Muslim girls are handicapped by the practice of enrolling them in Urdu-medium schools, for good Urdu texts are scarce, especially in the sciences.]

For Chakravartty, Gargi, see also entry 825.

148. Chakravarty, Basudha. *Sister Nivedita*. New Delhi: National Book Trust, 1975.
[This short popular biography of the famous Irishwoman turned *sannyasini* is principally interested in the portion of Nivedita's life that follows her encounter with Swami Vivekananda. The final chapter assesses Nivedita's impact.]

149. Chanana, Karuna, ed. *Socialisation, Education, and Women: Explorations in Gender Identity*. New Delhi: Orient Longman, 1988.
[Six of these fine papers from a 1985 symposium have some bearing on religion. Three on the history of education incorporate materials on the role of missions schools and/or Hindu constructions of women's education: Aparna Basu, "A Century's Journey: Women's Education in Western India"; Karuna Chanana: "Social Change or Social Reform: The Education of Women in Pre-Independence India"; and Malavika Karlekar, "Women's Nature and the Access to Education." Two discuss indoctrination of girls via rite and informal instruction: Leela Dube, "Socialization of Hindu Girls in Patrilineal India"; and Veena Das, "Femininity and the Orientation to the Body." Zarina Bhatty's "Socialization of the Muslim Child in Uttar Pradesh" treats inculcation of Muslim values; Meenakshi Mukherjee's "The Unperceived Self: A Study of Nineteenth-Century Autobiographies" adds some materials on Hindu women's religious experience and training.]

For Chanana, Karuna, see also entry 508, as well as Ahmad, Karuna and Ahmad, Karuna Chanana.

150. Chandola, Sudha. "Some Goddess Rituals in Non-Narrative Folk Song of India." *Asian Folklore Studies* 36, No. 1 (1977), 57–68.
[Significant for its attention to the ritual context in which goddess songs are sung, and to women's roles in the goddess rites.]

37

151.   Chandra, Sudhir. "Conflicted Beliefs and Men's Conscious-
        ness about Women: Widow Marriage in Later Nineteenth-
        Century Indian Literature." *Economic and Political Weekly*
        22, No. 44 (October 31, 1987), WS55–WS62.
        [Analyzes portrayals of the widow's predicament in novels
        by Bankimchandra Chatterjee and Govardhanram Madhav-
        ram Tripathi, showing how the dharmic ideal of the wife
        faithful beyond death left the concept of a happy widow
        marriage unthinkable for the two authors.]

152.   Chatterjee, B. "A Century of Social Reform for Women's
        Status." *The Indian Journal of Social Work* 41, No. 3 (Octo-
        ber 1980), 241–53.
        [Briefly surveys the history of nineteenth-century social re-
        form movements regarding female infanticide, abolition of
        sati, child marriages and enforced widowhood, and the over-
        all role of women. Cites religious precedents and the role of
        religious reform groups.]

153.   Chatterjee, Chachal Kumar. *Studies in the Rites and Ritu-
        als of Hindu Marriage in Ancient India.* Calcutta: Sanskrit
        Pustak Bhandar, 1978.
        [Based on the *Rg Veda*, on *dharmasastra*, and on shastric
        commentaries and digests, this study covers the concept of
        samskara and forms of marriage; it also furnishes a de-
        tailed description of marriage rites.]

154.   Chatterjee, Indrani. "The Bengali *Bhadramahila*: Forms of
        Organization in the Early Twentieth Century." *Manushi*
        No. 45 (March–April, 1988), 26–36.
        [Describes early women's organizations in Bengal, referring
        to the role of religion and participation by orthodox women.]

155.   Chatterjee, Partha. "Colonialism, Nationalism, and Coloni-
        alized Women: The Contest in India." *American Ethnologist*
        16, No. 4 (November 1989), 622–33.
        [Argues that Indian reformers responded to colonialism by

dividing their world into spiritual and material domains and permitting change in the material, while seeking to conserve their integrity via the spiritual; women were appointed custodians of the latter.]

For Chatterjee, Partha, see also entry 790.

156.   Chatterji, Jyotsna, ed. *Good News for Women*. Delhi: The Indian Society for Promoting Christian Knowledge, 1979.
[This series of Bible studies was created by women and intended for church women's groups in India. Study topics range from "The Position of Women in Biblical Times," to "Women in Ministry," to "Women and Men in the Image of God," to "Sisterhood with the Oppressed Persons." Contributors are Vimla Arengaden, Vimla Paulos, Sr. Celestine R.S.J.T., Alley Matthew, Leelamma Atyal, Corrine Scott, Mary Kness Kirkwood, Jasso Bose, Ellen Webster, Eunice Ancheas, and Jyotsna Chatterji.]

157.   ————, ed. *Women in Praise and Struggle*. Delhi: The Indian Society for Promoting Christian Knowledge, 1982.
[Another series of Bible studies created for women by women. Ranges from an examination of two important Biblical mothers (Hannah and Mary) and a woman prophet (Huldah) to "Women as Instruments of Transformation" and "Participation in Nation-Building." Contributors are Moala Peters, Usha Francis, Mrs. E. V. Mathew, Lakshmi Gonsalves, Saroj Sangha, V. B. Subbama, Vimala Arangaden, Miriam Chacko, and Jyotsna Chatterji.]

158.   ————, ed. *Changes in Christian Personal Laws*. Delhi: The Indian Society for Promoting Christian Knowledge, 1984.
[Calls for reforms in Christian marriage, divorce, inheritance, and maintenance laws.]

159.   ————, ed. *The Authority of the Religions and the Status*

of Women. New Delhi: Uppal Publishing House, for
WCSRC-CISRS Joint Women's Study Programme and the
William Carey Study and Research Centre, 1989; repub-
lished 1990 as *Religions and the Status of Women.*
[A collection of fourteen articles surveys the status of wom-
en in Hinduism, Islam, Christianity, Jainism, Sikhism,
Buddhism, and Zoroastrianism. Contributors are Ranjana
Kumari, K. V. K. Thampuran, Asghar Ali Engineer, Mu-
zammil Siddiqui, Mumtaz Ali Khan, Ramala M. Baxamusa,
Joseph Velacherry, Doris Franklin, A. R. Nagaraj, Chandra
Keerthi, P. S. Luthra, Surinder Suri, S. Rangaswamy, N. D.
Kamble, and Deenaz Damania. Selections are papers from
the 1985 Bangalore consultation on *Authority of the Relig-
ions and the Status of Women* (see also entries 58 and 750).]

For Chatterji, Jyotsna, see also entry 750.

160.   Chattopadhayay, Kamaladevi [OCLC lists as Chattopad-
hyaya]. *Indian Women's Battle for Freedom.* New Delhi:
Abhinav Publications, 1983.
[This history of Indian women's long struggle for social reform and political rights begins with a review of women's
heritage from the time of the Veda through the rise of Buddhism, Jainism, tantrism, the Hindu devotional traditions
(including the Lingayats and Sikhism), Islam, and Christianity. A second section covers nineteenth- and early
twentieth-century reform movements, including the anti-
sati campaign, the Brahmo Samaj, the Arya Samaj, and the
movements for widow remarriage, marriage reform, and
women's education, as well as reform in more secular areas.
The final section addresses issues of the later twentieth
century, including the child marriage campaign, the problem of inheritance for women, the predicament of Nam-
boodri brahmin daughters, and the multiplicity of personal
laws. A good introduction to women's issues, although by
now slightly outdated.]

161.   ————. *Inner Recesses, Outer Spaces: Memoirs*. New Delhi: Navrang, 1986.
[Recounts the autobiography of a towering personality who became successively a Gandhian crusader, social reformer, and patroness of handicrafts and theater. It has been called a "biography of the times," with Kamaladevi herself "more of a narrator than an actor"; Kamaladevi met many of the great religious reformers of her time, including Annie Besant and Aurobindo Ghose.]

For Chattopadhayay, Kamaladevi, see also entries 192 and 401.

162.   Chattopadhyay, Umanarayan. *Epic Anandamayee*. Kankhal, Haridwar, U.P.: Uma Chatterjee and N. K. Chatterjee, 1987.
[This slender book consists entirely of a poem celebrating the life of modern saint and guru Anandamayi Ma; it was written in commemoration of Anandamayi Ma's death.]

163.   Chaturvedi, Archana. "Muslim Women—A Political Profile." *Women's Oppression: Patterns and Perspectives*. Ed. Susheela Kaushik. New Delhi: Vikas Publishing House, 1985.
[Interviews with eleven Muslim women from a conservative community show that the subjects are more interested in political affairs and more open to change than is conventionally expected.]

164.   Chaudhary, Pratima Karuna. *Changing Values among Young Women*. Delhi: Amar Prakashan, 1988.
[Reports the results of surveys in a social-scientific mode; includes attitudes on family, marriage, dowry, divorce, and education of women.]

165.   Chaudhuri, A. B. *Witch-Killings amongst Santals*. New Delhi: Ashish Publishing House, 1984.
[The witches referred to are women. Discusses the socio-

religious context, divination of witchcraft, the concept of *fuskin* (witch), extraction of confessions, and reasons why only women are witches.]

166.   Chaudhuri, Maitrayee. *Indian Women's Movement: Reform and Revival*. Delhi: Radiant Publishers, 1993.
[This history of the women's movement in modern India extends from the nineteenth-century reform movements in Bengal, Bombay, and Madras through turn-of-the-century tension between reform and revival through the rise of women's organizations during the early twentieth century to the communalization of women's issues during the decade between 1927 and 1937. Covers both Muslim and Hindu movements and organizations.]

167.   Chaudhuri, Sushil. "*Sati* as Social Institution and the Mughals." *Proceedings of the Indian History Congress*. Calicut, 1976, pp. 218–22.
[Argues that Mughals held *sati* in disfavor but were cautious in opposing it and avoided the use of force to overcome it. Only Aurangzeb and Humayun took steps toward abolishing *sati*, and Humayun's modest effort was later itself abolished.]

168.   Chaudhury, Rafiqul Huda [OCLC lists as Chowdhury], and Nilufer Raihan Ahmed. *Female Status in Bangladesh*. Dacca: Bangladesh Institute of Development Studies, 1980.
[A chapter on religion and law includes a section on personal laws and changes brought about by the Muslim Family Laws ordinance of 1961.]

For Chaudhury, Rafiqul Huda, see also entry 651.

169.   Chawdhri, L. R. *Women and Astrology (Based on Hindu Predictive Astrology)*. New Delhi: Sagar Publications, 1987.
[Asserts the existence of mystical connections between women, the constellations, and the moon, and offers ensu-

ing advice about education, professions, pleasing husbands, avoiding divorce, widowhood, and poverty, acquiring children, and enjoying a satisfying sex life.]

170. Chawla, Janet. "The Rig Vedic Slaying of Vrtra: Menstruation Taboos in Mythology." *Manushi* No. 68 (April 1992), 29–31.
[Points to contradictions in the Hindu system of envisioning women's bodies and links them to an ancient myth and historical process.]

171. ————. *Child-Bearing and Culture: Women Centered Revisioning of the Traditional Midwife: The* Dai *as a Ritual Practitioner.* New Delhi: Indian Social Institute, 1994.
[Reexamines a number of traditional beliefs and practices surrounding childbirth in India, such as beliefs about pollution, female demons, the role of the *dai*, or traditional midwife, the rituals of childbirth, and celebrations following birth. The author blames Brahmanic discourse for the denigration of childbirth and other female bodily processes in India and points to the psychological value of non-Sanskritic childbirth rites currently being discarded.]

172. Chellappan, K. and Rani Rama Devi. "Individuation of Rights: A Comparative Study of Antigone, Draupadi and Kannaki." *Journal of Asian Studies* 3, No. 1 (March 1982), 13–30.
[Perceives these three heroic women as "individuals trying to wrest their lives from a personalized state." Without hope of securing justice, they must call up their spiritual reserves.]

173. Chetananda, Swami. "Gauri-Ma." *Prabuddha Bharata* 90 (September 1985), 393–98, also (October 1985), 424–29.
[Recounts the life of a woman disciple of Ramakrishna. Gauri-Ma refused to marry and ran away with wandering monks and nuns; she eventually took Ramakrishna as her

guru, but remained "a wanderer by nature." The article describes her family's efforts to bring her home, and her wanderings after Ramakrishna's death. In 1894, Gauri-Ma founded the Sri Sri Saradeshwari Ashrama for Women, an organization still in existence.]

174.   ————. "Lakshmi Devi." *Prabuddha Bharata* 91 (July 1986), 308–19.
[Ramakrishna's niece Lakshmi Devi was married at eleven and abandoned by her husband a few months later. She moved to Dakshineshwar, following Ramakrishna, and later became a noted religious teacher. Some information about Ramakrishna's mother is also included.]

175.   ————. "Yogin-Ma." *Prabuddha Bharata* 93 (September 1988), 347–54.
[The subject married a wealthy husband at age seven. Discovering he was a libertine and alcoholic, she left him and returned to her parents. She became a follower of Ramakrishna, a frequent visitor to Dakshineshwar, and a friend of Sarada Devi. After widowhood, she went to Dakshineshwar, and then to Vrindavan. Although she eventually took a secret *sannyasini* initiation, she kept the outward signs of a householder.]

176.   ————. *They Lived with God: Life Stories of Some Devotees of Sri Ramakrishna*. St. Louis: Vedanta Society of St. Louis, 1989.
[Short biographies of twenty-eight disciples of Ramakrishna include portrayals of Rani Rasmani, Lakshmi Devi, Yogin-Ma (Yogindra Mohini Biswas), Gauri-Ma, Gopaler-Ma (Aghoremani Devi), and Golap-Ma (Golap Sundrai Devi). Photographs or paintings of each subject are included.]

177.   Chetna. "'Who Can Stop a Man?'" *Manushi* No. 46 (May–June 1988), 11–13.
[On the continuation of polygamy among Hindus in a Maharashtrian village—mostly for the purpose of securing heirs.]

178.   Chhachhi, Amrita. "State Religious Fundamentalism and Women: Trends in South Asia." *Economic and Political Weekly* 24, No. 11 (March 18, 1989), 567–78.
[This complex study analyzes the Indian state's implication in the rise of "fundamentalism," the contributing role of backlash as women take up new economic roles that threaten patriarchal authority structures, and the ideal of "manliness" and control of women as a tool in the construction of communal identity. The author finds grounds for concern in covert state backing of fundamentalist groups, but also finds ground for hope in feminist counter-movements.]

179.   Chidvilasananda, Gurumayi. *Kindle My Heart: Wisdom and Inspiration from a Living Master.* 2 vols. New York: Prentice Hall, 1989.
[Compilation of public inspirational talks given by the present (female) guru of the Siddha Yoga tradition.]

For Chitnis, Suma, see entries 14 and 301.

180.   Chopra, Kuldip Singh. "O, Ye the Sikh Women." *Sikh Review* 25 (March 1977), 5–18.
[Approves a previous editorial that had rebuked Sikh women for neglecting religion; includes a review of Sikh history, with assertions at the end about the role of Sikh women—all very general and stressing women's importance for child-rearing.]

181.   Choudhary, Kameshwar. "Debunking the Call for Women's Slavery." *Economic and Political Weekly* 25, No. 51 (December 22, 1990), 2768–70.
[Criticizes a speech by Chief Justice of the Supreme Court, Ranganath Mishra, in which the latter argued that women's claim to equal rights is a dimunition of a former "superior status," and that constitutional articles extending equality to women should not be implemented.]

182. Chowdhry, Prem. "Socio-Economic Dimensions of Certain Customs and Attitudes: Women of Haryana in the Colonial Period." *Economic and Political Weekly* 22, No. 48 (November 28, 1987), 2060–66.
[Included for its references to the impact of the Arya Samaj on customs affecting women in Haryana—especially the sanctioning of levirate marriage, then a common practice among Jats of the area.]

183. ————. "An Alternative to the *Sati* Model: Perceptions of a Social Reality in Folklore." *Asian Folklore Studies* 49, No. 2 (1990), 259.
[Explores popular consciousness of widow remarriage in Haryana folklore, with much attention to levirate; sources are proverbs, popular beliefs, and festival practices.]

184. Chowdhuri, Naren. *Anandamayee Ma (As I Have Known Her)*. Varanasi: Shree Shree Anandamayee Charitable Society, 1978.
[A disciple's reminiscences and testimonial to an important twentieth-century woman saint.]

185. "A Christian Woman Demands Equal Succession Rights." *Manushi* 5, No. 1 (=No. 25; November–December 1984), 7.
[Mary Roy, a Syriac Christian, challenges the Travancore Christian Succession Act—in Kerala, different Christian laws of inheritance apply in different areas.]

186. "Christian Women Demand Reform—Joint Women's Programme." *Manushi* 6, No. 3 (=No. 33; March–April 1986), 16.
[A brief notice on a petition for change in Christian personal law; the issues at stake were minimum age for marriage and grounds for divorce.]

187. Clark, Elizabeth Ann. *Status of Women in the Religions of India: Hinduism, Sikhism, Islam and Chistianity*. Ottawa: National Library of Canada, 1987.

[A Canadian thesis published on microfiche; no further
information is available.]

188.   Claus, Peter J. "The Siri Myth and Ritual: A Mass Posses-
       sion Cult of India." *Ethnology* 14 (1975), 47–58.
       [Analyzes the myth and ritual of a *bhuta* cult popular
       among matrilineal Tulu speakers of South Kanara district
       in Mysore; the myth concerns problems of matrilineal kin-
       ship, the cult entails possession. Most of those possessed
       are women.]

189.   ————. "Mayndala: A Legend and Possession Cult of
       Tulunad, South Kanara, India." *Asian Folklore Studies* 38,
       No. 2 (1979) 95–130.
       [Although the functionaries of this ancient but newly popu-
       lar goddess cult are male, its principal patrons are women;
       the goddess has become "the women's champion, their pro-
       tector in a rapidly changing world."]

For Claus, Peter J., see also entry 41.

190.   Clementin-Ojha, Catherine. "The Tradition of Female
       Gurus." *Manushi* No. 31 (Vol. 6, No. 1; November–
       December 1985), 2–8.
       [Portrays four women gurus whom the author encountered
       during fieldwork in Banaras: Mataji Om Bharati, a *sannya-
       sini* of the Bharati section of Dasanami Sampraday; Mataji
       Ram Dulari Dasi, a *vairagini* of the Ramanandi Sampra-
       day; Saradvallabha Betiji, *mahant* of the Vallabhacharya
       Gopal Mandir (new); and Shobha Ma of the Nimbark
       Sampraday.]

191.   ————. "Outside the Norms: Women Ascetics in Hindu
       Society." *Economic and Political Weekly* 23, No. 18 (April
       30, 1988), WS34–WS36.
       [Hindu women ascetics are comparatively rare and the line
       of distinction between renouncing ascetics and widows re-

mains fuzzy. The author describes the lifestyle and motivations of women at three renouncers' monasteries at Banaras. She pronounces them rebels but not revolutionaries.]

For Clemintin-Ojha, Catherine, see also Ojha, Catherine.

192.   Cobb, Betsey. "Kamaladevi Chattopadhyaya." *Bulletin of Concerned Asian Scholars* 7, No. 1 (1975), 67–72.
[Summarizes the life of a celebrated freedom fighter, artist, socialist, and protectress of Indian handcrafts. Includes references to the Vedic learning of Kamaladevi's grandmother and her own conflicts with orthodoxy as she remarried after widowhood and later divorced this second husband.]

193.   Compton, Ruth. *Canadian Women and the Foreign Missionary Movement: A Case Study of Presbyterian Women's Involvement at the Home Base and in Central India, 1876–1914.* Ph.D. diss., York University (Canada), 1987.
[Three of this dissertation's six chapters discuss experiences of women who served as evangelistic, educational, or medical missionaries in Central India. Described *DAI* 48, No. 10 (April 1988), A-2746.]

194.   Copley, Antony. "Some Reflections by an Historian on Attitudes Towards Women in Indian Traditional Society." *South Asia Research* 1, No. 2 (November 1981), 22–33.
[Examines the roles of family and law to "see how in their contributions towards gender-formation they have helped to fashion the subservience of women in Indian traditional society."]

195.   Crawford, Cromwell. "Ram Mohan Roy on *Sati* and Sexism." *Indian Journal of Social Work* 41, No. 1 (April 1980), 73–91.
[Investigates Roy's historical role in the abolition of *sati* and explores his legacy for the Indian Women's Movement.]

196.   Cutler, Norman. *Songs of Experience: The Poetics of Tamil Devotion*. Bloomington: Indiana University Press, 1987.
[This collection of Tamil poems reflecting the quest for and experience of God includes eleven selections by the Shaiva saint Karaikkalammaiyar; translations are clear and very readable.]

197.   Dalal, Ajit K., et al. *"Sati* of Deorala: An Attributional Study of Social Reactions." *Indian Journal of Social Work* 49, No. 4 (October 1988), 348–58.
[Offers results of a survey conducted among 177 male and female residents of Allahabad, asking about awareness of and reactions to the Roop Kanwar *sati*. Includes categories of causal explanations (i.e., Who or what was responsible?) and affective reactions (i.e., How do you feel about it?). Respondents were also asked to suggest ways to prevent such incidents. Discovers significant differences in response both according to gender and according to socio-economic status.]

198.   Dalmia-Luderitz, Vasudha. *"Sati* as a Religious Rite: Parliamentary Papers on Religious Immolation, 1821–30." *Economic and Political Weekly* 27, No. 4 (January 25, 1992), PE58–PE64.
[The colonial papers on *sati* reveal not only denigration of both women and religion but also a series of ironies still having repercussions today. Women supposedly had no free will and were considered to be under the thumb of priests; yet most of the early restrictions on *sati* required authorities to determine whether or not a *sati*'s immolation was voluntary.]

199.   Dandekar, R. N., and P. D. Navathe, eds. *Proceedings of the Fifth World Sanskrit Conference* (Varanasi, India: October 21–26, 1981). New Delhi: Rashtriya Sanskrit Sansthan, 1985.
[Three articles of this collection bear on women and religion: B. N. Hazarika, "Women in the Brahmana Literature"; V. L. Sethuraman, "Widow-Remarriage—a View Point"; and

Kiran Kumari Singh, "Ideals of Womanhood as Reflected in the Works of Bhavabhuti."]

200.   Dandvate, Pramila, et al. *Widows, Abandoned and Destitute Women in India*. New Delhi: Radiant Publishers, 1989.
[This collection of essays includes a chapter titled "The *Devadasis*" by Ramesh and Nasreen Faiyaz, plus three on *sati*: Prahlad Singh Shekhawat, "*Sati* in Rajasthan"; Neera Mishra, "The Murder of Roop Kanwar"; and Indu Prakash Singh and Renuka Singh, "*Sati*: Its Patri-Politics." An additional chapter relevant to this listing traces the aftermath of the Delhi anti-Sikh riots of 1984: Jaya Srivastava, "The Widows of November 1984."]

201.   Dange, Sadashiv Ambadas. *Sexual Symbolism from the Vedic Ritual*. Delhi: Ajanta Publications, 1979.
[This series of essays on ritual imagery and practice contains an interesting portrayal of the sacrificer's wife as representation of all earthly femininity.]

202.   Dange, Sindhu. *Hindu Domestic Rituals: A Critical Glance*. New Delhi: Ajanta Publications, 1985.
[Principal sources for this study are the *grhya* (domestic) *sutra*s; discussed are norms regarding marriage rites, child-naming, and rites for female ancestors, along with others that have less bearing on women.]

For Dange, Sindhu, see also entry 646.

203.   Daniel, Ruby, assisted by Barbara C. Johnson. "Memories of a Cochin Jewish Woman." *Manushi* No. 67 (November–December 1991), 30–37.
[A daughter of Kerala's ancient Cochin Jewish community describes her early life, her education at a Christian school, her decision to work rather than marry, her career in the Indian civil service, her decision to emigrate to Israel, and her experience living in an Israeli *kibbutz*.]

204. Daniel, Sheryl. *Shifting Perspectives of Identity and Dharma in Tamil Culture.* Ph.D. diss., University of Chicago, 1981.
[No further information is available.]

For Daniel, Sheryl, see also entry 986.

205. Dar, Ghulam Mohiuddin. "Marriage Patterns among Muslims and Buddhists in Kargil," *Social Welfare* 32, No. 3 (June 1985), 8–16.
[Mostly concerns multiple marriages—i.e., polygamy and polyandry—but also covers child marriage, temporary marriage, dowry, and divorce.]

206. Das, Frieda Mathilda. *Purdah: The Status of Indian Women.* New Delhi: Ess Ess, 1979.
[This historical overview of the practice of secluding women includes chapters on the "Freedom of the Vedic Period," the *Laws of Manu*, women in the epic days, women under the Muslims, and Sister Nivedita.]

207. Das, J. L. "Mother Teresa: A Messenger of Mercy." *Sikh Review* 23 (October 1975), 31–33.
[Pays tribute to Mother Teresa on the occasion of the Silver Jubilee of the founding of her order.]

208. Das, Kamala. *My Story.* New Delhi: Sterling Publishers, 1976 and 1988.
[A Nair woman and accomplished poet recounts her autobiography; she includes her experiences as an Indian child in a Christian school.]

209. Das, Nilama. *Glimpses of the Mother's Life.* 2 vols. Pondicherry: Sri Aurobindo Ashram, 1978.
[Compiles autobiographical passages from the sayings of Mirra Alfassa Richard, "the Mother" of Pondicherry's Aurobindo Ashram.]

Bibliography

210.　Das, Veena. "The Body as Metaphor—Socialization of Women in Punjabi Urban Families." *Manushi* No. 28 (May–June 1985), 2–6.
[Shows how men and women construct the human body and how such constructions affect women's self-perception.]

211.　————. "The Goddess and the Demon: Analysis of *Devi Mahatmya.*" *Manushi* 5, No. 6 (=No. 30; September–October 1985), 28–31.
[Explores definitions of the feminine in a famous set of Hindu myths.]

212.　————. "Gender Studies, Cross-Cultural Comparison and the Colonial Organization of Knowledge." *Berkshire Review* 21 (1986), 58–75; followed by Gyan Prakash, "Comments on Das," pp. 76–79.
[Shows how nineteenth-century colonial discourse on *sati* served to distance rulers from ruled and thereby to further the imperialist project.]

213.　————. "On Female Body and Sexuality." *Contributions to Indian Sociology* N.S. 21, No. 1 (January–June 1987), 57–66.
[A response to interpretations of women's experience in Gananath Obeyesekere's *Medusa's Hair* and *Cult of the Goddess Pattini* compares his brahmin-based assertions about female predicaments and sexuality with materials reflecting women's perceptions of themselves.]

214.　————. "*Shakti* Versus *Sati*: A Reading of the Santoshi Ma Cult." *Manushi* No. 49 (November–December 1988), 26–30.
[This study of a goddess whose popularity was created by a Hindi film perceives her as marking a transition from *shakti* (power) to *sati* (suffering) based modes of refuge against evil.]

Bibliography

For Das, Veena, see also entries 149, 251, 401, and 789.

215. Dastur, Aloo J., and Usha H. Mehta. *Gandhi's Contribution to the Emancipation of Women*. Bombay: Popular Prakashan, 1991.
[A survey of 151 respondents assesses perceptions of Gandhi's impact on the current status of women in India. Participants include members of the Gandhi family, residents of his *ashram*, woman associates, Gandhian workers, women social workers, and converts to the Gandhi movement.]

216. Datta, V. N. *Sati: Widow Burning in India: A Historical, Social and Philosophical Enquiry into the Hindu Rite of Widow Burning*. New Delhi: Manohar, 1988.
[Topics addressed include British policy on *sati*, Christian missionary responses, the roles of Lord Bentinck and Ram Mohan Roy in the nineteenth-century Bengali anti-*sati* campaign, public responses to abolition of *sati*, records of *sati* practice in various states, the nature of the rite itself, and why Hindus burn women.]

217. David, S. Immanuel. *God's Messengers: Reformed Church in America Missionaries in South India, 1839–1938*. Th.D. diss., Lutheran School of Theology at Chicago, 1984.
[Examines the attitudes, goals, and accomplishments of Reformed Church in America missionaries, both male and female. A section of part II takes up the status of women in the mission. Described *DAI* 44, No. 5 (November 1983), A-1485.]

218. D'Cunha, S. *Mother of the Motherless: A Short Sketch of the Life and Work of Mother Teresa*. Bangalore: St. Paul Publications, 1975.
[A brief sketch of the life and work of Mother Teresa of Calcutta. The format is standard, except for a brief sketch of the training of Missionary of Charity nuns and a listing of

service provided by the organization called Co-Workers of Mother Teresa. Ends with quotes from Mother Teresa and a listing of her awards.]

219.   Dehejia, Vidya. *Slaves of the Lord: The Path of the Tamil Saints*. New Delhi: Munshiram Manoharlal Publishers, 1988.
[This study of poets of the *bhakti* movement includes one chapter on two women saints, the Vaishnava Andal and the Shaiva Karaikkal Ammaiyar. Includes fine translations of selected poems.]

220.   ————, ed. and trans. *Antal and Her Path of Love: Poems of a Woman Saint from South India*. Albany: State University of New York Press, 1990.
[Translates *Tiruppavai* and *Nacciyar Tirumoli*, the two extant works of the Tamil Vaishnava (Alvar) woman poet Antal (also Andal), into excellent, accessible, English. A thirty-six page introduction describes Antal's context and fame, the little that is known of her life, the image of Krishna in her work, the vow that inspires *Tiruppavai*, her relationship to the *Bhagavata Purana* and to Tamil Cankam Poetry, her mysticism, and the metrical structure of her work.]

221.   *Deorala Fire on Pyre*. Jodhpur: Sona Law House, 1988.
[Consists mostly of texts of Rajasthan High Court decisions from 1st December, 18th December, and 21st December, 1987, relating to the infamous Roop Kanwar *sati*.]

222.   Derrett, J. Duncan M. *The Death of a Marriage Law: Epitaph for the* Rishis. Durham: Carolina Academic Press, 1978; New Delhi: Vikas Publishing House, 1978.
[This volume by a long-time scholar of Hindu law in India describes changes in both the laws and concept of marriage that have occurred from the time of *dharmasastra*-established norms through the period of British colonialism until

the Marriage Laws (Amendment) Act of 1976. Derrett
charges that the new laws are a product of an elite class
out of touch with the assumptions and needs of the Hindu
masses; he concludes that Hindu marriage is no longer a
samskara (sacrament).]

223. Desai, A. R., ed. *Women's Liberation and Politics of Religious Personal Laws in India*. Bombay: C. G. Shah Memorial Trust, 1986; 2nd ed., 1990.
[Although India is a secular state, its constitution recognizes the validity of so-called "personal laws" that issue from within religious communities and govern their own members. Essays in this volume explore this provision's implications for women: A. R. Desai, "Women and Justice for All," "Impact of Religious Personal Laws on Status of Women in Independent India," and "Capitalist Patriarchal Assumptions of Indian State—Their Dangerous Implications for Women's Liberation"; Nandita Haksar, "Hindu Law has its Lapses" and "Campaign for a Uniform Code"; Jean D'Cunha, "The Antiquated Christian Law" and "The Muslim Law: A Woman is Half a Man"; Indira Jaising, "Why Must Hindu, Muslim, and Christian Women Be Governed by Different Personal Laws?"; Vibhuti Patel, "Shah Bano's Case and its Aftermath"; Divya Pande, "Religious Fundamentalism, a Threat to Women's Equality"; Neera Desai, "Protection or Punishment for Muslim Women"; and Madhu Kishwar, "Pro-Women or Anti-Muslim—the Shah Bano Controversy."]

224. Desai, Neera. *Women in Modern India*. 2nd ed. Bombay: Vora and Company, 1977; 1st ed., 1957.
[Includes one chapter on the *bhakti* movement and two on reform movements.]

225. ————. "Women and the Medieval Saints' Movement." Bombay: Research Centre for Women's Studies, SNDT Women's University, 1986.

[This typed manuscript, available through the SNDT Women's University Research Centre for Women's Studies, includes a general description of the saints' movement and its socio-economic background, focussing especially on the Rajasthani saint Meerabai. It concludes that Meerabai's life was important as a personal protest against oppression; her message, however, was not revolutionary.]

For Desai, Neera, see also entries 223, 789, and 811.

226. De Silva, Daya, and Chandra R. de Silva. *Sri Lanka Since Independence: A Reference Guide to the Literature.* New Delhi: Navrang, 1992.
[This bibliography of 2456 references contains sections both on women and on religion, although not on the combination of the two. Partially annotated.]

227. De Souza, Alfred, ed. *Women in Contemporary India and South Asia.* 2nd rev. ed. New Delhi: Manohar, 1980.
[Includes a village study by Zarina Bhatty, "Muslim Women in Uttar Pradesh: Social Mobility and Directions of Change," comparing upper- and lower-class Muslim groups, and a study by Ursula M. Sharma, *"Purdah* and Public Space," on spatial use and avoidance in two villages of H.P. Contains also a useful comprehensive article by British scholar Ursula King, "Women and Religion: The Status and Image of Women in Some Major Religious Traditions."]

228. Devadas, Nalini. "Mother India, Mother Goddess and Militancy in Neo-Hinduism: The Role of Sister Nivedita." *Annual Review of Women in World Religions II, Heroic Women.* Ed. Arvind Sharma and Katherine K. Young. Albany: State University of New York Press, 1992.
[Examines contributions of Vivekananda convert Sister Nivedita (nee Margaret Noble) to the Bengali revolutionary movement; includes Nivedita's conception of the Hindu Mother Church and other ideas expressed in her book *Kali the Mother.*]

229.   *The* Devadasi *Problem.* 2nd ed. Calcutta: Joint Women's Programme, Study and Research Centre, 1983.
[Studies the *devadasi* system and the Joint Women's Programme's work towards prohibition of *devadasi* dedications.]

230.   Devadason, E. D. *Christian Law in India: Law Applicable to Christians in India.* Madras: DSI Publications, 1974.
[Discusses personal law, divorce, succession, and consequences of conversion for both women and men.]

231.   Devadoss, T. S. *Hindu Family and Marriage: A Study of Social Institutions in India.* Madras: Dr. S. Radhakrishnan Institute for Advanced Study in Philosophy, 1979.
[Divided into three categories: "Social Philosophy—an Analysis," Family, and Marriage; the latter section attends extensively to status of women and ideals for women, but is not profound.]

232.   Devasia, Leelamma, and V. V. Devasia. *Girl Child in India.* Springfield, Va.: Nataraj Books, 1992.
[Eighteen articles on the predicaments of female children in India include two relating to religion: Joseph Benjamin, "Socio-Religious Status of Girl Child in India"; and M. Carol, "The Catholic Girl Child."]

233.   Devendra, Kiran. *Status and Position of Women in India: With Special Reference to Women in Contemporary India.* New Delhi: Shakti Books, 1985; New Delhi: Vikas Publishing House, 1990.
[Concentrating on changes in the status and roles of women after Independence, this book includes two chapters on the historical background and implications of the Hindu Code, as well as one, titled "A Redefinition of Womanhood in India," that deals in part with interreligious and inter-caste marriages. A chapter titled "Beyond the Middle Classes" has some materials on social service programs and homes for "needy women."]

234. Devi, Ratnamayi, and Madhu Kishwar. "Scholar, Fighter, Mother: The Life of Ratnamayi Devi as Narrated to Madhu Kishwar." *Manushi* No. 45 (March–April 1988), 2–18.
[Traces a Nair woman's long journey from wealth to poverty, through education and a disappointing early marriage, to work in Gandhi's *ashram*, to a literary career, and finally to appointment as an Indian cultural representative.]

235. Dhagamwar, Vasudha. "Women Who Use the Hindu Marriage Act: A Profile." *Indian International Centre Quarterly* 12, No. 1 (March 1985), 29–41.
[Reports on a survey undertaken between January 1973 and December 1977 to learn why women divorce and what they know of the divorce process; discovers considerable ignorance of law, even among educated women. The sample was sixty-five women.]

236. ———. "Uniform Civil Code: Don't We Have It Already?" *Mainstream* (July 6, 1985), 15–17, 34.
[This article is one of a 1985 *Mainstream* series that debated the Supreme Court decision in the Shah Bano case (on the right to maintenance of Muslim women divorcees). For others of the series, see Tara Ali Baig (May 18), Asghar Ali Engineer (May 25 and August 3), Syed Shahabuddin (June 1 and July 13), Nusrat Bano Ruhi (July 20), and Sakina Hyder (August 24). Note also Rumki Basu's two-part article "Divorce in India" published on March 2 and 9 of the same year.]

For Dhagamwar, Vasudha, see also 35, 68, and 799.

237. Dhar, Sodarshan, and M. K. Dhar. *Evolution of Hindu Family Law: Vedas to Vasistha*. Delhi: Deputy Publications, 1986.
[Covers marriage, marriage relationships, and inheritance (including exclusion of widows and provision for *niyoga*, bearing children by a dead spouse's brother).]

238. Dhruvarajan, Vanaja. *Hindu Women and the Power of Ideology*. New Delhi: Sage Publications, Vistaar Division, 1989; Granby, Mass.: Bergin and Garvey, 1989.
[This village study attends especially to the *pativrata* ideal and its repercussions in village behavior and experience.]

239. ————. "Religious Ideology, Hindu Women, and Development in India." *The Journal of Social Issues* 46, No. 3 (1990), 57–69.
[Argues that the ideology of *pativrata* has defeated efforts at aiding women because it encourages women towards submissiveness and dependency. Proposes programs aimed at diminishing "this oppressive ideology" and empowering women themselves to effect necessary changes.]

240. Dietrich, Gabriele. "Women's Movement and Religion." *Economic and Political Weekly* 21, No. 4 (January 25, 1986), 157–60.
[Calls upon the women's movement in India to take religion more seriously and to seize the lead in religious reform.]

241. Diwan, Paras. *Family Law: Law of Marriage and Divorce in India*. New Delhi: Sterling Publishers, 1983.
[No further information available at time of publication.]

242. Diwan, Paras, and Virendra Kumar, eds. *Law Towards Stable Marriages*. Delhi: Seema Publications, 1984.
[A collection of papers from an all-India conference on the theme of marriage and divorce laws.]

243. *Documentation Bulletins, Centre for Women's Development Studies* (New Delhi); issued monthly, January 1988 to present.
[This monthly listing, subdivided topically, of all news clippings placed on file by the New Delhi Centre for Women's Development Studies includes "Religion" and "Women and Religion" as topics. Available at CWDS itself and in most

women's research units; incomplete, sporadic issues are also available for 1987.]

244. Doig, Desmond. *Mother Teresa: Her People and Her Work.* New York: Harper and Row, Publishers, 1976; paperback ed., San Francisco: Harper and Row, 1980.
[This book on Calcutta's mother of the poor is more substantial than most; its focus is Mother Teresa's Calcutta Mission, and its sources are reminiscences of people close to her career—including the Bengali journalist who wrote it. The final chapter is a series of Mother Teresa's own assertions about conversion, belief, love, death, faith, prayer, sin, her own work, and her home for the destitute dying. Features many fine photographic illustrations.]

245. Dowman, Keith. *Sky Dancer: The Secret Life and Songs of the Lady Yeshe Tsogyel.* London: Routledge and Kegan Paul, 1984; New York: Dodd, Mead, 1988.
[A translation in readable English plus a 136-page commentary on the life of Tibetan Tantric Buddhism's most famous woman teacher. The songs referred to in the title are incorporated into the text.]

246. Dube, Leela. "Seed and Earth: The Symbolism of Biological Reproduction and Sexual Relations of Production." *Visibility and Power: Essays on Women in Society and Development.* Ed. Leela Dube, Eleanor Leacock, and Shirley Ardener. Delhi: Oxford University Press, 1986.
[Documents repercussions of the ancient and still active metaphor of impregnation as planting of seed in the mother's "field"; shows how this affects shastric regulations on ownership of children, land inheritance, and reckoning of kinship.]

247. ————. "On the Construction of Gender: Hindu Girls in Patrilineal India." *Economic and Political Weekly* 23, No. 18 (April 30, 1988), WS11–WS19.

Bibliography

[A long and rich paper examines the process of socialization to gender "through rituals and ceremonies, the use of language, and practices within and in relation to the family."]

For Dube, Leela, see also entries 38, 149, 507, and 920.

248.   Duggal, K. S. *Alien Heart*. Trans. Jai Ratan. New Delhi: Disha Books, 1990.
[A famous Punjabi novel traces the wrenching struggles of the Muslim widow of a patriot *sheikh* when partition forces her to choose between staying in India or fleeing to the newly-created Pakistan. Her problems are intensified by one daughter's love marriage to a Sikh, and a second's infatuation with a Muslim extremist.]

249.   Duvvury, Vasumathi Krishnaswamy. *Play and Symbolism in Rites of Passage of Tamil Brahmin Women: An Interpretation of Their Social Significance*. Ph.D diss., Rice University, 1987.
[Women subjects of this study are rural and urban Aiyar Brahmins; rites described include life-cycle rituals and *vratas* (*nombu*s in Tamil). Also discussed are symbolisms of color and food and the auspicious/inauspicious dichotomy. Described *DAI* 48, No. 5 (November 1987), A-1245. No opportunity to examine; prototype of *Play, Symbolism, and Ritual* (see entry 250 below).]

250.   ————. *Play, Symbolism, and Ritual: A Study of Tamil Brahmin Women's Rites of Passage*. New York: Peter Lang, 1991.
[Based on the author's doctoral fieldwork in a Tamilnadu Aiyar Brahmin village and an Aiyar community in Bangalore City, Karnataka, this volume treats primarily women's life-cycle rituals. The author argues that rites extending from puberty through first childhood must be treated as a continuous unit, effecting passage from childhood to adulthood incrementally. One chapter on *vratas* is also included,

treating the Savitri *vrata* (which includes unmarried girls), the Varamahalakshmi *vrata* performed by married women, and the Rishipanchami *vrata* for postmenopausal women. The volume's final chapter examines the special role of symbolic colors and foods in all rites described.]

251. Eck, Diana, and Devaki Jain. *Speaking of Faith: Global Perspectives on Women, Religion and Social Change.* New Delhi: Kali for Women, 1986; London: Women's Press, 1986. [Assembles papers from an international conference on Women, Religion, and Social Change held at Harvard University in 1981; most speakers were activists, asked to address the problem from the perspective of their own work and culture. Three Indian authors contributed: Radha Bhatt, "Lakshmi Ashram: A Gandhian Perspective in the Himalayan Foothills"; Devaki Jain, "Gandhian Contributions Toward a Feminist Ethic"; and Veena Das, "Notes on the Moral Foundation of the Debate on Abortion."]

252. Egnor, Margaret Trawick. *The Sacred Spell and Other Conceptions of Life in Tamil Culture.* Ph.D. diss., University of Chicago, 1978.
[Explores constructions of womanhood in Tamil culture via an analysis of language and practice; illuminates the concept of women's inner power and the paradoxes of practice resulting from this.]

253. ————. "The Changed Mother, or What the Smallpox Goddess Did When There Was No More Smallpox." *South Asian Systems of Healing: Contributions to Asian Studies* 18; ed. E. Valentine Daniel and Judy F. Pugh. Leiden: E.J. Brill, 1984, pp. 24–45.
[Cited here for its description of and interview with a woman "servant of the goddess" in Madras. Includes a long verbatim description of the woman's "trial by illness."]

254. Engels, Dagmar. "The Age of Consent Act of 1891: Colonial

Ideology in Bengal." *South Asia Research* 3, No. 2 (November 1983), 107–34.
[Treats the historical context of the act, the official debate and the public response, issues at stake in the opposition (including religious issues), and views of male sexuality and female honor that shaped British and Bengali perceptions of the issue.]

255. Engineer, Asghar Ali, ed. *The Status of Women in Islam.* Bombay: Institute of Islamic Studies, 1984; Delhi: Ajanta Publications, 1987.
[A liberal, critical assessment of women's status by Indian Muslim males takes the "degeneration after the prophet" approach to perceived abuses.]

256. ————."Divorce and Muslim Women," *Mainstream* (May 25, 1985), 17–19.
[This article and the one that follows were part of a 1985 *Mainstream* series that debated the Supreme Court decision in the Shah Bano case (on the right to maintenance of Muslim women divorcees). For others of the series, see Tara Ali Baig (May 18), Vasudha Dhagamwar (July 6), Syed Shahabuddin (June 1 and July 13), Nusrat Bano Ruhi (July 20), and Sakina Hyder (August 24). Note also Rumki Basu's two-part article "Divorce in India" published on March 2 and 9 of the same year.]

257. ————. "Muslim Personal Law and Shahabuddin." *Mainstream* (August 3, 1985), 22–24.
[See comment in entry 256 above.]

258. ————, ed. *The Shah Bano Controversy.* Bombay: Orient Longman, 1987.
[This collection of responses to the infamous Shah Bano controversy concerning Muslim women's right to maintenance includes not only articles but also interviews with prominent figures, survey results, editorials, reproduced

documents and letters; it appears to be the most complete source on this topic. Articles are: Asghar Ali Engineer, "Forces behind the Agitation"; P. Jaganmohan Reddy, "Shah Bano Verdict and Muslim Law"; Rafiullah Shehab, "Islamic Shariat and the Shah Bano Case"; Nusrat Bano Ruhi, "Revival of Islamic Fundamentalism"; Madhu Kishwar, "Pro-women or anti-Muslim?"; M. A. Latif, "Does the Judgement Justify Agitation?"; Seema Mustafa, "An Old Woman Deprived in the Name of God"; Irfan Engineer, "Leadership Exploiting Masses"; W. M. Shaikh, "Personal Law in Islamic Nations"; Ajoy Bose, "The Supreme Court Interpreted Muslim Personal Law"; V. K. Krishna Iyer, "The Bill is a Sin against the Quran"; L. K. Advani, "The Government Must not Capitulate"; Badar Durrez Ahmed, "Women's Rights Are Far Superior under the Shariat"; Danial Latifi, "The Muslim Women Bill"; Zarina Bhatty, "Muslim Women Bill Evades the Issues"; Seema Mustafa, "Behind the Veil"; Kuldip Nayar, "Separate Personal Laws Do Not Dilute Secularism"; and Nikhil Chakravartty, "Secularism Segregated in Rajiv's India." Interviewees include Rajiv Gandhi, Arif Mohammad Khan, Baharul Islam, Tahir Mahmood, Hemwati Nandan Bahuguna, and Mohammad Yunus Salim.]

259.　　　———. *Justice, Women, and Communal Harmony in Islam.* New Delhi: Indian Council of Social Science Research, 1989.
[Publishes a three-part lecture series sponsored by the ICSSR; the second lecture (chapter 3 of the volume) treats the "Rights of Women in Islam." This response to the Shah Bano furor examines Qur'an, *sunnah*, and juristic opinion to ascertain the actual rights of women in Islam regarding marriage, divorce, inheritance, maintenance, child custody, and right to property. It holds that Allah does not ordain sexual inequality, but modern law often fails to honor rights ceded to women in the Muslim past. Engineer is the most liberal of noted Muslim writers on women's rights in modern India.]

260.   ———. *Rights of Women in Islam*. New York: St. Martin's Press, 1992; New Delhi: Sterling Publishers, 1992.
[Distinguishing between the "contextual" and the "normative" in classic Islamic teachings, Engineer argues for the need to reinterpret these for the present age. His book treats the status of women during the pre-Islamic age, the Islamic concept of equality, marital rights, divorce, the need for reform in Personal Law, and the individual dignity of women in Islam.]

For Engineer, Asghar Ali, see also entries 58, 159, 354, 594, 739, 750, and 811.

261.   Erndl, Kathleen M(arie). *Victory to the Mother: The Goddess Cult of Northwest India*. Ph.D. diss., University of Wisconsin at Madison, 1987.
[Prototype for *Victory to the Mother* (see entry 263 below). Described *DAI* 48, No. 8 (February 1988), A-2083.]

262.   ———. "Fire and Wakefulness: The Devi *Jagrata* in Contemporary Panjabi Hinduism." *Journal of the American Academy of Religion* 59, No. 2 (Summer 1991), 339–60.
[All night vigils in honor on Seranvali, a lion-riding goddess, are growing in popularity among Punjabi Hindus; although this article is principally a description of rituals observed both by men and by women, it includes brief information on the role of possessed women honored as incarnations of the goddess (*Mata*s).]

263.   ———. *Victory to the Mother: The Hindu Goddess of Northwest India in Myth, Ritual, and Symbol*. New York: Oxford University Press, 1993.
[Explores both the nature of the goddess and the experience of her devotees, many of whom are women. Includes descriptions of goddess rituals, plus case studies and interviews with women whom the goddess possesses.]

264.   Eveland, Sandra Anne Newton. *The Divine Lover of Mira Bai and Mechthild von Magdeburg: A Study of Two Women's Literary Description of a Mystical Relationship with God*. Ph.D. diss., University of Texas at Austin, 1978. [Compares and contrasts the imagery of God as divine lover in the writings of the fifteenth-century Rajput poet-saint Mirabai and the thirteenth-century German beguine Mechthild. Described *DAI* 39, No. 11 (May 1979), A-6754.]

265.   Falk, Nancy Auer. "Women In-between: Conflicting Values in Delhi." *The Journal of Religion* 67, No. 2 (April 1987), 257–74. [Examines the dilemma of upper-class, English-educated, Hindu women who are pulled between traditional Hindu norms of subservience to family and Westernized ideals of self-determination.]

266.   ———. "Exemplary Donors of the Pali Tradition." *Ethics, Wealth, and Salvation: A Study in Buddhist Social Ethics*. Ed. Russell F. Sizemore and Donald K. Swearer. Columbia, S.C.: University of South Carolina Press, 1990. [Included for its materials on the paradigmatic female Buddhist donor Vishakha.]

267.   ———. "Women, Reform, and the Science of Religion in Nineteenth-Century Bengal." *Facing East/Facing West: North America and the Asia/Pacific Region in the 1990's*. Kalamazoo, Mich.: Western Michigan University Division of Continuing Education, 1990. [Examines a paradox in Keshub Chandra Sen's program of religious and social reform: why he wished to liberate women, but did not want them liberated too far.]

268.   ———. "Women's Experience of Religion: A Cross-Cultural Perspective." *Eclectic Streams in Women's Studies: Report on the RCWS Seminar Series, 1992*. Ed. Meera Kosambi and Veena Poonacha. Contribution to Women

Studies Series 8. Bombay: Research Centre for Women's Studies, SNDT University, 1993.
[Although it includes a few references to Indian practices and conversations, this published talk was intended to generate discussion via a series of sweeping cross-cultural generalizations. Its chief interest for the present bibliography is that it was tailored for an audience of Indian feminist scholars.]

269.   ———. "*Shakti* Ascending: Hindu Women, Politics, and Religious Leadership during the Nineteenth and Twentieth Centuries." *Religion in Modern India*. Ed. Robert Baird. 3rd rev. ed. New Delhi: Manohar, forthcoming.
[Reviews five male politically-driven initiatives of the colonial era that established preconditions for the rise of women as religious leaders in Hindu India.]

For Falk, Nancy Auer, see also entry 322.

270.   Falk, Nancy Auer, and Rita M. Gross, eds. *Unspoken Worlds: Women's Religious Lives in Non-Western Cultures*. San Francisco: Harper and Row, Publishers, 1980.
[Although this collection of case studies is cross-cultural in focus, six of its seventeen chapters pertain to India: Charles S. J. White, "Mother Guru: Jnanananda of Madras, India"; Doranne Jacobson, "Golden Handprints and Red-Painted Feet: Hindu Childbirth Rituals in Central India"; Susan S. Wadley, "Hindu Women's Family and Household Rites in a North Indian Village"; James M. Freeman, "The Ladies of Lord Krishna: Rituals of Middle-Aged Women in Eastern India"; Nancy Auer Falk, "The Case of the Vanishing Nuns: The Fruits of Ambivalence in Ancient Indian Buddhism"; and Reginald A. Ray, "Accomplished Women in Tantric Buddhism of Medieval India and Tibet."]

271.   ———, eds. *Unspoken Worlds: Women's Religious Lives*. Belmont, Calif.: Wadsworth Publishing Company, 1989.

[This second edition of the volume cited in entry 270 above adds seven new chapters, none of which concerns India, and an extensive bibliography on women in religion, with sections both on India and on Buddhism.]

272.   Fane, Hannah. "The Female Element in Indian Culture," *Asian Folklore Studies* 34, No. 1 (1975), 51–112.
[This ambitious survey, almost exclusively concerned with Hindu women, runs from the Indus Valley goddess through traces of matriarchy, through female elements in Saktism, Vaishnavism, and Shaivism, through village, low caste, and tribal India; it manages also to describe marriage ceremonies and *devadasis*. Despite a naive approach, it shows impressive coverage of the literature then available.]

273.   Fasano, Anthony Joseph. *The Religious Structure of Tantric Buddhism*. Ph.D. diss., Fordham University, 1981.
[Although principally concerned with a broader description of the tantric path, this volume includes a noteworthy translation of the commentary *Caturmudranniscaya,* which explains the Tantric role of women *mudras*. Described *DAI* 42, No. 5 (November 1981), A-2173.]

274.   Feldhaus, Anne. "Bahini Bai: Wife and Saint." *Journal of the American Academy of Religion* 50, No. 4 (December 1982), 591–604.
[The subject is a seventeenth-century Marathi saint who managed to be simultaneously a wife and devotee—but not without a struggle. Includes translations from several of Bahini Bai's poems.]

275.   *Fifth National Conference on Women's Studies*. Calcutta: Jadavpur University, 9–12 February, 1991.
[Available at Women's Studies and Development Centre, University of Delhi. The overall theme of this conference was "Religion, Culture, and Politics"; however, not all papers addressed this theme. Researchers should look espe-

cially at the following papers of Subtheme 5, titled "State
Policies and Their Implications: Reconstructing Secular-
ism": Chhaya Datar, "Reform? Or New Form of Patriarchy?
*Devadasi*s in Border Regions of Maharashtra and Karna-
taka"; Bavna Mehta, "Family Laws vis-a-vis women"; Mai-
treyi Chatterjee, (title same as section title); Swatija
Paranjpe, (title same as section title); and Vibhuti Patel,
"Patriarchal Prejudices of Personal Laws." See also papers
of Subtheme 6, titled "Women's Rights and Legal Systems":
Mary Roy, "Women and Law: Striking Down a Succession
Act"; P. K. Saru, "Women under Islamic Law"; and Flavia,
"Christian Women: The Struggle for Legal Reform." Under
Subtheme 8, titled "Political Use of Religious/Cultural Idi-
oms," see: Pratibha Ranade, "Role of Religion and Govern-
ment as Lawmaker with Reference to Women's Issues dur-
ing 19th Century in Maharashtra"; Divya Pandey, "Rise of
Religious Fundamentalism in Secular India—a Case of
Sati"; Rohini Gawankar, "National Movement and Emer-
gence of Women's Movements"; and Godavari D. Patil and
Anil G. Mudbiri, "The *Sati* Incident and Ethnic Identity in
Rajasthan." Under Subtheme 9, "Religious Organizations
and Institutions, Fundamentalism and Reformism," see:
Doopali Barua, "The Role of Assamese Women in the Free-
dom Movement and Post-Independence Politics"; and Dr. S.
Muthulakshmi, "The Impact of Religion and Society upon
Women." Finally, see the following three papers whose sec-
tion I could not determine: Vandana Dube, "Political Pat-
ronage and Religious Revivalism—the Shah Bano Case";
Indira Jain Singh and Kirti Singh, "Religious Trends in
Family Law as Reflected in Legislative Policy"; and Shud-
dhabrata Sengupta, "The Sexual Politics of Television
Mythology."]

276. Flemming, Leslie A., ed. *Women's Work for Women: Mission-
aries and Social Change in Asia.* Boulder: Westview, 1989.
[Three articles of this collection pertain to India: Ruth
Compton Brewer, "Opening Doors through Social Service:

Aspects of Women's Work in the Canadian Presbyterian Mission"; Leslie A. Flemming, "New Models, New Roles: U.S. Presbyterian Women Missionaries and Social Change in North India, 1870–1910"; and Geoffrey Burkhart, "Danish Women Missionaries: Personal Accounts of Work with South Indian Women."]

277. Flueckiger, Joyce. "*Bhojali*: Song, Goddess, Friend. A Chattisgarhi Women's Oral Tradition." *Asian Folklore Studies* 41/1 (1982), 27–44.
[*Bhojali* is a women's festival centering on the planting and worship of wheat seedlings; locale of the research is south central Madhya Pradesh. The article compares differences in performance in two areas.]

278. ————. *Study of a Central Indian Folklore Region: Chhattisgarh*. Ph.D. diss., University of Wisconsin at Madison, 1984.
[Three of this volume's six chapters describe traditions of women: one is the article cited in entry 277 above, the second concerns the *Sua Nac*, a dance and song tradition for adult women, and the third describes the *Dalkhai* festival for unmarried girls and the "Song of Suanbali," a narrative poem that expresses the festival's rationale.]

279. Forbes, Geraldine H. "Goddesses or Rebels: The Women Revolutionaries of Bengal." *Oracle* 2, No. 2 (April 1980), 1–15.
[The ideology of feminine self-sacrifice inspired young Bengali women who resisted the British Raj by revolutionary tactics. All had Hindu or Brahmo Samaj backgrounds and were well educated; many had been previously influenced by Gandhi's challenges to women.]

280. ————. "Caged Tigers: 'First Wave' Feminists in India." *Women's Studies International Forum* 5, No. 6 (1982), 525–36.

[Describes work to emancipate women from the end of the nineteenth century until the Second World War, including both religious and secular efforts and emphasizing child marriage, *purdah*, and the Hindu Code. Also discusses feminist ideology informing this work, its relationship to nationalism, the impact of the emancipation effort, and contrasts with Western feminism.]

281.   ————. "In Search of the 'Pure Heathen': Missionary Women in Nineteenth Century India." *Economic and Political Weekly* 21, No. 17 (April 26, 1986), WS2–WS33.
[During the latter half of the nineteenth century, British women sponsored by Ladies' Missionary Societies went to India to educate and hopefully to convert women living in *zenana*s. This plan had little impact on *zenana* women, but much on the missionaries themselves. Males in households where missionaries taught blocked efforts at conversion, while supporting attempts to change daughters and wives into English ladies. Education thus imparted was both sparse and superficial.]

For Forbes, Geraldine H., see also entries 569 and 570.

282.   Foster, Barbara M., and Michael Foster. *Forbidden Journey: The Life of Alexandra David-Neel*. San Francisco: Harper and Row, 1987.
[Traces the life of a celebrated French traveller and scholar of Tibetan religions from her birth in 1868 until her death in 1969; includes David-Neel's experiences in, and perceptions of, India.]

283.   Foster, Theodora Carroll. *Women, Religion, and Development in the Third World*. New York: Praeger, 1983.
[Treats Hinduism, Buddhism, Islam, and Christianity, giving an overview of each tradition and its impact on women, then following with implications for education and population. The author has worked in development agencies and has written extensively on development.]

71

Bibliography

284. *Fourth National Conference on Women's Studies.* Andhra University, December 28–31, 1988. Available at the Institute for Social Studies Trust, New Delhi.
[See especially, in subtheme 6, on violence: A. Suryakumari, "Violence in the Name of Religion: Torture Leading to Infirmity or Death Caused by Witchcraft, Sorcery, Mendicants, etc."; Saroj Gulati, *"Sati* Custom: A Historical Perspective"; Lalita Parihar, "Right to Maintenance of Muslim Divorcees: Judicial Benevolence and Legislative Despotism"; also in subtheme 9, see I. S. Gulati, *"Devadasis*: A Link between Religious Culture and Child Prostitution."]

285. Foxe, Barbara. *Long Journey Home: A Biography of Margaret Noble (Nivedita).* London: Rider and Co., 1975.
[A standard biography of the Irishwoman who followed Swami Vivekananda to India and became known as Sister Nivedita, based on Nivedita's writings and letters, the letters of other disciples, contemporary news accounts, interviews with her relatives, and surviving photographs. Coverage of the years before Noble meets Vivekananda is very sketchy. Has no footnotes and no Table of Contents.]

286. Fruzetti, Lina M. "Ritual Status of Muslim Women in Rural India." *Women in Contemporary Muslim Societies.* Ed. Jane I. Smith. Lewisburg, Pa.: Bucknell University Press, 1980.
[Shows how rural Bengali Muslim women create rank by performing certain rituals, how mobility is achieved within this system, and how women's ritual practice relates to the larger context of Bengali Muslim culture.]

287. ————. "Muslim Rituals: Household Rites vs. Public Festivals in Rural India." *Ritual and Religion among Muslims in India.* Ed. Imtiaz Ahmad. New Delhi: Manohar, 1981, pp. 91–112.
[Incorporates an extended description of childbirth rites and customs among rural West Bengali Muslims.]

288.   ———. "Food and Worship: An Account of Hindu and Muslim Birth Rituals." *Journal of the Indian Anthropological Society* 17, No. 1 (March 1982), 13–30.
[In the ritual domain of birth, "both Hindu and Muslim women act in a similar manner." Includes summaries of both Hindu and Muslim rites of parturition and birth; the context is West Bengal.]

289.   ———. *The Gift of a Virgin: Women, Marriage, and Ritual in a Bengali Society*. New Brunswick, N.J.: Rutgers University Press, 1982.
[Explores the rituals of women, especially those that complement and extend Brahmanic rites of marriage; includes detailed descriptions. Based on field research conducted in Vishnupur, West Bengal.]

290.   Fuller, C. J. *The Camphor Flame: Popular Hinduism and Society in India*. Princeton: Princeton University Press, 1992.
[Synthesizing findings from local studies by himself and other anthropologists, the author has constructed a very helpful overview of the popular religious milieux in which most Hindu women practice. Yet he has surprisingly little to say about women's practice itself; he is more concerned with the religion of public space (e.g., festivals, pilgrimage) than with the domestic spaces in which women celebrate. His chapter entitled "Devotionalism, Goddesses, and Women" attends, for example, mostly to festivals for the goddess Menakshi, although it does offer some material on women's roles within these festivals.]

291.   Gaitonde, Edila. *In Search of Tomorrow*. Ahmenabad: Allied Publishers, 1987.
[When the Portuguese author of this engrossing autobiography married a young Hindu doctor from Goa, she knew already of his deep longing for liberation of his region from Portuguese rule. She followed him to Goa, and eventually

into Indian exile, as he became a hero of the liberation struggle. Although mostly about the complexities of revolutionary life, this volume does include brief descriptions of a Ganesh festival, a post-childbirth ritual, a public showing of the undecayed body of St. Francis Xavier, a women's *haldi-kumkum* ceremony, and a Hindu marriage.]

292.   Gambhirananda, Swami. *Holy Mother Sri Sarada Devi*. 3rd ed. Mylapore: Sri Ramakrishna Math, 1977; 1st ed., 1940. [Recounts incidents from the life of the Ramakrishna Mission's Holy Mother Sri Sarada Devi. Issued in observance of the Holy Mother Centenary.]

293.   Gandhi, Nandita. "Impact of Religion on Women's Rights in Asia." *Economic and Political Weekly* 23, No. 47 (January 23, 1988), 127–29.
[Reports on the Asian Conference on Women, Religion and Family Laws, held in Bombay in December of 1987. Participants were from India, Pakistan, Bangladesh, Sri Lanka, Malaysia, Singapore, Hong Kong, Indonesia, Taiwan, Laos, the Philippines, and Algeria; topics described are principally the impact and nature of fundamentalism and the impact of colonialism on family laws and women's status.]

294.   Gandhi, Nandita, and Nandita Shah. *The Issues at Stake: Theory and Practice in the Contemporary Women's Movement in India*. New Delhi: Kali for Women, 1992.
[Principally addresses social, economic, and health-related issues, but contains some discussion of the historical connections between the women's movement and nineteenth-century religious reforms; also features a long section on personal laws and the controversies these have generated.]

295.   Ganesh, Kamala. *The Kottai Pillaimar of Srivaikuntam: A Socio-Historic Study*. Ph.D. diss., University of Bombay, 1982.

[The Tamilnadu community studied keeps its women in strictest seclusion for the purpose of maintaining caste purity.]

For Ganesh, Kamala, see also entries 508 and 611.

296.   Gatwood, Lynn. *Devi and the Spouse Goddess: Women, Sexuality, and Marriage in India*. Riverdale, Md.: Riverdale Co., 1985.
[Principally important for its demonstration of two distinct goddess types in India: the *devi* untamed by husbands and the domesticated "spouse goddess." Incorporates much information about the interplay of constructions of both goddess types with marital norms and with the status, economic roles, sexuality, religious life, and psychological characteristics of Hindu women. Also includes some description of women's roles in festivals that honor goddesses.]

297.   Gaur, Albertine. *Women in India*. London: The British Library, 1980.
[This booklet of twenty-eight pages is one of a series intended to introduce materials of the British Library to the public. Despite brevity, it manages to include sections on Parsi women, the Muslim family, Hindu marriage, Jewish, Christian, and Anglo-Indian women, daily life of Hindu women, wall paintings by Indian women, Indian women today, and legislation intended to improve the position of Hindu women—among other topics. Includes several fine reproductions of paintings featuring women. The author is a member of the British library staff.]

298.   Gaur, Meena. *Sati and Social Reforms in India*. Jaipur: Publication Scheme, 1989.
[Although this volume includes materials on *sati* in western India, much of it addresses social problems other than *sati*, viz., witchcraft, infanticide, and slavery. At times the volume reaches outside the Indian context.]

299. Gayatri Devi, Srimati. *One Life's Pilgrimage: Addresses, Letters, and Articles by the First Indian Woman to Teach Vedanta in the West.* Cohasset, Mass.: Vedanta Centre, 1977.
[Born in Dacca, East Bengal, as one of ten daughters in a comfortable but not wealthy family, the author was married at seventeen and widowed at twenty. Soon after, she received an opportunity to travel to the U.S. with her uncle, Swami Paramananda, who was founding a community of women dedicated to teaching Vedanta in the West. When her uncle and spiritual guide died, she became his successor as head of the women's *ashram* in Boston. This book contains her reminiscences and collected writings.]

300. Gellner, David N. "Hinduism, Tribalism and the Position of Women: The Problem of Newar Identity." *Man* 26 (March 1991), 105–25.
[Exposes a dichotomy (i.e., Hindu/tribal) that has led to distortion of academic studies of the Newar people; argues that Newars are autonomous, neither "Hindu" nor "tribal." Distinctive institutions affecting women are the key to Gellner's argument.]

301. Ghadially, Rehana, ed. *Women in Indian Society: A Reader.* New Delhi and Newbury Park Calif.: Sage Publications, 1988.
[Three articles by Indian authors in this fine anthology explore problems of women's self-construction in India: Sudhir Kakar, "Feminine Identity in India"; Ashis Nandy, "Woman versus Womanliness in India: An Essay in Social and Political Society"; and Suma Chitnis, "Feminism: Indian Ethos and Indian Convictions." Two by U.S. authors turn more explicitly to religion: Susan Wadley, "Women and the Hindu Tradition," and Lawrence A. Babb, "Indigenous Feminism in a Modern Hindu Sect." The volume has a total of twenty-one articles.]

302. Ghanananda, Swami, and Sir John Stewart-Wallace, eds. *Women Saints East and West.* Hollywood, Calif.: Vedanta Press, 1979; originally published as *Women Saints of East and West.* London: Ramakrishna Vedanta Centre, 1955.
[Twenty-six of this volume's twenty-eight essays concern the lives and teachings of specific female saints. Chapters pertinent to India are: T. S. Avinashilingam, "Avvaiyar"; S. Satchidanandam Pillai, "Karaikkal Ammaiyar"; Swami Paramatmananda, "Andal"; T. N. Sreekantaiya, "Akka Mahadevi"; Mrs. Lajwanti Madan, "Mira Bai"; B. G. Kher, "Maharashtra Women Saints"; Piroj Anandkar, "Bahinabai"; Mrs. Sarojini Mehta, "Gauribai"; P. Seshadri and Mahopadhyaya K. S. Nilakantan Unni, "Some Women Saints of Kerala"; Swami Chirantananda, "Tarigonda Venkamamba"; Mrs. Chandra Kumari Handoo, "Women Saints of Buddhism in India" and "Lalleswari or Lal Diddi of Kashmir"; and Swami Ghanananda, "Spiritual Tradition among Hindu Women: Introductory," "Sri Sarada Devi, the Holy Mother," "Some Holy Women Figuring in the Life of Sri Ramakrishna," "Improved Status of Women in Jainism and Buddhism: Introductory," and "Women Saints of Jainism."]

303. Ghosh, (Sri) Aurobindo, and the Mother. *On Women.* Pondicherry: Sri Aurobindo Society, 1978.
[Consists of selections from the writings of a very famous modern Indian guru-saint and his comparably celebrated female successor.]

304. Ghosh, S. K. *Women in a Changing Society.* New Delhi: Ashish Publishing House, 1984.
[This volume's principal focus is social ills; however, it includes one long section on family and marriage laws, subdivided into Hindu, Muslim, Sikh, tribal, Christian, and Parsee segments.]

305. ———. *Indian Women through the Ages.* New Delhi: Ashish Publishing House, 1989.

Bibliography

[Includes materials on Hindu, Muslim, Christian, Parsee, Sikh, and tribal family and marriage; also covered are intercaste, interreligious, and interracial marriage, widowhood, *sati*, witch-hunts, and *devadasi*s.]

306. Ghosh, Srabashi. "'Birds in a Cage': Changes in Bengali Social Life as Recorded in Autobiographies by Women." *Economic and Political Weekly* 21, No. 43 (October 25, 1986), WS88–WS96.
[Surveys a sampling of Bengali women's autobiographies published between 1876 and 1982 to document changes in the family status of women and in women's aspirations and access to education; included here for its information about the religious contexts of the subjects and their attitudes towards orthodox practice.]

307. Ghosha, Jogeshchandra. *Hindu Woman of India (Daughter of Hindustan)*. Delhi: Bimla Publishing House, 1982; repr. of 1928 volume.
[Begins with a chapter titled "The Victim of Power" and continues with sweeping indictments of Indian patriarchy and its attendant abuses of institutions such as marriage and widowhood. Plugs for Hindu schools, however, because Ghosha does not wish to see his Hindu women contaminated by too much exposure to the loose morals and impure values of other communities.]

308. Gilada, I. S., and Vijay Thakur. "*Devadasi*s: A Study of Socio-Cultural Factors and Sexual Exploitation." *Exploitation of Women: Its Causes and Effects*. New Delhi: Vishwa Yuvah Kendra, 1988.
[Surveys 480 *devadasi*s of the Yellama temple, with interest primarily in their relationship to prostitution.]

309. Gill, Kulwant. *Hindu Women's Right to Property in India*. New Delhi: Deep and Deep, 1986.
[Includes three chapters on *stridhan* and a sub-section on the alienation of a woman's estate for religious purposes.]

78

310. Gold, Ann Grodzins. *Life Aims and Fruitful Journeys: The Ways of Rajasthani Pilgrims*. Ph.D. diss., University of Chicago, 1984.
[Prototype for *Fruitful Journeys* (see entry 311 below).]

311. ————. *Fruitful Journeys: The Ways of Rajasthani Pilgrims*. Berkeley: University of California Press, 1988.
[A study of pilgrimages large and little, from the perspective of those who participate. Locating herself in a village of Ajmer district, the author not only joined pilgrims but also observed the village religious context in which these are set; she incorporates important information both on pilgrimages to secure offspring and on the significance of women's roles in village festivals.]

For Gold, Ann Grodzins, see also entries 41 and 721.

312. Good, Anthony. "The Female Bridegroom: Rituals of Puberty and Marriage in South India and Sri Lanka." *Social Analysis* No. 11 (October 1982), 35–55.
[Summarizes and analyzes in sociological categories women's rites from puberty through widowhood of two agricultural villages of Tirunelveli district, Tamil Nadu. A special feature of the puberty rite is a mock marriage to a female cross-cousin of the pubescent girl. Compares these rites with those of the Pramalai Kallar, the Kandyan Sinhalese, Nayars of Kerala, and groups described by Dube and Trautman in central India.]

313. Goonatilake, Herma. "The Position of Women in Buddhism from a Historical Perspective." *Logos* 21, No. 4 (November 1982), 33–41.
[Treats Buddhism as a liberating influence on women, citing access to education and to spiritual attainments, scriptural passages on women's worth, access to remarriage, contributions of women donors, and positive models in the literature; does acknowledge negative evidence also.]

314.   Gopalan, Gopalan V. *"Vrat*: Ceremonial Vows of Women in Gujarat, India." *Asian Folklore Studies* 37, No. 1 (1978), 101–29.
         [A long discussion of the process of "Wemosutization" (author's term) initiates this article; the author asserts that this process is now diluting life-cycle rites. Although discussion of *vrata*s is very general and sometimes patronizing, this essay contains a helpful summary of the annual *vrata* cycle.]

315.   ————. "The Marriage Ritual among the Nagar Brahmins of Gujarat." *Folklore* 21, No. 2 (1980), 29–36.
         [This detailed description of a marriage ceremony includes the role of the bride and texts of songs sung by women of both families.]

316.   Gopani, A. S. "Position of Women in Jaina Literature." *The Orient: The World of Jainism: Jaina History, Art, Literature, Philosophy and Religion.* Ed. Vishwanath Pandey. Bombay: Vishwanath Pandey, Himalaya Society, 1976.
         [Addressing the status of girls, wives, mothers, prostitutes, nuns, and princesses, this article admits that Jain women have been kept subordinate and sometimes slandered. The author pleads for their "equal and rightful place in the sanctuary of spiritualism."]

317.   *The Gospel of the Holy Mother.* Madras: Sri Ramakrishna Math, 1984.
         [This first full translation of the Bengali work *Sri Sri Mayer Katha* offers memories of the Ramakrishna Mission's Holy Mother Sri Sarada Devi by thirty-eight of her male and female disciples.]

318.   Goswami, Indira. *An Unfinished Autobiography.* New Delhi: Sterling Publishers, 1990.
         [A noted Assamese writer and landowner's daughter re-traces her own life. Includes a description of her meetings

with an astrologer, her (unwelcomed) participation in a sacrifice to Kali, her pilgrimage to Vrindavan, and a series of encounters with gurus and holy women.]

319. Gould, Ketayun. "Sex Inequalities in the Dual System of Education." *Economic and Political Weekly* 18, No. 39 (September 24, 1983), 1668–76.
[Challenges the common claim that Parsees do not discriminate against females in providing education, offering evidence of inequities in school enrollment and availability. Based on a survey of 551 households in Gujarat.]

320. Grimshaw, Anna. *Rizong: A Monastic Community in Ladakh*. Ph.D. diss., Cambridge University, 1983.
[Although not principally concerned with women, this dissertation contains some materials on links between monks of the community studied, laypersons, and nuns.]

321. ————. *Servants of the Buddha: Winter in a Himalayan Convent*. Cleveland: Pilgrim Press, 1994.
[A British anthropologist recounts her memories of a winter's sojourn in the Julichang Tibetan Buddhist convent of Ladakh, India. A prominent theme is the grinding round of work carried out by the nuns and their effective servitude to the monks of the nearby Rizong monastery. She shows as well how nuns mediate between the higher Buddhist practices carried out by the monks and the popular religion that remains so important to the laity.]

322. Gross, Rita M., ed. *Beyond Androcentrism: New Essays on Women and Religion*. Missoula, Mont.: Scholars Press, 1977.
[This collection of nineteen essays from an early phase of cross-cultural women's studies in the United States includes two essays featuring Indian materials. Nancy Auer Falk's "Draupadi and the Dharma" utilizes paradoxes in the Mahabharata's approach to its heroine Draupadi to illumine the epic's treatment of dharma. Arvind Sharma's "Ramakrsna Paramahamsa: A Study in a Mystic's Attitude

Towards Women" points to ambivalence in Ramakrishna's approach to women.]

323.   ————. *Buddhism after Patriarchy: A Feminist History, Analysis and Reconstruction of Buddhism*. Albany: State University of New York Press, 1993.
[This volume's three sections present a history of Buddhist roles and images of women, an analysis of basic Buddhist teachings' implication for gender, and a projection of changes required in theory and practice if a post-patriarchal Buddhism is to be achieved.]

For Gross, Rita M., see also entries 270, 997, and 998.

324.   Gross, Susan Hill, and Marjorie Wall Bingham. *Women in India: Vedic to Modern Times*. St. Louis Park, Minn.: Glenhurst Publications, 1980.
[The six short chapters of this work are intended as a text for high school social studies students. Among other topics, it covers the Vedas and the *Laws of Manu*, and the complexities of Hindu marriage, including wedding rituals, and problems associated with marriage, such as age of brides, widows' problems, *sati*, infanticide, and *purdah*. Also treats the religious roles of women and *devadasi*s. Includes textual selections and descriptions by first-hand observers; tends to stress Brahmanic ideals and sensational issues.]

325.   Grover, Verinder, ed. *Great Women of Modern India*. New Delhi: Deep and Deep, 1992.
[An eight-volume set covers distinguished women of all varieties, including those who have made outstanding contributions to religion, such as Annie Besant and Sister Nivedita.]

326.   Gulati, Leela. *Profiles in Female Poverty: A Study of Five Poor Working Women in Kerala*. Delhi: Hindustan Publishing Corporation, 1981; Oxford, Eng. and Elmsford, N.Y.: Pergamon Press, 1982.

[The women studied are an agricultural laborer, a brick worker, a fish vendor, a construction worker, and a coir worker. Sketches of Jayamma and Devaki include small segments on religious practice and weddings; the Devaki sketch also includes a puberty ceremony, and the Kalyani sketch has wedding material. Sara is a Christian; her sketch discusses the role of the church in her community.]

327. ————. "Coping with Male Migration." *Economic and Political Weekly* 22, No. 44 (October 31, 1987), WS41–WS46. [Concerns a variety of stresses and readjustments imposed on women of Kerala by migration of husbands and sons to the Middle East; one section describes how both Hindu and Muslim women turn to religion on such occasions.]

For Gulati, Leela, see also entry 507.

328. Gulati, Saroj. *Women and Society: Northern India in 11th and 12th Centuries.* Delhi: Chanakya Publications, 1985. [Includes chapters on family life, household rites, and the position of widows.]

329. ————. "*Sati*-Custom: A Survey from the Vedic Period to 1200 A.D." *Teaching Politics* 13, no. 2 (1987), 27–45. [Available at University of Delhi Department of Political Science. The title is self-descriptive. Mostly cites textual precepts approving *sati* and evidence for *sati* performance, but also sets the later custom in its social context and offers explanations for promotion of *sati*.]

For Gulati, Saroj, see also entry 284.

330. Gupta, A. R. *Women in Hindu Society: A Study of Tradition and Transition.* New Delhi: Jyotsna Prakashan, 1976. [Includes material on marriage customs, *sati*, widow-remarriage, sex, and contemporary patterns of change.]

331.   Gupta, Amulya Kumar Datta. *In Association with Sri Sri Anandamayi*. 3 vols. Calcutta: Shree Shree Anandamayee Charitable Society, 1987.
[Features personal reminiscences of the author's long acquaintance with a modern woman saint.]

332.   Gupta, Anirudha. "Raja Rammohan Roy and Rights of Women." *Mainstream* 23, No. 49 (3 August 1985), 29–30.
[Reflects on a volume honoring Rammohan Roy; includes a summary of Roy's argument about women's rights, with questions that this raises for the present day.]

333.   Gupta, Giri Raj. *Marriage, Religion and Society: Pattern of Change in a Village Society*. Delhi: Vikas Publishing House, 1974; New York: Wiley, 1974.
[This village study includes three chapters on marriage rituals; another chapter discusses the role of kin, including mothers, daughters, and aunts.]

334.   Gupta, Kamala. *Social Status of Hindu Women in Northern India, 1206–1707 A.D.* New Delhi: Inter-India Publications, 1987.
[Includes descriptions of birth and marriage rites, as well as women's dress and pastimes, festivals, education, widowhood, *sati, jauhar*, and public women, including *devadasi*s.]

335.   Gupta, Manjul. "Swami Dayananda: A Champion of Women's Cause." *Maharishi Dayanand University Research Journal (Arts)* 3, No. 2 (October 1988), 197–214.
[Cites the miseries of women before Dayananda's advent, and his proposed reforms regarding education and marriage. Describes his proposals on *niyoga* in some detail.]

336.   Gupta, Sanjukta, and Richard Gombrich. "Another View of Widow-Burning and Womanliness in Indian Public Culture." *Journal of Commonwealth and Comparative Politics* 22, No. 3 (November 1984), 262–74.

Bibliography

[From a symposium on Ashis Nandy's book *At the Edge of Psychology*; Gupta and Gombrich charge that Nandy does not have his facts straight for his article on *sati*.]

For Gupta, Sanjukta, see also entry 532.

337.   Gurupriya Devi. *Sri Sri Ma Anandamayi*. 3 vols. Calcutta: Shree Shree Anandamayee Charitable Society, 1984.
[This description of the life and wonders of the modern saint Anandamayi Ma was written by a female disciple who served the saint for more than fifty years. Unavailable in the U.S.; found at Nehru Memorial Library, New Delhi.]

338.   Haddad, Yvonne Yazbek, and Ellison Banks Findly. *Women, Religion, and Social Change*. Albany: State University of New York Press, 1985.
[Contains five essays pertaining to South Asian women: Ellison Banks Findly, "Gargi at the King's Court: Women and Philosophical Innovation in Ancient India"; Janice D. Willis, "Nuns and Benefactresses: The Role of Women in the Development of Buddhism"; Sandra P. Robinson, "Hindu Paradigms of Women: Images and Values"; Donna Marie Wulff, "Images and Roles of Women in Bengali Vaishnava *padavali kirtan*"; and Lou Ratte, "Goddesses, Mothers, and Heroines: Hindu Women and the Feminine in the Early Nationalist Movement."]

339.   Haksar, Nandita. "'*Ek Sata Ho, Hum Mandir Banayenge*': Countering Attempt to Revive *Sati*." *Manushi* No. 7 (1981), 32–33.
[A group of feminist workers attempts to stop a March by Marwari women honoring a princess who once committed *sati*.]

340.   ———. "Indian Women: The 'Image' Myth." *Mainstream* (Republic Day Issue, 1981), 63–65.
[This vigorous challenge to traditional views of women in India defends identification with the feminist movement.]

341.   ————. "The Nineteenth-Century Social Reform Movements in India and the Position of Women." *Man and Development* 3, No. 4 (December 1981), 119–33.
[Utilizes a handbook for social reformers published in 1889 to show contemporary perceptions of social and economic realities affecting women, and solutions being offered; points to limitations of those solutions and alternatives available at the time.]

For Haksar, Nandita, see also entries 145 and 223.

342.   Haksar, Nandita, and Anju Singh. *Demystification of Law for Women*. New Delhi: Lancer Press, 1986.
[In clever cartoons and simple laypersons' language, this booklet depicts the double standards inhering in sectarian personal laws in India; it pleads both for a uniform code and for united struggle among women.]

343.   Hamsa, N. "Impact of Regional Tradition on Muslim Women, with Special Reference to South India." *Islam and the Modern Age* 14, No. 1 (February 1983), 49–58.
[Cites differences between Muslims of Kerala and Tamilnadu with reference to practices such as claim to property, *mehr*, seclusion, veiling, and education; also cites differences in sub-communities of Muslims. Unfortunately, not a sophisticated treatment.]

344.   Hanchett, Suzanne. *Coloured Rice: Symbolic Structure in Hindu Family Festivals*. Delhi: Hindustan Publishing Corporation, 1988.
[Examines four folk festivals of Karnataka to show how they define the concept of family. Two are women's festivals: the Gauri festival known throughout India and a Lakshmi *puja* celebrated by just a single Brahman subcaste of two villages. Hanchett also cites other examples of significant women's activites, thus showing that women's import in family life is much greater than is usually thought.]

345.   Hancock, Mary Elizabeth. "Saintly Careers among South India's Urban Middle Classes." *Man* 25, No. 3 (September 1990), 505–20.
["The social construction of saintliness among urban Brahmans of Tamil South India is examined through the life histories of two such persons." One of the two cited examples is a married woman *sakta* named Rajalakshmi.]

346.   ————. *Women at Work: Ritual and Cultural Identity among Smarta Brahmans of Madras*. Ph.D. diss., University of Pennsylvania, 1990.
[The subjects of the author's fieldwork in Madras City were upper- and middle-class Smarta Brahmin women. Examining "the relation between women's ritual practice and gender and caste identity," this study finds that women are important ritual "doers," despite prescriptions to the contrary in Sanskrit texts; moreover "the symbolic efficacy of ritual depended on women's presence and their interventions in ritual practice." Cited from author's description, *DAI* 51, No. 12 (June 1991), A-4171–72.]

347.   Hansen, Kathryn. "The *Virangana* in North Indian History: Myth and Popular Culture." *Economic and Political Weekly* 23, No. 18 (April 30, 1988), WS25–WS33.
[The *virangana* is the heroic woman—the woman warrior. This article cites stories circulating about heroic women, describes varying uses made of the latters' stories and names, and cites folk dramas and films that have developed the *virangana* image.]

348.   ————. "Heroic Modes of Women in Indian Myth, Ritual and History: The *Tapasvini* and the *Virangana*." *Annual Review of Women in World Religions*, II: *Heroic Women*, ed. Arvind Sharma and Katherine K. Young. Albany: State University of New York Press, 1992, pp. 1–62.
[Describes two types of female heroism: the *tapasvini* is the self-denying woman who achieves power through self-morti-

fication, and the *virangana* is a woman warrior who exacts retribution for "politically and morally reprehensible deeds." The author promises exploration of further types in an article to come.]

349. Hardy, Friedhelm. "Diary of an Unknown Girl." *Religion* 10, No. 2 (Autumn 1980), 165–82.
[Summarizes the autobiography of Bahini Bai, seventeenth-century Maharashtrian poet-saint.]

350. Harishchandra. *A Unique Pilgrimage*. 1st ed. Varanasi: Sarva Seva Sangh Prakashan, 1975.
[Describes a twelve year journey through India on foot by four women spreading the message of Vinoba Bhave. Includes information on the women themselves and an extensive itinerary; however, much of its material is very vague and general.]

351. Harlan, Lindsey (Beth). "Caste and Gender Conflicts among Rajput Women." *Center for the Study of World Religions Bulletin, Harvard University* (Fall 1975), 36–41.
[Shows how Rajput women resolve conflicts between responsibilities derived from caste and those derived from gender; one example described concerns handling of young brides' loyalty to the *kuldevi* (clan goddess) of her natal family.]

352. ———. *The Ethic of Protection among Rajput Women: Religious Mediations of Caste and Gender*. Ph.D. diss., Harvard University, 1987.
[Prototype for *Religion and Rajput Women* (entry 353 below). Described *DAI* 48, No. 11 (May 1988), A-2903–04.]

353. ———. *Religion and Rajput Women: The Ethic of Protection in Contemporary Narratives*. Berkeley: University of California Press, 1992.
[The locus of Harlan's research is Mewar district; her sources range from queens to commoners, with emphasis on

the mid-range "noble" Rajputs. Stories that women tell about family goddesses (*kuldevis*), *satis*, and ancestral heroines (*viranganas*) reveal their ethos of caste duty and gender roles. Good bibliography.]

354.   Hasan, Zoya, ed. *Identity Politics: Community and Gender; the Construction of Muslim Women in pre- and post-Independence India*. New Delhi: Kali for Women, forthcoming. ["Through an examination of history, politics, work and culture, this collection attempts to explore how the construction of community identity has affected Muslim women in India; the processes by which such identities are constructed; how they are represented in the cultural domain; and how the ambivalence of women's multiple identities interacts with the above. Contributors include Barbara Metcalf, Farzana Sheikh, Feisal Devji, Paola Baccheta, Elizabeth Mann, Shahida Lateef, Farid ud din Kazmi, Nukul Kesavan, Zarina Bhatty, Uzra Kidwai, Asghar Ali Engineer and others" (from the publisher's catalogue description).]

For Hasan, Zoya, see also entry 719.

355.   Hasna, Begum [OCLC lists as Hasana, Begama]. *Women in the Developing World: Thoughts and Ideals*. New Delhi: Sterling Publishers, 1990.
[This study by a Bengali Muslim woman includes materials on the Muslim marriage code and analyses of male/female relations in folklore and fiction.]

356.   Hasnain, Nadeem, and Sheikh Abtar Hasnain. *Shias and Shia Islam in India: A Study in Society and Culture*. New Delhi: Harnam Publications, 1988.
[This sociological survey of one thousand respondents throughout India includes subsections on marriage, the status of women, perceptions of personal law, and perceptions of proposals for reform.]

357. Hatcher, Brian Allison. *The Religious Worldview of Pandit Isvarachandra Vidyasagar*. Ph.D. diss., Harvard University, 1992.
[Pandit Vidyasagar was the most articulate writer on behalf of women's rights during the mid- and later nineteenth century, as well as a noted educator; this dissertation explores his educational work, his pedagogy, and the convergence of "Modernist and Dharmic idioms" in his discourse. Described *DAI* 53, No. 6 (December 1992), A-1965.]

358. Havaldar, Pratima. "Changing Role of a Hindu Woman: Wife and Mother." *Dharma Marg* 3, No. 1 (April 1985), 45–46.
[The author states her opinion: changing times call for a changing understanding of the role of women.]

359. Havnevik, Hanna. *Tibetan Buddhist Nuns: History, Cultural Norms, and Social Reality*. Oslo: Norwegian University Press, 1989; Oxford and New York: Oxford University Press, 1989.
[Following an introductory chapter on women in Buddhist literature, the author examines the distribution and organization of nunneries in Tibet, accomplishments of distinguished nuns, and the founding, organization, practices, and everyday life of a Tibetan nunnery in exile. A concluding chapter examines the relationship between traditional norms of Tibetan culture and the contemporary situation of nuns—with citations from interviews.]

360. Hawley, John Stratton. "*Yoga* and *Viyoga*: Simple Religion in Hinduism." *Harvard Theological Review* 74, No. 1 (January 1981), 1–20.
[Hinduism, like other religions, incorporates a tension between those who tend to complicate religions and those who prize simplicity; this is demonstrated by the words and behavior of Krishna's *gopi*s (cowgirls) in the poetry of Sur Das. Hawley argues that taking these *gopi*s as models of ideal faith is equivalent to praising the simple religion of women.]

361.   ————. "Morality Beyond Morality in the Lives of Three
Hindu Saints." *Saints and Virtues.* Ed. John Stratton
Hawley. Berkeley: University of California Press, 1987.
[The eighteenth-century *Bhaktamal,* an anthology of lives
of great saints, cites its subjects as models of specific vir-
tues. Hawley examines the lives of Mira Bai, Narasai
Mehta, and Pipa Das, with the latter's wife Sita, to recover
the ethical concepts thus illustrated.]

362.   ————, ed. *Sati, the Blessing and the Curse: The Burning
of Wives in India.* New York: Oxford University Press, 1993.
[Twelve scholars—six Indian, six American—"consider the
many meanings of *sati* in India and the West: in literature,
art, and opera; in religion, psychology, economics and
politics" (quoted from the publisher's announcement).]

363.   ————, ed. *Fundamentalism and Gender.* New York:
Oxford University Press, 1994.
[Two case studies treat materials pertinent for South Asian-
ists: Peter J. Awn "The Shah Bano Affair"; and John
Stratton Hawley, "Hinduism: *Sati* and Its Defenders."]

For Hawley, John Stratton, see also entry 127.

364.   Hawley, John Stratton, and Mark Juergensmeyer. *Songs of
the Saints of India.* New York: Oxford University Press,
1988.
[Six of northern India's most celebrated Hindi-speaking
saints are featured in this anthology of well-translated poems; one of them is the Rajput princess and lover of Krishna, Mirabai. Includes a solid fifteen-page introduction to
the poet, her fame, her life, and the themes of her poetry.]

365.   Hawley, John Stratton, and Donna Marie Wulff, eds. *The
Divine Consort: Radha and the Goddesses of India.*
Berkeley: Graduate Theological Union, 1982; Boston:
Beacon Press, 1986.

[The twenty-two excellent articles in this volume tend to focus much more on divinity than humanity; however, see Frédérique Apffel Marglin, "Types of Sexual Union and Their Implicit Meanings," and A. K. Ramanujan, "On Women Saints."]

366. Hazra, R. C. *Studies in the Puranic Records on Hindu Rites and Customs*. 2nd ed. Delhi: Motilal Banarsidass, 1975; original ed. 1940.
[The first half of this volume is an analysis of the chronology of individual Puranas; the second traces developments in ideology and practice, basing conclusions on the preceding chronological analysis. References to women and *vrata*s are scattered throughout.]

367. Hejib, Alaka. "Wife or Widow? The Ambiguity and the Problems Regarding the Marital Status of the Renounced Wife of a *Sannyasi*." *Yoga Life* 13, No. 11 (1982), 3–14.
[A woman whose husband has renounced home and family to take up the wandering *sannyasi*'s life is in a peculiar dilemma, according to Hindu precepts and tales. This article analyzes both dilemma and proffered solutions.]

368. Henry, Edward O. "North Indian Wedding Songs." *Journal of South Asian Literature* 11, Nos. 1–2 (Fall–Winter 1975), 77–93.
[The Hindu women's wedding songs translated here were collected by the author in a village of Uttar Pradesh. Includes a verse-by-verse commentary on central imagery of the songs, a description of performance, and a concluding thematic analysis.]

369. Hess, Linda. "The Poet, the People, and the Western Scholar: Influence of a Sacred Drama and Text on Social Values in North India." *Theatre Journal* 40, No. 2 (May 1988), 236–53.

[Attempts to discover how the values of Tulsidas, as presented in the Ramlila, shape views of women and caste among those who attend it. Based on interviews with Ramlila attenders in Ramnagar, Uttar Pradesh.]

370. Hettiaratchi, S. B. *Social and Cultural History of Ancient Sri Lanka*. Delhi: Sri Satguru Publications, 1988.
[Includes a chapter on marriage and another on "The Position of Women"; the latter includes materials on nuns and nunneries. Sources are both literary and epigraphic.]

371. Hiltebeitel, Alf. *The Cult of Draupadi*. 2 vols. Chicago: University of Chicago Press, 1988, 1991.
[Draupadi is both an epic heroine and a South Indian goddess; these first two volumes of a projected three-volume series trace her mythology (volume 1) and the performance of her story during lengthy festivals in and around the "Gingee country" of Tamilnadu.]

372. *Hindu Laws Acts*. Allahabad: Central Law Agency, 1985.
[Contains texts of the Hindu Marriage Act (1955), the Hindu Succession Act (1956), the Hindu Minority Guardianship Act (1956), and the Hindu Adoptions and Maintenance Act (1956).]

373. *Hindu Widows Remarriage Act, 1856*.
[Cites text of the law on Widow Remarriage as modified on April 1, 1982.]

374. Hobson, Sarah. *Family Web: A Story of India*. London: John Murray, 1978; Chicago: Academy Press, 1982.
[The author tells the story of a family with whom she and her husband lived while he was making a film in Karnataka. Descriptions include women's activities during a temple visit, menstrual prohibitions, marriage preparations and rites, the concept of a virtuous wife, rites and prohibitions at birth, and a woman's experience with possession.

Although ritual information is not detailed, the whole gives a good picture of women's everyday life.]

375. Holden, Pat, ed. *Women's Religious Experience: Cross-Cultural Perspectives.* Totowa, N.J.: Barnes and Noble, 1983.
[Of the eleven studies in this volume, two pertain to India. Julia Leslie's "Essence and Existence: Women and Religion in Ancient Indian Texts" searches Sanskrit and devotional literature of Hinduism for women's roles and women's voice; Catherine Thompson's "Women, Fertility and the Worship of Gods in a Hindu Village" surveys religious practices of women in a village of Malwa region, Madhya Pradesh.]

376. Horner, I. B. *Women under Primitive Buddhism: Laywomen and Almswomen.* Delhi: Motilal Banarsidass, 1975; originally published London: G. Routledge, 1930.
[A classic work, now reissued, assembles references to women in the Buddhist Pali Canon. Horner treats the laywoman as mother, daughter, wife, widow, and worker, as well as admission, rules for, and life in the women's order, relations between nuns and laity, and the collection of women's stanzas known as *Therigatha.*]

377. Husain, Shahanara. *The Social Life of Women in Early Medieval Bengal.* Dhaka: Asiatic Society of Bangladesh, 1985.
[Includes a chapter on religion and women.]

378. Husain, Sheikh Abram. *Marriage Customs among Muslims in India: A Sociological Study of the Shia Marriage Customs.* New Delhi: Sterling Publishers, 1976.
[Describes marriage customs of the Shi'a community; includes a section on rites.]

379. Hutheesing, M. O. L. Klein. "The *Thiratee Kalyanam* Ceremony among South Indian Hindu Communities of Malaysia: A Changing Female Initiation Rite." *The Eastern Anthropologist* 36, No. 1 (January–March 1983), 131–47.

[Describes modifications of puberty rites for girls still being practiced among South Indians of Malaysia.]

380. Hyder, Sakina. "Maintenance of Divorcee: Some Questions." *Mainstream* (August 24, 1985), 26–29.
[This article is one of a 1985 *Mainstream* series that debated the Supreme Court decision in the Shah Bano case (on the right to maintenance of Muslim women divorcees). For others of the series, see Tara Ali Baig (May 18), Asghar Ali Engineer (May 25 and August 3), Vasudha Dhagamwar (July 6), Syed Shahabuddin (June 1 and July 13), and Nusrat Bano Ruhi (July 20). Note also Rumki Basu's two-part article "Divorce in India" published on March 2 and 9 of the same year.]

381. *I Am Ever with You: Matri Lila. Vol. I (1952–62)*. Calcutta: Shree Shree Anandamayi Charitable Society, 1985.
[Offers an anecdotal biography and reconstruction of modern saint Anandamayi Ma's life during the decade cited.]

382. Ifeka, Caroline. "Spiritual and Statistical Models of the Sexes in British India, 1871–1931." *South Asia* 1 (June 1982), 16–28.
[Shows a relationship between three seemingly disparate phenomena: the Hindu concept of marriage, the symbolism of right and left, and "lost" women of the Indian census reports.]

383. Iltis, Linda Louise. *The Swasthani* Vrata: *Newar Women and Ritual in Nepal*. Ph.D. diss., University of Wisconsin at Madison, 1985.
[Investigates stories and worship of Swasthani, the Goddess of Own Place; argues that representations of women in these sources are "independent, initiatory, positive, and integrative," and offer "new models of female participation in Newar society." Cited from author's description, *DAI* 47, No. 1 (July 1986), A-184.]

384.   "Impact of Ahmedabad Disturbances on Women: A Report."
        Economic and Political Weekly 20, No. 41 (October 12,
        1985), 1726–31.
        [Representatives of the Bombay Women and Media group
        report following their interviews of women affected by the
        1985 Hindu/Muslim rioting in Ahmedabad.]

385.   *Indian Women: Marriage and Social Status: Report of the
        Age of Consent Committee, 1928–29.* New Delhi: Usha, 1984.
        [Traces implementation and test cases of legislation on age
        of consent and law of rape as amended in 1925.]

386.   Indira, M. K. *Phaniyamma—a Novel.* Trans. from Kannada
        by Tejaswini Niranjana. New Delhi: Kali for Women, 1989.
        ["This award-winning novel tells the story of Phaniyamma,
        a child widow of 13 who lived to be 112 years old. . . . How
        a young girl confronts the grim reality of widowhood . . . in
        a society which regards it as the ultimate pollution and
        how, through sheer will power, she survives and grows to
        abhor the moral perversions practiced against women, are
        movingly told" (from the publisher's announcement).]

387.   Indiradevi, M. *Women, Education, Employment, Family
        Living: A Study of Emerging Hindu Wives in Urban India.*
        Delhi: Gian Publishing House, 1987.
        [This sociological survey of eighty Hindu families, half with
        educated non-working wives and half with educated work-
        ing wives, reports on family structure, role performance, de-
        cision making, and husband-wife interaction. The research
        site is Visakhapatnam, Andhra Pradesh.]

388.   Indrajeet. *Letters from a Husband to His Wife.* New
        Barrackpur: Sabita Press, 1980.
        [The letters compiled here are mostly devoted to the reli-
        gious concepts of the husband, a Bengali much influenced
        by Ramakrishna. But they also reveal his relationship to
        his wife and the female models he holds up to her.]

389. *In the Company of the Holy Mother.* 2nd ed. Calcutta: Advaita Ashrama, 1980; first published 1963.
[Consists of anecdotes from the life of the Ramakrishna Movement's Holy Mother Sri Sarada Devi, as recorded originally in Bengali by her disciples.]

390. "In the International Women's Year." *Sikh Review* 24 (May 1976), 2–4.
[An editorial from a Sikh publication charges that women have become too absorbed in their "domestic affairs, coffee parties, and fashion" to bother about religion. Recounts how women reinspired and saved religion in the past, and issues a call to mothers: "Save the straying race!"]

391. Iqbal, Safia. *Women and Islamic Law.* Delhi: Al-Asr Publications, 1988.
[Treats contemporary issues affecting women, such as divorce, maintenance, family planning, succession, and the impact of women's liberation; charges that games of oppression and suppression have been played against women. Offers evidence both for and against women's rights.]

For Ishwaran, K., see entries 57 and 960.

392. Israel, Milton, and N. K. Wagle, eds. *Islamic Society and Culture: Essays in Honour of Professor Aziz Ahmad.* New Delhi: Manohar, 1983.
[Three articles of this *Festschrift* address aspects of Muslim women's lives: Barbara D. Metcalf, "The Making of a Muslim Lady: Maulana Thanawi's *Bihishti Zewar*"; Gail Minault, "Hali's *Majalis Un-Nissa: Purdah* and Woman Power in Nineteenth Century India"; and Annemarie Schimmel, "A Nineteenth Century Anthology of Poetesses."]

393. Iyengar, K. R. Srinivasa [OCLC lists as Srinivasa Iyengar, K. R.]. *On the Mother: The Chronicle of a Manifestation and Ministry.* 2nd ed. Pondicherry: Sri Aurobindo International Centre of Education, 1978.

["The Mother" of this volume is the Aurobindo Ashram's Mirra Alfassa Richard; the work is a biography with records of the Mother's teachings and conversations.]

394. Jacobson, Doranne. "The Chaste Wife." *American Studies in the Anthropology of India*. Ed. Sylvia Vatuk. New Delhi: Manohar, 1978.
[Examines the theme of "wifely fidelity and its central place in the life of Bhuribai, a (high caste) woman of Nimkhera" in Madhya Pradesh. Bhurabai recounts her discipline of chastity, her troubles with an errant daughter, her experience of widowhood, and her views on *sati*.]

395. ————. "Studying the Changing Roles of Women in Rural India." *Signs* 8, No. 1 (Autumn 1982), 132–37.
[Principally describes the author's experiences as participant-observer researcher in a village of central India, including the limitations that local custom imposed upon her; includes brief references to practice that maintains purity and the refusal of a young Brahmin widow to remarry.]

For Jacobson, Doranne, see also entries 10, 270, 271, and 679.

396. Jacobson, Doranne, and Susan S. Wadley, eds. *Women in India: Two Perspectives*. 2nd, enl., ed. New Delhi: Manohar Book Service, 1992; original ed. Manohar, 1977.
[Two anthropologists of distinction combine a selection of their articles to introduce the practices and predicaments of Indian women. Articles included are Doranne Jacobson, "The Women of North and Central India: Goddesses and Wives," and "Golden Handprints and Red-Painted Feet: Hindu Childbirth Rituals in Central India"; also Susan Wadley, "Women and the Hindu Tradition" and "Hindu Women's Family and Household Rites in a North Indian Village."]

397. Jagannathachariar, C. *The* Tiruppavai *of Sri Andal: Textual, Literary, and Critical Study*. Madras: Arulmigu Parthasarathy Swami Devasthanam, 1982.

[A distinguished retired Professor of Tamil offers a stanza-by-stanza close commentary and analysis of Tamilnadu's most celebrated devotional poem by a woman. The thirty-stanza *Tiruppavai* portrays a celebration of the *nonbu* festival in the month of Margali by virgin cowgirls who adore Lord Krishna. More than half the volume is notes; transliterations of the text are offered in both Roman script and *devanagari*.]

398. Jahan, H. H. Nawab Sultan Begam Sahiba. *Muslim Married Couple*. New Delhi: Award Publishing House, 1980.
[Summarizes Quranic injunctions on marriage, nuptial rights, separation and divorce, *izzat*, and inheritance; a simple book, with a conservative approach.]

399. Jahan, Roushan, ed. and trans. *Inside Seclusion: The* Avarodhbasini *of Rokeya Sakhawat Hossain*. Dacca: Women for Women, 1981.
[Introduces the author and translates the text of a very early book on *purdah* practices written in Bengali by a Muslim woman. Rokeya Sakhawat Hossain was born in 1880 to a zamindar's family and educated secretly with the aid of her older brother; she became a writer, with her husband's encouragement, but was widowed after eleven years of marriage. She later worked on women's behalf and started a girls' school. Her book describes forty-seven examples of women's suffering under *purdah*.]

For Jahan, Roushan, see also entry 767.

400. Jai, Janak Raj, ed. *Shah Bano*. New Delhi: Rajiv Publications, 1986.
[A collection of articles responding to a very controversial case in which a seventy-five year old Muslim woman sued her husband for maintenance—and lost. Authors include both Hindus and Muslims.]

401. Jain, Devaki, ed. *Indian Women*. New Delhi: Government of India, 1975.
[A pioneering early collaborative work offers a general overview of Indian women's problems and lives. Nine contributions have potential importance for religionists: Kamaladevi Chattopadhyay, "The Women's Movement, Then and Now"; Romila Thapar, "Looking Back in History"; Ashok Rudra, "Cultural and Religious Influences"; M. A. Sreenivasan, *"Panchakanya*—an Age-Old Benediction"; Veena Das, "Marriage among the Hindus"; Qurratulain Hyder, "Muslim Women of India"; Verrier Elwin, "Tribal Women"; Gita Aravamudan, "Nurses and Nuns of Kerala"; and Mina Swaminathan, "Chellama: A Portrait."]

402. ————. "Journey of a Woman Freedom Fighter." *Mainstream* (August 22, 1981), 9–10, 28–29.
[Recounts the story of a Jain housewife who went to jail in the freedom struggle along with her husband—and later returned to household life.]

403. ————. "Development as if Women Mattered: Can Women Build a New Paradigm?"
[Lecture Delivered at OECD/DAC meeting, Paris, January 26, 1983; available at the Institute for the Social Studies Trust, New Delhi. Criticizes contemporary development strategies from a woman-centered perspective, and suggests a new model of development. Included here for its Gandhian philosophical basis.]

404. ————. "Women and Religion: Issues and Possibilities—an Indian Presentation."
[Paper presented at International Conference on Women, Religion and Social Change, Harvard University, 1983; available at the Institute for Social Studies Trust, New Delhi. A later version of this paper has been published under the title of "Gandhian Contributions Towards a Feminist Ethic" in Diana Eck and Devaki Jain, *Speaking of Faith*, entry 251.]

405. ————. "Women, Religion and Social Change: The Indian Women's Movement."
[In Devaki Jain, *Articles on Religion*, a file of the Institute for Social Studies Trust, New Delhi. Presented originally at Harvard University in 1983, this paper is primarily concerned with responses to poverty in the women's movement; the coverage is very general.]

For Jain, Devaki, see also entries 251 and 920.

406. Jain, Jagdish Chandra, and Margaret Walter. *Women in Ancient Indian Tales*. Delhi: Mittal Publications, 1987.
[Tales of virtuous and evil wives and courtesans are featured in this simple retelling of stories from Sanskrit and Prakrit sources.]

407. Jain, L. C. "Kamaladevi: A *Karmayogi.*" *Indian International Centre Quarterly* 15, No. 3 (Monsoon 1988), 6–8.
[An obituary article celebrates the life of Kamaladevi Chattopadhyay, Gandhian freedom fighter, social crusader, and patroness of Indian handicrafts and theater.]

408. ————. "Kamaladevi: An Epochal Life." *Manushi* No. 53 (July–August 1989), 10–17
[Remembers Kamaladevi Chattopadhyay; see the description in entry 407 above.]

409. Jain, Sagar Chand. *The Law Relating to Marriage and Divorce: Based on Latest Amendments and Up-to-date Case Law*.Delhi: Surjeet Book Depot, 1983.
[Reproduces the Hindu Marriage Act of 1955, with commentaries on each clause and procedures for implementation.]

410. Jain, Sharada, Nirja Misra, and Kavita Srivastava. "Deorala Episode: Women's Protest in Rajasthan." *Economic and Political Weekly* 22, No. 45 (November 7, 1987), 1891–94.

[Assembles a chronology of responses to the Roop Kanwar *sati*; asks why the incident was never simply described as murder and calls for systematic dialogue on the status of widows.]

411. Jain, Shashi. *Status and Role Perception of Middle Class Women*. New Delhi: Puja Publishers, 1988.
[This sociological survey of four hundred working women in Agra, Kanpur, Lucknow, and Varanasi includes a sub-section on religious activities and commitments and another on invitations extended to others at festival time.]

412. Jain, Sushila. *Muslims and Modernization: A Study of Their Changing Role, Structure, and Norms in an Urban Setting*. Jaipur: Rawat Publications, 1986.
[Included in this sociological survey of 375 Sunni Muslims in Jaipur City are chapters on "Modernization and the Institutions of Family and Marriage" and the "Position of Women."]

413. Jaini, Padmanabh S. "*Padipadanajataka*: Gautama's Last Female Incarnation." *Amala Prajna: Aspects of Buddhist Studies. Professor P. V. Bapat Felicitation Volume*. Ed. N. H. Samtani and H. S. Prasad. Delhi: Sri Satguru Publications, 1989.
[Relates a unique story from the *Pannasa Jataka*, describing a birth of the future Gautama as a woman at a time prior to the outset of his *bodhisattva* career; compares this with a similar story from the Chinese canon. Both women, expressing the wish to be a Buddha in the future, are told that Buddhahood is off limits to women. But in the future, born as a man, each will achieve her aim and will receive a Buddha predication.]

414. ———. *Gender and Salvation: Jaina Debates on the Spiritual Liberation of Women*. Berkeley: University of California Press, 1991.

[Traces a long-lived argument between Svetambara and Digambara Jains about the capacity of women for achieving liberation; the body of the text consists primarily of translations from six works on the subject, extending from 150 C.E. to the turn of the eighteenth century. Introductions are comprehensive and clear and can stand as works in their own right. Good bibliography.]

415. Jaiswal, Suvira. "Women in Early India: Problems and Perspectives." *Proceedings of the Indian History Congress.* Bodh Gaya: University of Magadha, 1981, pp. 54–60.
[Reconstructs prevailing portrayals of the Vedic period, basing hypotheses on ethnographic parallels between Aryas and groups living under similar economic conditions.]

416. James, V. "Marriage Customs of Christian Son Kolis." *Asian Folklore Studies* 36, No. 2 (1977), 131–48.
[The Son Kolis are a Bombay fishing community. A straightforward description of their marriage rites and customs attends to contributions both of women and of men.]

417. Javed, Arifa Kulsoom. *Muslim Society in Transition.* New Delhi: Commonwealth Publishers, 1990.
[This study of wealthy Shi'a Muslim families of Hyderabad tracks the effects of political change and economic duress over three generations. Includes some description of marriage customs and *purdah*; also includes a chapter titled "Muslim Life-Style, Family, and Status of Women."]

418. Jayakar, Pupul. *The Earth Mother.* New York and New Delhi: Penguin Books, 1989; San Francisco: Harper and Row, 1990 [title extended to *The Earth Mother: Legends, Goddesses, and Ritual Arts of India*]; originally published New Delhi: The National Museum, 1980, as *The Earthen Drum.*
[Describes the ritual arts and crafts of India, with extensive materials on women's creations, including a chapter on Mithila paintings and another on *vrata mandala*s.]

103

419. Jayawardena, Kumari. *Feminism and Nationalism in the Third World*. New Delhi: Kali for Women, 1986; London: Zed Books, 1986.
[A section titled "Women, Social Reform, and Nationalism" includes a summary of religion-based social reform movements of the nineteenth century, as well as a summary of Gandhi's teachings on women. A section titled "Emancipation and Subordination of Women in Sri Lanka" includes a segment on Buddhism and women.]

420. Jeffery, Patricia. *Frogs in a Well: Indian Women in* Purdah. London: Zed Press, 1979.
[This book explores the phenomenon of women's seclusion from the perspective of those who experience it. Although problems of domestic dependence and terrors of the outer world receive the most attention, ideologies underlying its subjects' predicaments are also addressed. See, for example, subsections titled "Islam and the Seclusion of Women," "Polluting Women," and "Ideological Subordination." The village studied is located beside the shrine of the Sufi *pir* Hazrat Nizamuddin Auliya, near Old Delhi.]

421. Jethmalani, Rani. "Politics and Pathology of *Sati*." *Teaching Politics* 12, no. 1 (1987), 47–64.
[Describes the context and questions raised by the Roop Kanwar *sati* case of 1987; includes a recounting of the author's own experiences as part of a fact-finding team that visited the site.]

422. Jhabvala, Renara. "A Story of Courage—the Lives of Muslim Women in Ahmedabad." *Manushi* 5, No. 4 (=No. 29; July–August 1985), 2–9.
[Describes the lives and day-to-day struggles of poor women of a minority religious community. Incorporates much case material and citations from interviews, revealing not only economic ills but also stresses arising from marriage; describes movements towards unity among women and the pitfalls these encounter.]

423.   Jhabvala, Ruth Prawer. "How I Became a Holy Mother."
         How I Became a Holy Mother and Other Stories. London: J.
         Murray, 1976; Middlesex: Penguin Books, 1981.
         [A twice-divorced *ashram*-hopping British girl finds a Hima-
         layan haven and a lover in the person of its junior guru-
         designate. The problem of their relationship is solved by ap-
         pointing her as Holy Mother to join her lover on his West-
         ern tour. Short story.]

424.   Joardar, Biswanath. *Prostitution in Nineteenth and Early
         Twentieth Century Calcutta.* New Delhi: Inter-India Publi-
         cations, 1985.
         [Two pages of this slim volume describe the role of "prosti-
         tutes" in *puja*s and festivals.]

425.   Johnsen, Linda. "Women Saints of India." *Yoga Journal*
         (July–August, 1988), 52–109.
         [Among the new wave of spiritual leaders emerging in
         India, the "new wave is women." Describes especially three
         female teachers from India who have toured the United
         States: Gurumayi Chidvilasananda, Asha Ma, and Amritan-
         andamayi Ma.]

426.   Jones, Kenneth W. *Arya Dharm: Hindu Consciousness in
         19th-Century Punjab.* Berkeley: University of California
         Press, 1976.
         [This definitive history of northwestern India's most prom-
         inent nineteenth-century Hindu nationalist group incorpo-
         rates throughout information on the Arya Samaj's work to
         alter the status and roles of women. Especially important
         were Arya Samaj efforts to found and support girls' and
         women's education.]

427.   Jones, V. R., and L. Bevan Jones. *Woman in Islam: A
         Manual with Special Reference to Conditions in India.*
         Westport, Conn.: Hyperion Press, 1981; originally published
         by Lucknow Publishing House, 1941.

[Prepared as a manual of information for women missionaries working in India, this volume describes an impressive array of practice. Covers home and family life, several aspects of betrothal and marriage, polygamy, concubinage, *purdah*, rights and duties of wives and mothers, religious meetings and duties, knowledge of the faith, the cult of Sufi saints, vows and offerings, spirits and exorcisms, charms and divination, festivals, rites of passage, and effects of conversion.]

428.   Jordan, Kay Kirkpatrick. *From Sacred Servant to Profane Prostitute: A Study of the Changing Legal Status of the* Devadasis*, 1857–1947*. Ph.D. diss., State University of Iowa, 1990.
["Examines reform legislation affecting the status of *devadasis* who were women 'married' to a deity and expected to perform temple service. Analysis of the changing perception of *devadasis* between 1857 and 1947 highlights some of the major shifts in Indian thought and political structure." Based principally on records from court cases and legislative debates. Quotes are from author's description, *DAI* 50, No. 9 (March 1990), A-2939.]

For Jordan, Kay Kirkpatrick, see also entry 68.

429.   Joseph, Ammu. "Political Parties and '*Sati*'." *Economic and Political Weekly* 26, No. 16 (April 20, 1991), 1025–26.
[Support for *sati* brings a minister to his downfall.]

430.   Joshi, Hari Ram. *Ma Anandamayi Lila: Memoirs of Sri Hari Ram Joshi*. 2nd ed. Calcutta Shree Shree Anandamayee Charitable Society, 1981; original edition, 1974.
[After telling of this modern Hindu saint and guru's childhood, marriage, and *sadhanas*, the author-disciple continues with personal memories of her. Contains many tales of miracles, especially healings. The author, a government employee, first met Anandamayi Ma in 1933.]

431. Joshi, Kireet. *Sri Aurobindo and the Mother: Glimpses of Their Experiments, Experiences, and Realisations.* Delhi: Mother's Institute of Research, in association with Motilal Banarsidass, 1989.
[Describes yogic experiments and experiences of the two spiritual masters of the Aurobindo Ashram. Sketches early supramundane experiences for both Aurobindo and his helper and successor Mirra Alfassa Richard ("The Mother"), then describes their meeting, their work together, and Richard's continued experiments after Aurobindo's death, including her efforts in old age to transmute her own body. Makes extensive use of quotations from work of the two leaders.]

432. Joshi, Pushpa. *Gandhi on Women: Collection of Mahatma Gandhi's Writings and Speeches on Women.* New Delhi: Centre for Women's Development Studies, 1988; Ahmedabad: Navajivan Publishing House, 1988.
[Four hundred sixteen short pieces are assembled here, including extracts from letters, news citations, and speeches. Arranged chronologically.]

433. Joshi, Svati. "Torn Up by the Roots." *Manushi* No. 48 (September–October 1988), 14–16.
[Summarizes memoirs in Gujarati by Kamalaben Patel, who worked in refugee camps for Hindu and Sikh women displaced by the 1947 partition riots.]

434. Joshi, Umashankar. "Four Women Poet-Saints of India." *Panjab University Journal of Medieval Indian Literature* 5, Nos. 1–2 (March–September 1981), 3–11.
[Briefly introduces the works and devotional styles of four celebrated women of the *bhakti* tradition. Subjects are Andal of Tamil Nadu, Mahadeviyakka of Karnataka, Lall Yogini of Kashmir, and Mirabai of Rajasthan.]

435. Jung, Anees. *Unveiling India: A Woman's Journey.* New Delhi: Penguin Books India, 1987; New York: Viking Penguin, 1987.

[Commissioned to explore the nature of India's population problem, the journalist author of this volume determined to "look for the faces behind the figures." She interweaves her own experiences as a Muslim woman reared in *purdah* with dozens of interviews touching on religion, marriage, mother-hood, and male-female relations. Interviewees include not only other Muslim women but also Hindu untouchables and brahmins, city and village women, Jain *sadhvis*, Christian nuns and doctors, a *devadasi*, Vrindavan widows, and the attendant of a goddess temple for women only; includes also some sketchy descriptions of women's rites and festivals.]

436. Jung, Mahomed Ullah ibn Saruland. *The Muslim Law of Marriage: Compiled from the Original Arabic Authorities.* New Delhi: Kitab Bhavan, 1986.
[Covers marriage in ancient Arabia, polyandry, the concept of marriage and prohibited partners, the Qur'an and various legal systems on marriage, establishing of parentage in the case of children born from illicit unions, *mahr*, maintenance, and divorce.]

437. Junghare, Indira Y. "Songs of the Goddess Shitala: Religio-Cultural and Linguistic Features." *Man in India* 55, No. 4 (October–December 1975), 298–316.
[The songs are sung by women to the goddess of smallpox; though this article does not focus on religious features, it cites several songs and describes the ritual contexts in which they are sung.]

438. ———. "Position of Women as Reflected in Marathi Folk Songs." *Man in India* 61, No. 3 (September 1981), 237–53.
[Presents images of the wife, daughter, sister, daughter-in-law, mother-in-law, and widow; challenges claims that Marathi women are equal partners with males.]

439. Junghare, Indira Y., and Judy Frater. "The *Ramayana* in Maharashtrian Women's Folk Songs." *Man in India* 56, No. 4 (October–December 1976), 289–305.

108

Bibliography

[Examines portrayals of the Indian epic *Ramayana* in women's work songs, showing special interest in values and ideals portrayed and their implications for contemporary India.]

440. Jyoti, Surinder K. *Marriage Practices of the Sikhs: A Study of Intergenerational Differences*. New Delhi: Deep and Deep, 1983.
[Most materials of this volume concern mate selection, but one chapter lays out normative precepts and rules.]

441. Kabeer, Naila. "The Quest for National Identity: Women, Islam and the State in Bangladesh." *Feminist Review* 37 (Spring 1991), 38–58.
[Claims that women of Bangladesh have been beneficiaries of an incomplete merger between Islamic beliefs and Bengali culture.]

442. Kabilsingh, Chatsumarn. *A Comparative Study of* Bhikkuni Patimokkha. Varanasi: Chaukhambha Orientalia, 1984.
[A distinguished Thai scholar compares rules for nuns in texts originating from six Buddhist schools. Includes a thirty-seven-page introduction on the pre-Buddhist status of women, the Buddha's attitude towards women, and the formation of the *bhikkuni samgha* (the order of nuns).]

For Kabilsingh, Chatsumarn, see also entry 951.

443. Kabiraj, Sibnarayan. "Significance of Durga Worship: Its Antiquity and Present Development in Bengal." *Folklore* 32, No. 10 (October, 1991), 169–76.
[Principally describes the mythology and festivals of Durga; acquires significance for this listing principally via the concept that Durga is a married daughter returning to her parents' home for the festival season.]

109

444.   Kakar, Sudhir. *Shamans, Mystics and Doctors: A Psychological Inquiry into India and Its Healing Traditions*. Boston: Beacon Press, 1982; New York: Knopf, 1982; Chicago: University of Chicago Press, 1991.
        [This examination of traditional Indian healing techniques from a Westernized psychoanalytic perspective includes one Tantric *mataji* among practitioners interviewed, as well as several possessed women who are subjects of various styles of treatment.]

For Kakar, Sudhir, see also entry 301.

445.   Kalanidhi, M. S., and S. Hemalatha. "Prepuberty and Puberty Rites among Three Tribal Communities of Nilgiris," *Folklore* 32, No. 11–12 (November–December 1991), 199–201.
        [Briefly describes variations in prepuberty and puberty rites, as practiced by Kotas, Todas, and Trulas; while all presuppose that menstruation is polluting, they articulate this expectation differently.]

446.   Kalyanav, V. I. "The Image of the Indian Woman in the Mahabharata." *Annals of the Bhandarkar Oriental Research Society* 58–59 (1977–78), 161–72.
        [Surveys tales of epic women whom the author finds to be heroic, worthy, and deserving.]

447.   Kanga, Firdaus. *Trying to Grow*. Delhi: Ravi Dayal Publishers, 1990.
        [The upbringing of a Parsee girl is described in this autobiography.]

448.   Kapadia, Kanailal Motilal. *Marriage and Family in India*. 3rd ed. Calcutta: Oxford University Press, 1988; original edition Bombay: Oxford University Press, 1955.
        [Includes both Hindu and Muslim materials and treats among its topics the sacramental character of Hindu mar-

riage, the status of women in marriage, and matrilineal family structures.]

449. Kapoor, Nina. "The Ritual Murder." *Seminar* 331 (March 1987), 28–32.
[From dowry deaths to abuse of child brides to *sati,* this article principally cites grisly examples of sanctioned destruction of women. But it also explores cultural precedents and rationales for such practices.]

450. Kapur, Jyotsna. "Putting Herself into the Picture—Women's Accounts of the Social Reform Campaign in Maharashtra, Mid Nineteenth to Early Twentieth Centuries." *Manushi* No. 56 (January–February, 1990), 28–37.
[The title is self-explanatory: women described are Lakshmibai Tilak, Pandita Ramabai, Anandibai Karve, Parvati Athavale, Ramabai Ranade, Leelabai Patwardhan, and Dosebai Cowasjee.]

451. Kapur, Tribhuwan. *Religion and Ritual in Rural India: A Case Study in Kumaon.* New Delhi: Abhinav Publications, 1988.
[A chapter on "life-cycle rituals" includes some material on women's roles, especially in childbirth, and describes childhood and marriage rites.]

452. Karaka, Dosabhai Framji. *History of the Parsees, including Their Manners, Customs, Religion and Present Position.* 2 vols. Delhi: Discovery Publishing House, 1986; repr. of 1884 edition.
[Chapter III in volume 1 discusses "liberty of women"; Chapter IV describes domestic life; Chapter VI includes a segment on female education.]

453. Karkaria, Bachi J. "Parsee Women: Are They Really More Liberated?" *Illustrated Weekly of India* 96, No. 36 (September 7, 1975), 30–33.

[The author's answer is a qualified "Yes," with a carefully documented argument.]

454. Karlekar, Malavika. "Kadambini and the *Bhadralok*: Early Debates over Women's Education in Bengal." *Economic and Political Weekly*, 21, No. 17 (April 26, 1986), WS25–WS39.
[Describes the threefold debate about education appropriate for women that occurred in Bengal during the later nineteenth century. Included because much of the debate occurred within the Brahmo Samaj; the opposition likewise arose within religious groups.]

455. ————. "Hinduism Re-Visited: The Relevance of Gandhi Today." Occasional Paper No. 18. New Delhi: Centre for Women's Development Studies, 1991.
[This response to the pro-*sati* movement and the ideology of sacrifice that informs it shows Gandhi's complex relationship to the *sati* problem, both as one who reaffirmed the sacrifice ideology, and as one who sought to empower women. It concludes that the stress on male authority characteristic of *sati* supporters represents a major change from Gandhi.]

456. ————. *Voices from Within: Early Personal Narratives of Bengali Women*. Delhi: Oxford University Press, 1991.
[Cites letters and autobiographical accounts to reveal women's values and responses to education; shows how religion could motivate women to acquire literacy. Includes an account by the wife of Keshab Chander Sen.]

For Karlekar, Malavika, see also entry 149.

457. Kasturi, N. *Easwaramma: The Chosen Mother*. Prasanthi Nilayam: Sri Sathya Sai Books and Publications Trust, 1984.
[Pays tribute to the mother of contemporary saint and guru

Sathya Sai Baba by reviewing her life with her famous son. Portrays her early visits to temples, her rites and prayers for his protection, her memories of his unusual childhood, her initial resistance to his transformation and proclamation of his divinity, her subsequent discipleship, services to women at the *ashram*, and pilgrimage journeys with her son.]

458. Katagade, N. T., and C. G. Kolhatar. *"Sadgati?*—The Deaths of 'Blessed Women'."* (Translated extracts from the authors' autobiographies). *Manushi* No. 47 (July–August 1988), 25–27.
[Tells of two brahmin women of the early twentieth century who committed suicide to escape maltreatment by in-laws; shows parallels between their deaths and *sati*.]

459. Kaul, Ikbar. "The Origin of *Sati*." *Illustrated Weekly of India* 102, No. 3 (January 18, 1981), 28–29.
[Traces references to *sati* throughout Indian history.]

460. Kaul, Jayalal [OCLC lists as Jai Lal]. *Lal Ded*. New Delhi: Sahitya Akademi, 1973.
[Addresses the life, times, and verses of a celebrated devotional saint of Kashmir who lived—perhaps—during the fourteenth century. Includes forty-three pages of translations from Lal Ded's poetry, in a somewhat archaic style.]

461. Kaur, Inderjeet. *Status of Hindu Women in India*. Allahabad: Chugh Publications, 1983.
[This small social-scientific survey of three hundred educated Hindu women of Gorakhpur, Uttar Pradesh, includes a chapter on "changing religious outlook," as well as new views on marriage and male/female relationships.]

462. Kausar, Zinat. *Muslim Women in Medieval India*. Patna and New Delhi: Janaki Prakashan, 1992.
[Includes, among others, chapters on "Birth, Marriage and Other Allied Customs," "Games, Sports, Amusements, and

Feasts, Festivals, and Fairs," "Polygamy and Harem Life," and "Dower, Divorce, *Purdah*, Child Marriage, Unmatched Marriages and Widows' Position in India."]

463. Kelkar, Govind, and Dev Nathan. *Gender and Tribe: Women, Land, and Forests in Jharkand*. New Delhi: Kali for Women, 1991; London: Zed Books, 1991.
[This study of *adivasi* (aboriginal) tribes in a region of eastern India is included for its chapter titled "Women, Witches and Land Rights," which confirms that witch-hunting becomes prevalent where widows have claims to inherit land. Also has a perceptive interpretation of local versions of the story of how women lost their power to men.]

464. Kelkar, Indumati, and Madhu Kishwar. "Trying to Live by her Principles," *Manushi* No. 48 (September–October 1988), 30–38.
[A Brahmin woman whose mother was an early *satyagrahi* tells the story of her own immersion in activism. The daughter picked up the standard when the mother grew ill, later became a socialist, and is now a writer. Rich in information about women's roles in the *satyagraha* movement.]

465. Kelker, Shanta. *The Sage and the Housewife*. Bangalore: Sowmya Publishers, 1990.
[Offers vignettes from the author's encounters with guru U. G. Krishnamurti.]

466. Kerkhoff, Kathinka Renata. "Missionaries, Brahmos and the Issue of Female Education: Calcutta in the Nineteenth Century." *Gender, Caste and Power in South Asia: Social Status and Mobility in a Transitional Society*. Ed. John P. Neelsen. New Delhi: Manohar, 1991, pp. 103–26.
[Treats the historical context, the British missionaries, the latters' concepts of women's status and educational ideology, *bhadralok* rationales for women's education, and roles and ideologies both of female missionaries and of

Brahmo Sadharans. Charges that older patriarchal forces thwarted intended goals for both the missionaries and the Brahmos.]

467. Kersenboom, Saskia Cornelia. *Nitya Sumangali: Towards the Semiosis of the Devadasi Tradition*. Ph.D. diss., University of Utrecht, 1984.
[Could not examine; assumed to be prototype for Kersenboom-Story, *Nityasumangali* (see entry 468 below).]

For Kersenboom, Saskia Cornelia, see also Kersenboom-Story, Saskia C. (below) and entry 532.

468. Kersenboom-Story, Saskia C. *Nityasumangali: Devadasi Tradition in South India*. Delhi: Motilal Banarsidass, 1987.
[This comprehensive study of *devadasi* traditions in South India is divided into three sections: "*Devadasis* in the Cultural History of South India"; "Function and Form of the *Devadasi* Tradition within Temple Ritual in Tamilnadu"; and "Rites of Passage of the *Devadasis* of Tamilnadu." Includes samples of choreography for *devadasi* performances.]

469. ———. "*Devadasi Murai*." *Sangeet Natak*, No. 96 (April–June 1990), 44–54.
[Attempts to set straight a number of confusions that have arisen in regard to *devadasis*, women dedicated for service to a god; argues that a *devadasi*'s *murai* (function) is to be perpetually auspicious.]

470. ———. *Devadasi Heritage: Ritual Songs and Dances of the* Devadasis *of Tiruttani*. Delhi: Motilal Banarsidass, forthcoming.
[No further information was available at time of publication.]

For Kersenboom-Story, Saskia C., see also Kersenboom, Saskia Cornelia (entry 467 above) and entry 532.

471. Khan, Mazharul Haq [OCLC lists as Mazhar-ul-Haq]. *Purdah and Polygamy.* New Delhi: Harnam Publications, 1983; original edition Peshawar: Nashiran-e-Ilm-o-Tara-qiyet, 1972 [with the title of *Purdah and Polygamy: A Study in the Social Pathology of the Muslim Society*].
    [Discusses the theory and history of *purdah* and its effect on women, girls, and family life. Highly critical.]

For Khan, Mazharul Haq, see also entry 768.

472. Khan, Muniza Rafiq. *Socio-Legal Status of Muslim Women.* New Delhi: Radiant Publishers, 1993.
    [Based on interviews with two-hundred women of Mirzapur City, U.P., this study's chief objective was to discover the impact of new laws and legal decisions upon Indian Muslim women; it pays special attention to issues arising from the Shah Bano case. Includes twenty-five brief case histories of divorced or separated women.]

For Khan, Muniza Rafiq, see also entry 1001.

473. Khan, Qamaruddin [OCLC lists as Qamar-ud-Din]. *Status of Women in Islam.* New Delhi: Sterling Publishers, 1990; original edition, Lahore: Islamic Book Foundation, 1988.
    [A distinguished Muslim professor offers a liberal critique of the Muslim status quo.]

474. Khan, Raja Said Akbar. *Mahommedan Law Containing the Law Relating to Succession and Status Compiled from Authorities in the Original Arabic.* New Delhi: Kitab Bhavan, 1984.
    [This massive study, clearly a reference work, covers inheritance, marriage, the rights and duties of spouses in marriage, divorce, and the effect of conversion on marriage.]

475. Khare, R. S. *Culture and Reality: Essays on the Hindu System of Managing Foods.* Simla: Indian Institute of Advanced Study, 1976.

116

[Treats the symbolic significance of food in Hindu thought and practice, covering cooked and uncooked foods, the food cycle (including a bride's first cooking), fasts and festivals, *prasad*, and other related topics.]

476.   ————. *The Hindu Hearth and Home.* New Delhi: Vikas Publishing House, 1976; Durham, N.C.: Carolina Academic Press, 1976.
[Treats the uses of food in Hindu households, including domestic rituals, taking a descriptive ethnographic approach. Different from and complementary to the volume cited in entry 475.]

477.   ————. "From *Kanya* to *Mata*: Aspects of the Cultural Language of Kinship in Northern India." *Concepts of Person: Kinship, Caste, and Marriage in India.* Ed. Akos Oster, Lina Fruzetti, and Steve Barnett. Cambridge: Harvard University Press, 1982, pp. 143–71.
[Three focal terms are analyzed to reveal underlying cultural constructs of womanhood.]

478.   Khatoon, Aisha. "The Anguished Cry of Muslim Women." *Social Welfare* 23, No. 1 (April 1976), 4–5, 12.
[Protests the right of a Muslim husband to divorce his wife by saying *"Talaq"* three times; recounts tales of a much-abused privilege.]

479.   Khokar, Mohan. "A Momentous Transition." *Sangeet Natak: Journal of the Sangeet Natak Akademi* 84 (April–June, 1987), 41–47.
[Describes the campaign for abolition of *devadasi* dedication, including Muthulakshmi Reddy's role. The "transition" cited in the title is the *devadasis'* subsequent shift to the professional stage.]

480.   Kidwai, Shaikh Mushir Hosain (of Gadi'a). *Woman under Different Social and Religious Laws, Buddhism, Judaism, Christianity, Islam.* Delhi: Seema Publications, 1976.

[Catalogues the legal status of women in traditions cited by its title.]

481. King, Ursula. "Women and Religion: Image and Status of Women in Some Major Religious Traditions." *Social Action* 25 (July–September 1975), 277–91.
[Covers the widespread presence of women in ancient religions, the "regressive trend" that came with institutionalization, householders, nuns, and *bhakta*s of Indian religions, images of women and ascetic misogyny in Christianity, and the impact of contemporary social change on women.]

482. ———. "Women and Religion: The Status and Role of Women in Major Religious Traditions." *Women in India: Traditional Images and Changing Roles.* Ed. Alfred De Souza. New Delhi: Manohar, 1975.
[Identical with the piece cited in entry 481 above.]

483. ———. "Effect of Social Change on Religious Self-Understanding: Women Ascetics in Modern Hinduism." *Changing South Asia: Religion and Society.* Ed. K. Ballhatchet and D. Taylor. Hong Kong: Asian Research Service, for the Centre of South Asian Studies in the School of Oriental and African Studies, University of London, 1984, pp. 69–84.
[Effects of social change on images and roles of women are shown by examining contemporary ascetic practice. Treats the relationship of women to asceticism in traditional Hinduism, social changes affecting the image and status of women in modern Hinduism, and women ascetics of modern Hinduism, with special attention to women of Sri Sarada Math and Mission.]

484. ———. *Women in the World's Religions, Past and Present.* New York: Paragon House, 1987.
[Two essays from this collection have some bearing on India. Anne Bancroft's survey "Women in Buddhism" includes

Indian Theravadin and Mahayanist materials. Kim Knott's "Men and Women, or Devotees? Krishna Consciousness and the Role of Women" combines a discussion of Krishna Consciousness teachings with field materials from American branches of the movement.]

For King, Ursula, see also entry 227.

485. Kinsley, David. "Devotion as an Alternative to Marriage in the Lives of Some Hindu Women Devotees." *Journal of Asian and African Studies* 15, Nos. 1–2 (January–April, 1980), 83–93.
[Discusses women saints who found devotion incompatible with worldly marriage; subjects are Mahadeviyakka, Lallesvari, Mirabai (and Radha as their model). Incorporates translations from the poetry that reflects their dilemmas and choices.]

486. Kishwar, Madhu. "She Dared to Dream—an Interview with Asha Apradh." *Manushi* 4, No. 3 (=No. 21; March–April 1984), 2–7.
[A Sunni Muslim girl, married at the age of fourteen and a mother at fifteen, tells how she struggled to gain higher education against her family's and community's opposition.]

487. ———. "Gandhi on Women." *Economic and Political Weekly.* Part I: Vol. 20. No. 40 (October 5, 1985), 1691–1701; Part II: Vol. 20, No. 41 (October 12, 1985), 1753–58.
[This two-part "article" is substantial enough to be a small book. According to the author, it "reviews and analyses the role of Gandhi in drawing a large number of women into the mainstream of the freedom movement." Subheadings are "Gandhi's Views on Nature of Women's Oppression," "Women's Role in the Struggle for Swaraj," and "Gandhi's Personal Relationships with Women." The author maintains that repercussions of the "moral legitimacy" Gandhi

brought to the cause of women go "far beyond his own views and pronouncements of women's role and place in society."]

488.   ————. "Pro Women or Anti Muslim? The Shabano Controversy." *Manushi* 6, No. 2 (=No. 32; January–February 1986), 4–13.
[The subject is a Supreme Court decision that overruled Muslim law and its communalistic implications.]

489.   ————. "Arya Samaj and Women's Education: Kanya Mahavidyalaya, Jalandhar." *Economic and Political Weekly* 21, No. 17 (April 26, 1986), WS9–WS24.
[Offers a long and rich case study of a successful school for girls founded in the 1890s by a famous reform movement of northwestern India. Describes the place of the school in the history of Punjabi education, the career of its founder, its curriculum, its attempts to reform women's practices and attitudes, its justifications for teaching English, its role models, its relationship to the nationalist movement, its fund-raising, critics, and its impact both on its founding organization and on its students' self-perceptions. Concludes that the Arya Samaj movement was intended to reform women rather than to reform the social conditions which oppressed them.]

490.   ————. "Rethinking Dowry Boycott." *Manushi* No. 48 (September–October 1988), 10–13.
[This controversial editorial questions the benefit of continued efforts to do away with dowry; it argues that securing effective inheritance rights would offer much more fundamental protection for women.]

491.   ————. "Towards More Just Norms for Marriage: Continuing the Dowry Debate." *Manushi* No. 53 (July–August 1989), 2–9.
[Responds to the outcry prompted by the previous article; criticizes the cultural ideal of endless giving in marriage and proposes a model contract for an egalitarian marriage.]

492. ————. "In Defence of our *Dharma.*" *Manushi* No. 60
(September–October 1990), 2–14.
[Eloquently protests the divisiveness of the Ram Mandir
movement.]

For Kishwar, Madhu, see also entries 223, 234, 258, 464, 506, 937,
1002, and 1011.

493. Kishwar, Madhu, and Ruth Vanita, eds. *In Search of An-
swers: Indian Women's Voices from* Manushi. London: Zed
Books, 1984.
[This collection of articles from the magazine *Manushi*'s
first five years concentrates predominantly on social and
economic issues. However, a collection on violence against
women includes a young woman's petition to the supreme
court documenting her father's harassment of her after
learning of her plans to marry a Muslim (Kiran Singh, "It's
Only a Family Affair!"). Several letters selected challenge
inherited practice and values, especially with regard to
marriage. Finally, *Manushi* tells the story of its own
struggle to come to birth.]

494. ————. "The Burning of Roop Kanwar." *Manushi* No.
42–43 (September–December 1987), 15–25.
[Describes the infamous 1987 case of *sati* in Rajasthan, and
analyzes the state's failure to prevent it.]

495. ————. "Inheritance Rights for Women: A Response to
Some Commonly Expressed Fears." *Manushi* No. 57
(March–April 1990), 2–15.
[Summarizes Hindu, Christian, Parsi, Muslim, and tribal
laws of succession, and rebuts arguments commonly raised
against equal right to inheritance for women; an unusually
thorough and thoughtful job.]

496. Kohli, Yash, ed. *The Women of Punjab*. Bombay: Chic
Publications, 1983.

[This picture book is light in content, but offers some information about women in Sikhism.]

497.   Kolenda, Pauline. "Women as Tribute, Woman as Flower: Images of 'Woman' in Weddings in North and South India." *American Ethnologist* 11, No. 1 (February 1984), 98–117.
[Compares upper-caste Rajput weddings of North India with those of the lower-caste *sudra* Nattati Nadars of Tamilnadu; beyond surprising similarities in structure and ritual structure lie striking differences in images of women projected; the southern, lower-caste, version seems far more appreciative.]

498.   Kondos, Vivienne. "Images of the Fierce Goddess and Portrayals of Hindu Women." *Contributions to Indian Sociology*, N.S. 20, No. 2 (July–December 1986), 173–98.
[Challenges psychoanalytic interpretations of fierce goddesses that perceive them as "evidence of psychic disturbance" and interprets Nepali tantric rituals to present a more complex picture; also shows how such images and rituals are used to perpetuate male power over women.]

499.   ————. "Subjection and the Ethics of Anguish: The Nepalese Parbatya Parent-Daughter Relationship." *Contributions to Indian Sociology* N.S. 25, No. 1 (1991), 113–33.
[Interprets menstrual seclusion in light of the three-*guna* theory and its context of social experience and obligations.]

500.   Kopf, David. *The Brahmo Samaj and the Shaping of the Modern Indian Mind*. Princeton: Princeton University Press, 1979.
[Materials concerning reform efforts on behalf of girls and women are found throughout this definitive work on the nineteenth century's most influential Indian reform movement. Women's education and aid for young widows were high Brahmo Samaj priorities.]

501. Kosambi, Meera. "Women, Emancipation and Equality: Pandita Ramabai's Contribution to Women's Cause." *Economic and Political Weekly* 23, No. 44 (October 29, 1988), 38–48.
[This major article on India's first independent woman to work for women's emancipation covers not only Pandita Ramabai's life and views but also the social context within which she worked. Contains a valuable overview of the nineteenth-century Maharashtrian debate regarding women's issues.]

502. ————. "Girl-Brides and Socio-Legal Change: Age of Consent Bill (1891) Controversy." *Economic and Political Weekly*, 26, Nos. 31–32 (August 3–10, 1991), 1857–68.
[This review of the debate between orthodox factions and reformers on the proposal to set a minimum age of twelve years for cohabitation with girl-brides is important for its analyses of both the uses of sacred texts and the problem of government interference in religion. Includes some discussion of cases tried under the Act after passage and of the Act's political repercussions.]

For Kozlowski, Gregory C., see entries 68 and 506.

503. Krishna Iyer, V. R. *Woman Unbound: A Plea for Gender Justice*. Madurai: Society for Community Organisation Trust, 1984.
[Treats discrimination by sex in various religious law codes of India.]

For Krishna Iyer, V. R., see also entries 35 and 956.

504. Krishnamurthi, N. Putali. *The Changing Condition of Women in Andhra: From the Middle of the 19th Century to the Middle of the 20th Century*. Hyderabad: Navayuga, 1987.
[A chapter titled "Moral and Material Uplift" treats the *devadasi* problem, the issue of Hindu, Christian, and Mus-

lim property rights, and movements for founding and maintaining homes for widows.]

505.   Krishnamurthy, S. *The Dowry Problem: A Legal and Social Perspective*. Bangalore: IBH Prakashana, 1981.
[Includes limited discussion of the *stridhana* concept as a source for dowry.]

506.   Krishnamurty, J., ed. *Women in Colonial India: Essays on Survival, Work, and the State*. Delhi: Oxford University Press, 1989.
[This collection of eleven essays on Indian women's economic and social experience under colonialism includes three with materials related to religion. Madhu Kishwar's "The Daughters of Aryavarta" examines the Punjabi context of Arya Samajists' attention to women's education and women's issues. Gregory C. Kozlowski's "Muslim Women and the Control of Property in North India" traces the history of Muslim women's access to property rights from the early sixteenth century to the modern period. Lucy Carroll's "Law, Custom and Statutory Social Reform in the Hindu Widow's Remarriage Act of 1856" analyzes a famous reform act; this latter article is identical with that of entry 132.]

507.   Krishnaraj, Maithreyi, ed. *Evolving New Methodologies in Research on Women's Studies*. Contribution to Women Studies Series-3. Bombay: Research Centre for Women's Studies, 1988.
[Consists of sixteen articles by various authors on aspects of the research process; none focus specifically on religion, but several have tangential importance, viz., Nirmala Banerjee, "Methodology for Historical Research"; Leela Gulati, "Case Studies—How to Do Them"; C. S. Lakshmi, "Interpretation in Oral History Methods"; Sumitra Bhava, "Constructing of Self Images of Women"; and Leela Dube, "The Use of Folk Material."]

508. Krishnaraj, Maithreyi, and Karuna Chanana. *Gender and the Household Domain: Social and Cultural Dimensions.* Women and the Household in Asia, Vol. 4. New Delhi and Newbury Park, Calif.: Sage, 1989.
[Two articles of this largely social-scientific collection have some bearing on religion: K. M. A. Aziz's "Gender Creation from Birth to Adolescence in Rural Bangladesh" examines the process of female socialization among rural Muslims; Kamala Ganesh's "Seclusion of Women and the Structure of Caste" shows how a high subcaste of Tamilnadu, the Kottai Pillaimar, seclude women to maintain their community's ritual purity.]

509. Krishnaswamy, Revathi. "Subversive Spirituality: Woman as Poet-Saint in Medieval India." *Women's Studies International Forum* 16, No. 2 (1993), 139–47.
[Focussing on the work of Mahadeviyakka, a twelfth-century poet-saint from Karnataka, this article argues that her choice of metaphors subverts prevailing sexual stereotypes.]

510. Ku, Cheng-Mei. *The Mahayanic View of Women: A Doctrinal Study.* Ph.D. diss., University of Wisconsin at Madison, 1984.
[This study in the history of Buddhist doctrine examines North Indian texts from the Mahasangika, Mahisasaka, Sarvastivadin, and early Mahayanist schools to reconstruct conflicting views on women. Mahayanist views are the central focus. Described *DAI* 46, No. 1 (July 1985), A-176–77.]

511. Kullar, K. K. "The Women in the Life of Maharaja Ranjit Singh." *Sikh Review* 30 (August 1982), 44–48.
[Cites wives, courtesans, and the Amazon army contingent of the greatest Sikh king, and describes the self-immolation of his four wives and five slaves at his death.]

512. Kumar, Dharmendra. "Easier Divorce." *Quest* 96 (July–August 1975), 31–37.

[Criticizes an amendment to the Hindu Marriage and Special Marriage Acts that was intended to make divorce more accessible to women. The author calls this "patchwork reform."]

513. Kumar, Nita. "Widows, Education and Social Change in 20th Century Banaras." *Economic and Political Weekly* 26, No. 17 (April 27, 1991), WS19–WS25.
[Describes a series of widows who became "goddess-like" by founding schools for women during the early and mid-twentieth century. Includes a discussion of contemporary understandings of dharma and the roles of women within it.]

514. Kumar, Radha. "The Women's Movement." *Seminar* 355 (March 1989), 21–25.
[Principally describes developments in the Indian women's movement since the early 1970s. Shows, on the one hand, the movement's search for resources and models in myths, epics, and folktales, and, on the other, complications introduced by communalism and the effort to co-opt women's issues to serve communalist ends.]

515. Kumar, Raj. *Annie Besant's Rise to Power in Indian Politics, 1914–1917*. New Delhi: Concept Publishing Company, 1981.
[Included for a chapter on Besant's "Political Ideology" that reveals her distinctive mix of Theosophy and politics.]

516. Kumari, Ranjana. *Female Sexuality in Hinduism*. Delhi: For the Joint Women's Programme by ISPCK, 1988.
[This pamphlet cites sources from the Veda, epics, Puranas, and *dharmasastra* on the power of female sexuality and the need to control it; it treats also the *pativrat* ideal, the concept of marriage, and female biology.]

For Kumari, Ranjana, see also entries 58, 159, and 750.

517.   Kumari, Rekha. "The Role of Women—a Sarvodaya View."
        Gandhi Marg 6, No. 7 (February 1985), 794–803.
        [Presents a Gandhian view of women, arguing woman's dig-
        nity and equality and her ability to will changes in her own
        destiny. Woman is an incarnation of *ahimsa*; married
        couples should be partners.]

518.   Kuppuswamy, B. *Dharma and Society: A Study in Social
        Values*. Delhi: Macmillan, 1977; Columbia, Mo.: South Asia
        Books, 1977.
        [Includes an appendix on "The Position of Women in An-
        cient India."]

519.   Kurian, George, and Mariam John. "Women and Social
        Customs within the Family: A Case Study of Attitudes in
        Kerala, India." *Being Female: Reproduction, Power, and
        Change*. Ed. Dana Raphael. The Hague: Mouton, 1975, pp.
        255–66.
        [This survey of sixty Christians, sixty Hindus, and thirty
        Muslims, balanced for age, assesses attitudes towards mar-
        riage rituals and dowry, aspirations for children, and open-
        ness to honoring children's decisions. It finds significant dif-
        ferences among religious groups only in attitudes towards
        wedding rites.]

For Kurian, George, see also entry 57.

520.   Lakshmi, C. S. "Symbols, Women and Tamil Nadu Politics."
        Economic and Political Weekly 18, No. 3 (January 15, 1983),
        54–55.
        [Criticizes the putative progressivism of South Indian poet
        and editor Bharti; asserts that his statements about women
        reveal him to be just another liberal but limited Brahmin.]

For Lakshmi, C. S., see also entries 507 and 611.

521.   Lakshminarayana, H. D. "Dimensions of Religiosity among College Students." *Man in India* 59, No. 4 (October–December 1979), 350–60.
[Examines "the extent of religiosity among college students who are subject to the forces of modernization and westernization." The sample responding to the study's questionnaires consisted of 256 students of Bangalore City. The analysis is broken down by sex and concludes that the women were far more interested in religion than the men.]

For Lakshminarayana, H. D., see also entry 57.

522.   Lalleshwari. *Lalleshwari: Spiritual Poems by a Great Siddha Yogini*. As rendered by Swami Muktananda. Ganeshpur: Gurudev Siddha Peeth, 1981; South Fallsberg, N.Y.: SYDA Foundation, 1981.
[Very readable translations of the work of a great Kashmiri woman saint of the fourteenth century are offered by a noted twentieth-century guru who claimed Lalleshwari as part of his own spiritual lineage.]

523.   Lang, Karen Christina. "Lord Death's Share: Gender-Related Imagery in the *Theragatha* and *Therigatha*." *Journal of Feminist Studies in Religion* 2, No. 2 (Fall, 1986) 63–79.
[Differences in monks' and nuns' use of the phrase "Lord Death's share" reveal differences between men's and women's self-perceptions.]

524.   Lateef, Shahida. *The Status and Role of Women in a Minority Community: The Case of Muslims in India*. Ph.D. diss., University of Sussex, 1983.
[No further information is available; the work is assumed to be a prototype for *Muslim Women in India* (see entry 525 below).]

525.   ————. *Muslim Women in India: Political and Private Realities, 1890s–1980s*. New Delhi: Kali for Women, 1990. [Covers education, social legislation, the women's movement, marriage, family and *purdah*, as well as Muslim women's responses to change. Includes results of surveys covering more than 1300 respondents from nine Indian cities.]

For Lateef, Shahida, see also entries 14 and 354.

526.   Law, Bimala Churn. *Women in Buddhist Literature*. Varanasi: India Book House, 1981; repr. from 1927 edition. [This composite of references to women in the Pali Buddhist canon is arranged according to topic. Topics include married women, slave girls, dancing girls and courtesans, comments on female character, education of women, women's relationship to Buddhism, the *bhikkuni-samgha* (community of nuns), and prominent Buddhist women.]

527.   *The Law, the Oppressed, and Women*. Special Issue, *Religion and Society* 31, No. 1 (March 1984). [Includes five relevant articles: Lotika Sarkar, "Women's Rights" (pp. 2–7); Noorjehan Razak, "Muslims and the Civil Code" (pp. 8–11); Sutupa Sarkar, "Oppression of Women and Apathy of the Government" (pp. 38–41); Sister Leela and Sister Magdalene, "*Devadasi* Practice Still Prevalent in Manvi" (pp. 42–47); and Aley Matthew, "Bible Study: Administration of Law and the Oppressed, Particularly Women" (pp. 48–52).]

528.   *Legal Status of Women in India*. Bhagalpur: Sundarvati Mahavidyalaya, 1984. [Covers the social, legal, economic, religious, and political status of women, approached from a historical perspective.]

529.   Leslie, Julia. *The Religious Role of Women in Ancient India: A Discussion of the* Stridharmapaddhati *of Tryambakayajvan*. D. Phil. diss., Oxford University, 1983.

[Not available for examination; assumed to be prototype for *The Perfect Wife* (see entry 531 below).]

530.   ————. *"Strisvabhava*: The Inherent Nature of Women." *Oxford University Papers on India* I, Part I. Ed. N. J. Allen et al. Delhi: Oxford University Press, 1986.
[How can religious instructions help a woman if she is naturally sinful? This essay cites Tryambaka on this problem, and continues with Leslie's reflections on Indian teachings about wicked women and virtuous wives.]

531.   ————. *The Perfect Wife: The Orthodox Hindu Woman according to the* Stridharmapaddhati *of Tryambakayajvan*. Delhi and New York: Oxford University Press, 1989.
[According to Leslie, this eighteenth-century text from Thanjavur is the only extant writing of the orthodox Hindu tradition exclusively devoted to women's *dharma* (duty). Leslie provides a blend of translation, commentary, and summary, treating three chapters of the original text in detail, and the remaining two more briefly. Most novel are the work's detailed prescriptions for a woman's daily round of activities, and a brief chapter about Tryambaka's views on the nature of women. Includes reproductions of manuscript illustrations, done in Thanjavur style. Good bibliography.]

532.   ————, ed. *Roles and Rituals for Hindu Women*. London: Pinter Publishers, 1991; Rutherford: Fairleigh Dickenson University Press, 1991; Delhi: Motilal Banarsidass, 1992.
[Contents are as follows: In Section I (The Ritual Wife): Frederick M. Smith, "Indra's Curse, Varuna's Noose, and the Suppression of Women in the Vedic Srauta Ritual"; and Werner F. Menski, "Marital Expectations as Dramatized in Hindu Marriage Rituals"; in Section II (Power in the Home): Mary McGee, "Desired Fruits: Motive and Intention in the Votive Rites of Hindu Women"; Helene Stork, "Mothering Rituals in Tamilnadu: Some Magico-Religious Beliefs"; and Julia Leslie, "Sri and Jyestha: Ambivalent

Role Models for Women"; in Section III (The Ritual of Dance): Saskia C. Kersenboom, "The Traditional Repertoire of the Tiruttani Temple Dancers"; and Anne-Marie Gaston, "Dance and the Hindu Woman: *Bharatnatyam* Re-Ritualized"; in Section IV (The Pursuit of Salvation): Julia Leslie, "Suttee or *Sati*: Victim or Victor?"; Sanjukta Gupta, "Women in the Saiva/Sakta Ethos"; and Lynn Teskey Denton, "Varieties of Hindu Female Asceticism." Good bibliography.]

533.   ———, ed. *Rules and Remedies in Classical Indian Law.* Leiden, E.J. Brill, 1991.
[Two essays of this collection pertain to women. Richard W. Lariviere's "Matrimonial Remedies for Women in Classical Indian Law: Alternatives to Divorce" discusses the possibility of supercession, taking another spouse, as raised in the text *Naradasmriti.* Editor Julia Leslie's "A Problem of Choice: The Heroic *Sati* or the Widow-Ascetic" discusses the two classic options for a widow, and compares the latter with the Hindu male's path of renunciation.]

For Leslie, Julia, see also entries 79 and 375.

534.   Liddle, Joanna, and Rama Joshi. *Daughters of Independence: Gender, Caste, and Class in India.* New Delhi: Kali for Women, 1986; London: Zed Press, 1986; New Brunswick, N.J.: Rutgers University Press, 1989.
[This sociological study of 120 educated middle-class working women is based both on historical contextual research and on contemporary interviews. The historical component contains materials on *sati*, the matriarchal religious heritage, and the impact of Aryan concepts, including purity and pollution. The contemporary component contains a very brief chapter on experiences of orthodoxy. Subjects were from all traditions, although Hindus are clearly dominant; the study was based in Delhi, although subjects came from regions throughout India.]

535.   Lind, Mary Ann. *The Raj Made Personal: Welfare Activities of British Women in India, 1900–1947*. Ph.D. diss., University of Colorado at Boulder, 1985.
[Studies the activities and motivations of fifteen British *memsahibs* who performed welfare work in India during the designated period. Motivations seem to have been "a combination of religious principles, *noblesse oblige*, and boredom." Quotes are from author's description in *DAI* 45, No. 8 (February 1986), A-2411]

536.   Lindsay, Carolina Sara. *Upholding the Veil: Hindu Women's Perceptions of Gender and Caste Identity in Rural Pakistan*. Ph.D. diss., University of Edinburgh, 1985.
[No further information is available.]

537.   Lipske, A. *Life and Teachings of Sri Anandamayi Ma*. Delhi: Motilal Banarsidass, 1977.
[This tribute to a modern Hindu saint sketches her life, personality, and teachings, and offers selected sayings, the saint's advice for daily living, her understanding of the *chakras* experienced in meditation, and a selection of poems and songs dedicated to her by her disciples. The latter four topics are addressed in appendices. Despite the ambitious coverage, a very small book.]

538.   Logan, Penelope. *Domestic Worship and the Festival Cycle in the South Indian City of Madurai*. Ph.D. diss., University of Manchester, 1980.
[No further information is available.]

539.   Mabry, H. P., et al. "Theologically Trained Women." *Religion and Society* 31, No. 3 (September 1984), 3–25.
[Presents the results of a questionnaire sent to all women of theological training whose addresses were available to the Association of Theologically Trained Women in India. Subjects were asked for their age, denomination, social

origins, level and type of non-theological education, marital status, motivation for seeking theological education, aspirations and values, and for factors that they had found helpful or hindering.]

540. MacMillan, Margaret. *Women of the Raj.* New York: Thames and Hudson, 1988.
[Primarily describes everyday social life under the British rule in India—courtship, marriage, children, and obstacles encountered; however, a chapter titled "Unconventional Women" includes both Christian missionaries and women such as Nivedita who became workers for Indian movements.]

541. Madan, T. N. *Non-Renunciation: Themes and Interpretations of Hindu Culture.* Delhi and New York: Oxford University Press, 1987.
[This collection of Madan's essays includes "Domesticity and Detachment," "Auspiciousness and Purity," "Asceticism and Eroticism," "The Desired and the Good," and "Living and Dying."]

542. Madhok, Sujata. "She Struggled for Dignity: Interview with Shanta Devi." *Manushi* 5, No. 5 (=No. 30; September–October 1985), 35–36.
[Shanta Devi is a woman who works with slum children; the interview describes her early values and encounters with religions.]

543. Mahadevan, T. M. P. "Indian Culture and Womanhood." In two parts. *Samvit* 3 (March 1981), 12–15, and 4 (September 1981), 22–30.
[Restates classical conceptions of excellence in women, citing Sita as an example.]

544. Mahale, Prabha. *"Basavis* of Karnatak—the Daughters Endowed with Masculine Privileges." *The Eastern Anthropologist* 39, No. 2 (April–June 1986), 125–30.

[Describes the practice of dedicating girls to deities among lower-caste *sudra*s of Karnataka; these *basavi*s are distinguished from *devadasi*s. *Basavi*s never marry; they may live in concubinage, inherit family property, and perform their parents' funeral oblations. The institution lets a sonless family keep its inheritance in the family line.]

545.   Mahmood, Tahir, ed. *Family Law and Social Change: A Festschrift for Asaf A. A. Fyzee.* Bombay: N. M. Tripathi, 1975.
[Family law is essentially women's law; therefore cases cited in this *festschrift* often refer to women's predicaments, and several authors are women. Articles include: M. Hidayatullah, "Muslim Law: A Suggested Reform"; Upendra Baxi, "Muslim Law Reform, Uniform Civil Code and the Crisis of Commonsense"; David Pearl, "Intersect Conflict of Laws among Muslims in the Indian Sub-Continent"; Deena Ahmadullah, "Prohibited Relationship under the Special Marriage Act: A Lacuna"; Sujata Manohar, "On a Secular Law of Adoption"; A. B. Shah, "Meaning of Secularism for India"; Tahir Mahmood, "Family Law Reform: Perspective in Modern India"; Rajkumari Agrawala, "Uniform Civil Code: A Formula, Not a Solution"; and B. Sivaramayya, "Towards a Secular Concept of Family."]

546.   ————. "Indian Legislation on Muslim Marriage and Divorce." *Social Legislation in India.* Ed. K. D. Gangrade. New Delhi: Concept Publishing Company, 1978, pp. 16–29.
[Treats Muslim law in British India, matrimonial legislation under the British, and Muslims after independence.]

547.   ————. *The Muslim Law of India.* Allahabad: Law Book Company, 1980.
[This large book clearly intended for technical use is divided into three parts. The first describes the scope and application of Muslim law, addressing itself to the "Place of Muslim Law in the Indian Legal Order," the "Courts' Authority

to Apply Muslim Law," and "Muslims of India: Their Schools of Law and Classes." The second takes up principles and precedents on ten subjects, running from aspects of marriage, through divorce, through widowhood, through the parent-child relationship, through debts, inheritance, and *wakf*s. The third consists of verbatim texts of relevant enactments.]

548.   ————. "Womanhood and Islam." *Studies in Islamic Law, Religion, and Society.* Ed. H. S. Bhatia. New Delhi: Deep and Deep, 1989.
[Argues that once-noble Islamic laws pertaining to women have been distorted over the course of Muslim history.

For Mahmood, Tahir, see also entries 68 and 258.

549.   Maithri Forum for Women. "Fight for Prostitutes' Rights as Citizens." *Manushi* No. 58 (May–June 1990), 35–36.
[Muslim women who sing and dance in an annual Sufi saint's festival are hounded by moralists from right-wing Hindu movements.]

550.   Maity, Pradyot Kumar. "Children Protecting Deities and Rituals of Bengal—a Study." *Folklore* 22 (April, 1981), 77–89.
[Cites the deities worshipped for child-protection, the occasions of their worship, and distinctive features of the rites performed. Some practices are pan-Bengali, others are regional.]

551.   ————. "Image of Mother and Wife in Mediaeval Bengal, as Depicted in Folklore and Vernacular Literature of Bengal." *Folklore* 25 (July 1984), 135–43.
[Proverbs and stories provide images of loved and unloved mothers, and of wives both in their natal and in-laws' houses.]

552. ———. *Folk-Rituals of Eastern India.* New Delhi: Abhinav Publications, 1988.
[This small book focuses entirely on *vrata*s, with rich information on women's practice throughout. *Vrata*s for rain, healing, and agricultural and human fertility are stressed. Materials are primarily from Bengal.]

553. ———. *Human Fertility Cults and Rituals of Bengal: A Comparative Study.* New Delhi: Abhinav Publications, 1989.
[This woman-centered work discusses sociological, religious, and economic backgrounds for fertility cults, the deities thus honored, *vrata*s associated with human fertility, and trees, plants, and other species connected to fertility.]

554. Mallinson, F. A. "A Note on Holiness Allowed to Women: *Pativrata* and *Sati.*" *Ludwig Sternback Felicitation Volume.* Lucknow: Akhila Bharatiya Sanskrit Parishad, 1979.
[Perfecting her role as wife is said to be the Hindu woman's path to holiness. *Dharmasastra* assigns to women responsibility for fully realizing *dharma*.]

555. Mandal, Pratibha. "Where the Bride-Groom Sends for the Bride: A Study on the Haijong Marriage Rites." *Journal of the Indian Anthropological Society* 23 (1988), 103–12.
[Describes marriage rites of an agricultural tribe in Megalaya; these reveal many traits adopted from Bengali Hindus, but include possible vestiges of bride-price practice.]

556. Mandlebaum, David G. *Women's Seclusion and Men's Honor: Sex Roles in North India, Bangladesh, and Pakistan.* Tucson: University of Arizona Press, 1988.
[This synthesis of existing scholarship on seclusion shows differences between Hindu and Muslim *purdah*, and includes a chapter on "Effects and Meanings of *Purdah-Izzat*"; in general, however, it attends very little to relationships between *purdah* and religious ideologies.]

Bibliography

557. Mani, Lata. "Production of an Official Discourse on *Sati* in Early Nineteenth Century Bengal." *Economic and Political Weekly* 21, No. 7 (April 26, 1986), WS32–WS40.
[A long and careful paper examines assumptions underlying British authorities' discussions regarding abolition of *sati*; it describes the historical context, the British positions, and uses made of statements by brahmin *pandits*. Complements the author's paper by a similar title published in Kumkum Sangari and Sudesh Vaid, *Recasting Women* (see entry 790 below).]

558. ———. *Contentious Traditions: The Debate on* Sati *in Colonial India, 1780–1833*. Ph.D. diss., University of California at Santa Cruz, 1989.
[Examines representations of *sati* and debates over its prohibition among British officials, missionaries, and the Indian male elite to reveal the modes of colonial discourse that informed them. Argues "although *sati* became an alibi for colonialism's civilising mission, the women who burned were neither subjects, not even objects of concern in the debate, but rather the ground for struggles over Indian society and definitions of tradition" (*DAI* 50, No. 12 [June 1990], A-4066). Includes an analysis of women's own testimonials at their pyres and an epilogue on current debates about widow burning.]

559. ———. "Multiple Mediations: Feminist Scholarship in the Age of Multinational Reception." *Predicaments of Theory*; special issue of *Inscriptions* (1989), 1–23.
[Scrutinizes the relationship between context and discourse; the author reflects on the issue informing her own dissertation (see entry 558 above), and on differing receptions to her work in India and in the West which themselves are a product of the differing contexts of her audiences. A concluding analysis of debates in India that followed the Roop Kanwar *sati* shows how these debates simultaneously reflect the context established by previous colonial discourse

137

and change the context within which talk about *sati* is now occurring.]

For Mani, Lata, see also entry 790.

560.   Manimala. "Because They Were Women." *Manushi* No. 23 (July–August, 1984), 19–21.
[Four women of Munger district, Bihar, are charged with witchcraft after failing a diviner's test—and are promptly stripped and beaten to death.]

561.   Manjushree. *The Position of Women in the* Yajnavalkyas-mrti. New Delhi: Prachi Publishers, 1990.
[Summarizes a work of *dharmasastra* that is second in prestige and age only to *Manusmriti*. Covers the *Yajnavalk-yasmrti*'s concept of womanhood, marriage regulations, property rights of women and *stridhana*, precepts for widows, and punishments and penances.]

562.   March, Kathryn S. *The Intermediacy of Women: Female Gender Symbolism and the Social Position of Women among Tamangs and Sherpas of Highland Nepal.* Ph.D. diss., Cornell University, 1979.
["Explores the relation between gender symbolism and the position of sexed individuals in the world . . . investigates the importance of women as social links between clans, villages, households, and individuals, and the importance of female symbols as mediators within the gender belief system." The female religious symbolism described is of shamanic and Buddhist origin. Cited from the author's description, *DAI* 40, No. 9 (March 1980), A-501.]

563.   Marglin, Frédérique Apffel. "Types of Oppositions in Hindu Culture." *Purity and Auspiciousness.* Ed. Carman and Frédérique Marglin. Special Issue, *Journal of Developing Societies* I (1985), 65–83.
[The terms in Hindu dichotomies are not necessarily exclu-

sive of one another; examples are the terms pure/impure and auspicious/inauspicious. *Devadasi/daita* roles in rituals of the annual car festival at Puri are cited as examples.]

564. ————. *Wives of the God-King: The Rituals of the* Deva-dasis *of Puri*. Delhi and New York: Oxford University Press, 1985.
[Some dancers married to Lord Jagannath of Puri survive, despite the Indian government ban on new *devadasi* dedications. Marglin explores the *devadasis'* relationship to married women, their sexuality and its relationship to Indian concepts of purity and auspiciousness, their relationship to kingship, and their ritual duties at both the palace and Lord Jagannath's temple. This book has brought significant new understanding to Hindu conceptions of auspiciousness.]

565. Maryam Jameelah. *Islam and the Muslim Woman Today*. 3rd ed. Lahore: Mohammad Yusuf Khan and Sons, 1988.
[According to the author, "The purpose of this essay is to demonstrate the inherent superiority of those Islamic teachings pertaining to women and why to tamper with them is mischief-making of the first magnitude." This forty-eight-page defense of the status quo treats the Muslim woman's role in society, the duties of a Muslim mother, and the fallacies of various Muslim and feminist efforts to emancipate the women of Islam.]

566. Mathew, P. M. "Liberation Theology in Practice." *Mainstream* (August 3, 1985), 17–21.
[References to Christian nuns' activities in this article mention two who undertook a fast unto death.]

567. Mathrani, Kala. "Sri Sri Ma, the Holy Mother." *Samvit* 5 (March 1982), 7–13.
[A Sarada Math devotee reflects on the role of Sarada Devi, Holy Mother of the Ramakrishna and Sarada Missions.]

568. Maurya, Sahab Deen, ed. *Women in India*. Allahabad: Chugh Publications, 1988.
[Most of this book's sixteen articles address social and economic issues; three, however, have some bearing on religion: Gayatri Devi's "Emancipation of Women in India" discusses dowry, widow remarriage, and *sati*; Amitabh Tewari's "Economic Status and Socio-Religious Attitude of Indian Women" includes results of a survey of daily *puja* performance and temple attendance; and Gayatri Devi and Smt. Madhuri's "Marriage and Hindu Women" has some information on the impact of marriage on ritual status.]

569. Mazumdar, Shudha. *A Pattern of Life: The Memoirs of an Indian Woman*. Trans. and ed. Geraldine H. Forbes. New Delhi: Manohar, 1975; Columbia, Mo.: South Asia Books, 1977.
[The author was raised in *purdah*, but ceased to observe it following her marriage to a civil servant of the Raj. Includes several fine descriptions of *vrata*s Mazumdar performed as a young girl. The time frame is early twentieth century.]

570. ————. *Memoirs of an Indian Woman*. Ed. Geraldine Forbes. Armonk, N.Y.: M. E. Sharpe, 1989.
[A new U.S. edition of the work cited above; includes an afterword on the author's life following her memoir's close.]

571. McClean, M. D. "Women as Aspects of the Mother Goddess in India: A Case Study of Ramakrishna." *Religion* 19, No. 1 (January 1989), 13–25.
[Argues that Ramakrishna's teachings do not reflect a "high view on women," despite his instructions to view all women as the goddess.]

572. McCormack, Manjit Kaur. "The Sikh Marriage Ceremony." *Sikh Review* 29 (August 1981), 35–39.

[This comprehensive treatment, with definitions, procedures, and a semi-detailed description, includes a translation of verses accompanying the ceremony and an interpretive commentary.]

573. McDaniel, June. *Bhava: Religious Ecstasy and Madness in Bengal*. Ph.D. diss., University of Chicago, 1986.
[Prototype for *The Madness of the Saints* (see entry 574 below).]

574. ————. *The Madness of the Saints: Ecstatic Religion in Bengal*. Chicago: The University of Chicago Press, 1989.
[Saints mad for god are studied here, in four varieties: one is the Bengali Holy Woman. Six such women selected for individual discussion are Anandamayi Ma, Sarada Devi, Arcanapuri Ma, Laksmi Ma, Yogesvari Devi and Siddhimata.]

575. McGee, Mary. *Feasting and Fasting: The* Vrata *Tradition and its Significance for Hindu Women*. 2 vols. Th.D. diss., Cambridge, Mass.: Harvard University, 1987.
[Examines both texts and practice of Hindu women in the Pune district of Maharashtra to discover women's motivations for performing *vrata*s. Finds a discrepancy between texts that treat *vrata*s as optional and on-the-ground practice which treats them as a prerequisite for being a truly responsible wife. Furnishes valuable information about *vrata* performance—especially concerning when and for what purpose individual *vrata*s are enacted. Described *DAI* 49, No. 10 (April 1989), A-3057–58.]

For McGee, Mary, see also entry 532.

576. McGilvray, Dennis B. "Sexual Power and Fertility in Sri Lanka: Batticaloa Tamils and Moors." *Ethnography of Fertility and Birth*. Ed. Carol P. MacCormack. New York: Academic Press, 1982, pp. 25–73.

[Describes in some detail the rituals of first menstruation among both groups, as well as standard practice for ordinary menstruation, observances during and after childbirth, strategies against barrenness, and attitudes towards contraception.]

577. ————. "The 1987 Stirling Award Essay: Sex, Repression, and Sanskritization in Sri Lanka?" *Ethos* 16, No. 2 (June 1988), 99–127.
[A response to Gananath Obeyesekere's *Cult of the Goddess Pattini* suggests Obeyesekere has oversimplified his model of Sri Lankan families and has skipped over the influence of Tamil concepts of female power and auspiciousness.]

578. Mehta, Anjali D. "*Sati*: A Psychological Analysis." *The Secularist* 115 (January–February, 1989), 5–11, 17.
[A psychologist utilizes the concepts of internalization and cathexis to shed light on *sati*, locating these in the context of beliefs that a wife can cause her husband's death by failing in ritual performance.]

579. Mehta, Bavna. "Family Laws vis-a-vis Women." *Fifth National Conference of the Indian Association for Women's Studies*. Calcutta: Jadavpur University, 1991.
[A duplicated typescript, housed at the Research Centre for Women's Studies, SNDT Women's University, Bombay, summarizes provisions destructive to women in religious personal laws.]

For Mehta, Bavna, see also entry 275.

580. Mehta, Hamsa. *Indian Women*. Delhi: Butala, 1981.
[Includes one section on Gandhi and women and another on the Hindu marriage code.]

581. Mehta, Rama. *Divorced Hindu Woman*. Delhi: Vikas Publishing House, 1975.

[A sociological analysis reveals the impact of social change on women's values, especially receptivity to divorce and acceptance of separated and divorced women. Tolerance for marital breakups increases among women who live in nuclear families. Groups studied are urban and "middle class"; the latter category is again divided into "lower-middle" and "upper-middle" clusters.]

582.   ———. *Inside the Haveli*. New Delhi: Arnold-Heinemann, 1977.
[The heroine of this award-winning novel is a Western-educated urban woman who must adjust to *purdah* after marrying the only son of a conservative Rajput family. Describes the reception given the new bride, the celebration at the birth of her first child, mourning following the death of the household's senior wife, prostrations to Saraswati when a child starts school, arrangements and celebration for the marriage of a servant's daughter, and restrictions placed upon widows.]

583.   Mehta, Ved. *Mamaji*. New York: Oxford University Press, 1979.
[An expatriate Punjabi who is now a well-known U.S. author traces the life and social milieu of his mother, whose father was the noted Arya Samajist Durga Das. Includes some reflection on Arya Samaj politics, and the rules that Mamaji's father imposed regarding household rites; also incorporates a five-page description of Mamaji's stripped-down Arya Samaj wedding.]

584.   Menon, M. Indu. "Educational Backwardness of Muslim Women in Kerala." *Social Welfare* 25, Nos. 2–3 (May–June 1978), 17–18, 39.
[Based on a survey of four Kerala districts with the state's largest concentration of Muslims, this study finds a persistence of early marriage, low educational levels, continued practice of seclusion and veiling, little work outside the

home, and a high level of religious education. Time devoted to religious education correlates inversely with time spent on formal school education.]

585.   ————. *Status of Muslim Women in India: A Case Study of Kerala*. New Delhi: Uppal Publishing House, 1981.
[Initially the author's Ph.D. thesis, in Sociology, this volume uses survey methods to study the realities of education, marriage, divorce, occupation, politics, and male attitudes towards women.]

586.   Menski, Werner F. *Role and Ritual in the Hindu Marriage*. Ph.D. Thesis, University of London, 1984.
[No further information is available.]

For Menski, Werner F., see also entry 532.

587.   Metcalf, Barbara Daly, trans., with commentary. *Perfecting Women: Maulana Ashraf 'Ali Thanawi's* Bihishti Zewar. Berkeley: University of California Press, 1990.
[Partially translates and comments on a work by the leader of the late nineteenth-century Muslim Deobandi reform movement of northern India. Written to offer a "basic education" for Muslim women, Thanawi's book became a classic gift for Muslim brides. Selections cover categories of custom, comportment and character, stories of good women, and a chapter on miscellaneous activities of women, covering a range of topics from approved books and pursuit of religious knowledge to recipes and instructions for posting parcels.]

For Metcalf, Barbara Daly, see also entries 354 and 392.

588.   Michael, R. Blake. "Women of the *Sunyasampadane*: Housewives and Saints in Virasaivism." *Journal of the American Oriental Society* 103, No. 2 (1983), 361–68.

[Qualifies the vaunted sexual egalitarianism of Virasaivas by analyzing stories from a fifteenth-century text about the career and spiritual debates of a prominent male saint. Although five women whom the saint encounters demonstrate spiritual prowess equal to that of males, they attain this within a social context that presupposes women's subordination.]

589. Mies, Maria. "Indian Women and Leadership." *Bulletin of Concerned Asian Scholars* 7, No. 1 (January–March 1975), 56–66.
[Explores a paradox of Indian leadership: while the *pativrata* ideal and all its attendant abuses persist, more women are found in leadership roles there than in Western countries—and women leaders are less likely to suffer from male counterparts' aggression and resentment.]

590. ————. *Indian Women and Patriarchy: Conflicts and Dilemmas of Students and Working Women*. Trans. Saral K. Sarkar. New Delhi: Concept Publishing Company, 1980.
[A chapter on "Historical, Cultural, and Social Determinants of Female Roles" traces the impact of Brahmanical law and includes a subsection on *devadasis*. Mies stresses the relative independence and self-determination of *devadasis* and questions the anti-*devadasi* movement.]

591. Minault, Gail. "*Begamati Zuban*: Women's Language and Culture in Nineteenth Century Delhi." *Indian International Centre Quarterly* 11, No. 2 (July 1984), 204–22.
[Offers limited information about Muslim women's practices for warding off evil and about women's vows.]

592. ————. "Making Invisible Women Visible: Studying the History of Muslim Women in South Asia." *South Asia: Journal of South Asian Studies* 9, No. 1 (June 1986), 1–14.
[Reviews and characterizes the resources available for study of a still nearly invisible group.]

593.   ———. "Urdu Women's Magazines in the Early Twentieth
        Century." *Manushi* No. 48 (September–October 1988), 2–9.
        [Describes three early magazines that offered Muslim wom-
        en a "place where their voices could be heard."]

594.   ———. "Legal and Scholarly Activism: Recent Women's
        Studies on India—a Review Article." *Journal of Asian
        Studies* 47, No. 4 (November 1988), 814–20.
        [Reviews seven works on women's studies from India, rang-
        ing in date from 1985–87; two concern the Shah Bano case
        (Ali Asghar Engineer, *The Shah Bano Controversy,* and
        Janak Raj Jai, *Shah Bano*). Included principally for its
        lucid summary of issues underlying the Shah Bano re-
        sponse.]

For Minault, Gail, see also entries 14, 392, and 679.

595.   Minturn, Leigh. *Sita's Daughters: Coming Out of* Purdah:
        The Rajput Women of Khalapur Revisited. New York:
        Oxford University Press, 1993.
        [Returning after twenty years to a village site where she
        had formerly participated in a group research project on so-
        cialization, the author of this volume explored changes in
        practice and attitudes of families she had studied earlier.
        Selected chapters cover topics such as "Ritual and Recrea-
        tion," "Women's Nature: Honour and *Shakti*," "Widows,"
        "*Sati, Rand, Bhaktani*," and "Socialization", the author's
        conclusions pay special attention to religion.]

596.   Mishra, Kiran. *Hearths and Fields: Changing Lives of Nish-
        ing Women of Arunachal Pradesh.* New Delhi: Satvahan,
        1985.
        [Describes the life of women of a hill tribe of Arunachal
        Pradesh; includes a chapter on "Customs, Norms, and Ritu-
        als."]

597. Mishra, V. B. "The Practice of *Niyoga* in Ancient Literature of India: A Sociological Study." *Annals of the Bhandarkar Oriental Research Institute* 58–59 (1977–78), 773–76.
      [Examines stipulations governing the practice whereby the brother of a dead husband begets a child on a sonless widow. Includes evidence showing that neither women nor law codifiers liked this practice.]

598. Misra, Gitanjali. "*Puspunei*: A Festival of the Juangs of the Hills of Keonjhar District of Orissa." *Folklore* 24 (October 1983), 211–14.
      [A priestess known as *boitani* plays the central role in this festival.]

599. Misra, Ish Narain. "The Women's Question in Communal Ideologies: A Study of the Ideology of Rashtriya Swayam Sevak Sangh and Jamat-e-Islami." *Teaching Politics* 13, No. 1 (1987), 7–34.
      [Analyzes the stated ideologies of two extremely right-wing communalist movements, one Hindu, one Muslim, with reference to the issue of gender equality. Both offer remarkably similar opposition to egalitarian ideals, charging that these will destabilize families and "lead to sexual anarchy." Both prefer to keep women in the domestic sphere.]

600. Mitra, Kana. "Women in Hinduism." *Journal of Ecumenical Studies* 20 (Fall 1983), 585–601.
      [Describes models of ideal female roles that women are taught to emulate and repercussions of following such models. Models cited include wives, mothers, daughters, and women of intellectual and spiritual achievements.]

601. ————. "Women and the Hindu Tradition." *Women's and Men's Liberation: Testimonies of Spirit*. Ed. Leonard Grob, Riffat Hassan, and Haim Gordon. New York: Greenwood Press, 1991.

[Examines the impact of normative precepts and models on the self-perceptions and values of contemporary Hindu women. Shows how a woman imbibes the former as she "grows up female."]

602. Mitter, Dwarkanath. *The Position of Women in Hindu Law*. New Delhi: Inter-India Publications, 1984; originally published in 1913.
[A massive historical survey covers the status of women in general, the status of wives, marriage, the status of widows, rights of inheritance, *stridhan*, and the status of courtesans and dancing girls.]

603. Mitter, Kaushik. "Mother Teresa—a Living Saint." *Sikh Review* (August 1988), 42–44.
[This testimony to Mother Teresa on the occasion of her seventy-eighth birthday consists solely of brief biographical anecdotes.]

604. Mody, Nawaz B. "The Press in India: The Shah Bano Judgment and Its Aftermath." *Asian Survey* 27 (August 1987), 935–53.
[The press played a crucial role in articulating the different opinions on the Shah Bano case—but it often oversimplified the issues, describing them in black-and-white terms. Charges that such portrayals undercut reformist tendencies and strengthen the hand of communalists.]

605. Mokhal, Bhagwan Singh. "The Influence of Religion on Raj Kumar in *Rana Surat Singh*." *Sikh Review* 28 (December 1980), 28–35.
[Describes the spiritual journey of the heroine of a Sikh epic.]

606. Mondal, Sekh Rahim. "*Parda* among Muslim Women: A Study in a West Bengal Village." *Man in India*, 59, No. 4 (October–December 1979), 342–49.

[Describes the extent and details of *purdah* in a village where almost all women observe it, but Muslims observe it most intensely.]

607. Mookerjee, Nanda, ed. *Sri Sarada Devi: Consort of Sri Ramakrishna*. Calcutta: Firma KLM, 1978.
[A collection of essays, many by contemporaries. Several are very short and written in testimonial style.]

608. Moore, Melinda A. "Symbol and Meaning in Nayar Marriage Ritual." *American Ethnologist* 15, No. 2 (May 1988), 254–73.
[Examines three rituals affecting women of a much-examined matrilineal group: rites are the *tali*-tying ceremony, first menstruation rite, and the ceremony that begins a sexual relationship. Combines informants' interpretations with written source materials.]

609. Moses, Jane, and Grace Aaron. "Thirty Years of the C.S.I. Order for Women." *The South Indian Churchman* (January 1980), 8–9.
[A brief history of the Order for Women of the Church of South India.]

610. "Mother Teresa and the Poorest of the Poor." *Parabola* 16 (February 1991), 22–23.
[Consists of five quotations from Mother Teresa, with descriptions of the situations that evoked them and a single photograph.]

611. *Motherhood in India*. Review of Women's Studies Supplement, *Economic and Political Weekly* 25, Nos. 42–43 (October 20–29, 1990), WS50–WS116.
[Features seven articles on the imagery and ideology of motherhood in past and present India: Sukumari Bhattacharji, "Motherhood in Ancient India"; Kamala Ganesh, "Mother Who is Not a Mother: In Search of the Great

Indian Goddess"; Jasodhara Bagchi, "Representing Nation-
alism: Ideology of Motherhood in Colonial Bengal"; C. S.
Lakshmi, "Mother, Mother-Community and Mother-Politics
in Tamil Nadu"; Sangeeta Dutta, "Relinquishing the Halo:
Portrayal of Mother in Indian Writing in English"; Shanta
Gokhale, "Mother in Sane Guruji's *Shyamchi Ai*"; and
Prabha Krishnan, "In the Idiom of Loss: Ideology of Mother-
hood in Television Serials."]

612.   Motiwala, Shailbala. "Muslim Women's Inheritance Law—
the Case of Zubeda Bibi." *Manushi* No. 23 (July–August,
1984), pp. 41–42.
[An attorney tells the story of a Muslim widow's battle to
collect her husband's benefits.]

613.   Mowli, V. Chandra. *"Jogin" Girl-Child Labour Studies*. New
Delhi: Sterling Publishers, 1992.
[The first section of this two-part volume is a study of the
jogin system in Andhra Pradesh; low-caste girls here are
"married" to a god, then become concubines of the "feudal
gentry" in their villages. The author distinguishes these
girls from *devadasi*s, although the two institutions seem
very similar. The same section discusses the role of voluntary organizations in releasing girls from their dedication,
including fifty brief case-studies. The second section surveys
the international struggle on behalf of female children.]

614.   Mukhopadhyay, Carol. *"Sati* or *Shakti*: Women, Culture and
Politics in India." *Perspectives on Power: Women in Africa,
Asia, and Latin America*. Ed. Jean F. O'Barr. Durham:
Duke University Center for International Studies, 1982.
[Here *sati* is taken as a trope for the oppressed woman and
shakti for the woman who is powerful; the article seeks to
explain the presence of the powerful woman Indira Gandhi
in a context where women are more typically oppressed.
The author cites four aspects of the Hindu religious and
philosophical tradition which validate women's claims to
political power.]

615.   Mukhopadhyay, Maitrayee. *Silver Shackles: Women and
       Development in India*. Oxford: Oxfam, 1984.
       [Contains an introductory chapter titled "Culture and
       Tradition: Women's Place Ordained"; a section of this chap-
       ter titled "Religion and Women's Status" covers Hinduism,
       Islam, Christianity, and other religious traditions of India,
       including those of tribal women. The book as a whole is
       short, and the sections described are simple; however, they
       are careful and accurate.]

616.   Muktiprana, Pravrajika. "The Holy Mother." *Samvit* 1
       (March 1990), 16–22.
       [The General Secretary of Sri Sarada Math reflects on the
       life and significance of Holy Mother Sarada Devi.]

617.   ———. "Sister Nivedita, Sister Christine and Their
       School." In two parts. *Samvit* 23 (March 1991), 13–19, and
       24 (September 1991), 27–33.
       [Describes dedicated efforts by two Western disciples of
       Swami Vivekananda to open and run a school for girls in
       Calcutta.]

618.   Mullatti, Leela. "Marriage and the Status of Women in
       Veerasaivism." *Society and Culture: in Honour of Late Dr.
       Radhakamal Mukerjee*. Ed. R. M. Loomba and G. R. Madan.
       Ahmedabad: Allied Publishers, 1987.
       [Based on a survey of one-hundred Virasaiva families from
       Dharwar district, Karnataka, this article appears to be a
       pilot study for the author's book on Virasaivism (entry 619
       below); Mullati finds that twelfth-century Virasaiva mar-
       riage reforms still enhance women's status today.]

619.   ———. *The Bhakti Movement and the Status of Women:
       A Case Study of Virasaivism*. New Delhi: Abhinav Pub-
       lishers, 1989.
       [This study of contemporary practice in a once-radical tradi-
       tion includes chapters on the Virasaiva image of women,

training of children, marriage and family practice, economic
life, and "socio/religious life." Sources are both textual analysis and findings from field surveys conducted in the state
of Karnataka.]

620.   Murcott, Susan. *The First Buddhist Women: Translations
and Commentaries on the* Therigatha. Berkeley, Calif.:
Parallax Press, 1991.
[This new translation of a rare record of stanzas by ancient
Buddhist women of high spiritual attainments features
sixty-one of the seventy-three poems from the original work.
The translator has summarized stories of the Pali commentary that tell of each poem's author and the circumstances
in which her poem was composed. Poems are grouped topically, thus changing the order of the original.]

621.   Murshid, Ghulam. *Reluctant Debutante: Response of Bengali Women to Modernization, 1849–1905*. Rajshahi, Bangladesh: Sahitya Samsad, Rajshahi University, 1983.
[Drawing on women's writings in Bengali women's magazines, the author examines the "modernization" of nineteenth-century Bengali women. He traces early attitudes towards women's education, men's work to "free" women, and
women's own concepts of freedom, finding that women's approaches towards reform closely reflected ideals that had
been framed by men.]

622.   Murshid, Tazeen Mahnaz. *The Bengal Muslim Intelligent-
sia, 1937–1977: The Tension between the Religious and the
Secular*. Ph.D. diss., Oxford University, 1985.
[Although this dissertation is principally interested in the
male Bengali elite, its seventh chapter "discusses the debates on the role of religion in social life, especially attitudes to social mores, family laws, the position of women,
and the fine arts." Cited from author's description, *DAI* 50,
No. 6 (December 1989), A-1773–74.]

623. "Muslim Personal Law: Evading the Issue." *Economic and Political Weekly* 20, No. 48 (November 30, 1985), 2096.
[This editorial summarizes responses to the Shah Bano case; "evading the issue" are those who argue that initiative for reforming Muslim personal law must come from Muslims themselves.]

624. "Muslim Women Launch Agitation." *Manushi* 5, No. 6 (=No. 30; September–October 1985), 33–34.
[The issue prompting this "agitation" was verbal divorce.]

625. *Muslim Women (Protection of Rights on Divorce) Act, 1986, Together with Muslim Women (Protection of Rights on Divorce) Rules, 1986.* Lucknow: Eastern Book Company, 1986.
[A pamphlet explains the two laws referred to in the title.]

626. Muthanna, I. M. *Mother Besant and Mahatma Gandhi.* Vellore: Thenpulam, 1986.
[Describes the rivalry between two famous leaders who combined politics with spiritual discipline; this was based in part on personality clashes and in part on differences in political and religious convictions. Locates both Besant and Gandhi in the context of the nationalist movement, with generous description of their aims, methods, and accomplishments.]

627. Nagamma, Suri. *My Life at Sri Ramanasramam.* Tiruvannamalai: Sri Ramanasramam, 1975.
[Orphaned at ten and widowed at twelve, the troubled author finally found solace at the *ashram* of the Brahmin saint Ramana Maharishi; she was a permanent resident there from 1941 until 1953. Her volume portrays *ashram* life, events affecting the community, the author's own *ashram* activities, pilgrim excursions, and writings, and progression of the cancer that finally caused the Maharishi's death.]

628.   Nahar, Sujata. *Mother's Chronicles. Mirra*. Paris: Institut
       de Recherches Evolutives, 1979.
       [Five volumes recount the life of Mirra Alfassa Richard,
       Holy Mother of the Sri Aurobindo Ashram.]

629.   Nair, Janaki. "Reconstructing and Reinterpreting the His-
       tory of Women in India." *Journal of Women's History* 3, No.
       1 (Spring 1991), 131–36.
       [This review essay of Sangari and Vaid, *Recasting Women*,
       Krishnamurti, *Women in Colonial India*, and Lalita, *We
       Were Making History,* offers a helpful characterization of
       three models for reconstructing history reflected in these
       three volumes.]

630.   Nair, K. Chandrasekharan. *Devadasi Tradition in Kerala:
       A Study, with Special Reference to Literature, Dance, and
       Music*. Trivandrum: Kerala Historical Society, 1987.
       [A very brief volume includes materials on *devadasi* history,
       devadasi performances, and the end of the *devadasi* tradi-
       tion.]

631.   Nair, Lalitha. "Abolition of *Devadasi* System in Kerala."
       Journal of Kerala Studies 7, Nos. 1–4 (March–December,
       1980), 61–75.
       [Argues that *devadasi*s of Kerala once enjoyed a "high and
       esteemed" position; their downfall began after the thir-
       teenth century. Also describes the drive to prohibit *deva-
       dasi* dedications, including texts of several relevant docu-
       ments.]

632.   Nam-mkha'i snying-po. *Mother of Knowledge: The Enlight-
       enment of Ye-shes mTsho-rgyal*. Trans. Tarthang Tulku.
       Berkeley, Calif.: Dharma Publishing, 1983.
       [Translates the Tibetan biography of the most important
       woman teacher in Tibetan Buddhism's rNying-ma lineage.]

633.   Nanavutty, Piloo. "Parsi Women: Their Contribution to In-
         dian Public Life." *The Sugar in the Milk: The Parsis of In-
         dia*. Ed. Nancy Singh and Ram Singh. Delhi: ISPCK, for the
         Institute for Development Education, 1986.
         [Consists principally of short biographical sketches of Parsi
         women from the independence movement and in social
         work, education, the media, commerce, the arts, and
         sports.]

634.   Nand, Lokesh Chandra. *Women in Delhi Sultanate*. Allaha-
         bad: Vohra Publishers, 1989.
         [Includes chapters titled "Women in Islam," "Women and
         Bhakti Saints," and "Women and Sufis," plus miscellaneous
         materials on rites, beliefs, and issues confronting women.]

635.   Nanda, B. R. *Indian Women, from* Purdah *to Modernity*.
         New Delhi: Vikas Publishing House, 1976.
         [Contains three articles with bearing on religion: Zarina
         Bhatty, "Status of Muslim Women and Social Change"; Vina
         Mazumdar, "The Social Reform Movement in India, from
         Ranade to Nehru"; and Lotika Sarkar, "Jawarharlal Nehru
         and the Hindu Code Bill."]

636.   Nandan, Justice Deoki. *Hindu Law: Marriage and Divorce*.
         Allahabad: University Book Agency, 1989.
         [This massive study of marriage, marriage rights, annul-
         ment, divorce, legitimacy of children, and property rights is
         clearly intended as a resource for the Indian courts. It in-
         cludes citations of pertinent cases, treats the history of cen-
         tral issues, and offers the author's own opinions on these.]

637.   Nandy, Ashis. *At the Edge of Psychology: Essays in Politics
         and Culture*. Delhi: Oxford University Press, 1980.
         [Two of six essays in this volume relate to women: "*Sati*: A
         Nineteenth Century Tale of Women, Violence and Protest,"
         and "Woman versus Womanliness in India: An Essay in

Cultural and Political Psychology." The first and more influential of the two contends that the *sati* "epidemic" of the late 1700s and early 1800s was a product of British colonialism and a response to the environmental and social changes this brought; it interprets Ram Mohan Roy as a product of a society attempting to "work through its ambivalences towards this rite." Nandy's second pertinent essay calls upon the model of the "cosmic feminine principle" to explain connections between creativity and womanliness in India.]

638. ———. "The Human Factor." *The Illustrated Weekly of India* (January 17, 1988), 20–23.
[Responds to the Roop Kanwar *sati*. Nandy "argues that neither self-immolation nor murder is uncommon in India, particularly that of women, and that the reaction to this *sati* tells us more about Indian journalists, social activists, and the dominant political culture of the Indian bourgeoisie than about the suffering of the victim."]

639. ———. "*Sati* in Kaliyuga." *Economic and Political Weekly* 23, No. 38 (September 17, 1988), 1976.
[Defends the author's position on *sati* against charges that he has created a covert rationalization for a grisly practice.]

For Nandy, Ashis, see also entries 35, 301, 336, and 719.

640. Narang, Gokul Chand. "Hinduism and Women." *Dharma Marg* 2, No. 4 (January 1985), 31–38.
[Defends Manu's restrictions on women, claiming that women are not suited to the "rough and tumble" of public life; also asserts that the Vedas knew no *sati* and no prohibition on widow remarriage—and that the Hindu *shastras* recognized women's right to hold property.]

641. Narasinha, Sakuntala. *Born Unfree: A Selection of Articles on Practices and Policies Affecting Women in India.* Banga-

lore: Samanvitha Department of Women's Studies, NMKRV First Grade College for Women, 1989.
[These selections from the author's column in the *Deccan Herald* include, among others, columns on "Son-in-Law Worship," "*Sati*—Glorifying a Gory Death," "Gandhi on Women," "Women and Religious Observances," and "Discrimination against Christian Women."]

642.   ———. *Sati: A Study of Widow Burning in India*. New Delhi: Viking, 1990.
[This response to the Roop Kanwar incident cites the latter's precedents, social context, the historical frequency of *sati* incidents, and pro-*sati* arguments. It perceives the pro-*sati* campaign as a manifestation of religious fundamentalism and, hence, also identifies social factors contributing to the rise of fundamentalist movements.]

643.   Narayan, Kiran. "Birds on a Branch. Girlfriends and Wedding Songs in Kangra." *Ethos* 14, No. 1 (Spring 1986), 47–75.
[Explores friendship among women as a recurring theme in auspicious wedding songs from Kangra, Himachal Pradesh; tells much about weddings themselves and the wrenching transitions they effect.]

644.   Narayana, Gita. "*Sati* is Not for Worship." *Illustrated Weekly of India* 102, No. 3 (January 18, 1981), 21.
[Addresses controversy surrounding a proposal to build a temple to a Rajasthani *sati* in New Delhi.]

645.   Narayana, V. "Meeting Sri Sarada Devi." *Samvit* 1 (March 1980), 6–9.
[Describes the author's experiences as a child and youth with the Ramakrishna Mission's Holy Mother.]

646.   *The* Nartaki *in Indian Dance*. Special issue, *Sangeet Natak* 97 (July–September 1990).

[This entire issue devoted to traditional dance in India includes the following articles on *devadasis*: Sindhu S. Dange, "The Institutions of *Ganika* and *Devadasi* from Ancient to Medieval Times"; Kalpana Desai, "The *Devadasi* in the Socio-Religious Context"; R. Nagaswamy, "The *Devadasis* of Tamil Nadu: A Study"; D. N. Patnaik, "The *Devadasi* Tradition in Orissa"; R. Sathyanarayana, "Temple Dance and the *Devadasi* in Karnataka"; and Kavalam Narayana Panikkarm, "*Devadasi* System Unknown to Kerala."]

647. Naseem, Mohammad Farogh. *The Shah Bano Case X-rayed*. Karachi: Karachi Legal Research Centre, 1988.
[A Pakistani lawyer trained in London analyzes the Shah Bano judgment, concluding that it was an attempt to destroy Muslim personal law. Includes the text of the judgment, together with that of a related case, Zohara Khatoom v. Mohd. Ibrahim, and several brief extracts from published responses to Shah Bano.]

648. Nath, Alokananda. "Women in Folklore of North-East India: Some Focus on the Position and Status." *Folklore* 28, No. 6 (June 1987), 120–25.
[Household duties, choice in marriage, love affairs, stepmothers, and the intellectual capacities of women are depicted in story and in song.]

649. Nath, Jhorna. "Beliefs and Customs Observed by Muslim Rural Women during Their Life Cycle." *The Endless Day: Some Case Material on Asian Rural Women*. Ed. T. Scarlett Epstein and Rosemary A. Watts. Oxford, England, and New York: Pergamon Press, 1981.
[The site is Bangladesh; the chapter describes rites and beliefs surrounding infancy, sex-differentiated socialization during childhood, sex segregation during adolescence, premarital sex, marriage, divorce, remarriage, and procreation; the latter section treats the respective roles of daughter-in-law, mother, mother-in-law and grandmother.]

650. Nath, Rakhal Chandra. *The New Hindu Movement, 1886–1911*. Calcutta: Minerva, 1981.
[Includes materials on the "woman question" and the reform movement.]

651. *National Conference on Women's Studies*. Bombay, 1981. Available at the Institute for Social Studies Trust, New Delhi.
[Bound in three volumes; one includes reports and review papers. This first conference of a distinguished series focussed principally on development, but also includes extensive materials on education and the media. See especially: M. Sen, "Religion and Social Change—an Analysis of Anti-Feminist/Feminist Trends in Early Buddhism"; Rafiqul Huda Chaudhury, "Patriarchy, Religion and Women's Work in Bangladesh"; and Sudha R. Desai, "Women in Folklore of Gujarat" (with special reference to folk songs).]

652. *National Seminar on the Status of Women in Islam*. New Delhi: Bait-al-Hikmat, 1983.
[Housed at Jamia Millia Islamia University library. No further information is available.]

653. *The National Situation* and *A Biblical Response from Women*. Madras: All India Council of Christian Women, n.d.
[Two papers are bound together to form this small booklet; the first describes the current situation of crisis in India: economic imbalance, political chaos, and rising communalism. The second offers a "Biblical response" specifically directed towards the problem of communalism.]

654. Neff, Deborah L. "Aesthetics and Power in *Pambin Tullah*: A Possession Ritual of Rural Kerala." *Ethnology* 26 (January 1987), 63–71.
[Describes a ritual sponsored by Nayyars in which men of a lower caste perform the ritual itself; however, Nayyar women of the sponsoring family are possessed by, and speak for, the family's serpent deities.]

655.   Nirankarj, Man Singh. "Genesis of Anand Marriage." *Sikh Review* 30 (March 1982), 49–55.
[Traces the evolution of today's Sikh marriage ceremony, citing names of the early couples who performed and modified it.]

656.   Nivedita, Sister (Margaret Noble). *Sister Nivedita's Lectures and Writings: Hitherto Unpublished Collection of Lectures and Writings of Sister Nivedita on Education, Hindu Life, Thought and so on.* Calcutta: Sister Nivedita's Girls' School, 1975.
[Assembles miscellaneous talks and writings discovered after publication of Nivedita's *Complete Works.* Section headings are "On Education," "On Hindu Life, Thought, and Religion," "On Political, Economic and Social Problems," "Biographical Sketches and Reviews," "Newspaper Reports of Speeches and Interviews," and "Miscellaneous Articles Written before Meeting Swami Vivekananda."]

657.   ———. *Letters of Sister Nivedita.* 2 vols. Ed. Bimal Kumar Basu. Calcutta: Nababharat Publishers, 1982.
[The title is self-descriptive.]

658.   ———. *Kali the Mother.* Mayavati: Swami Ananyananda, Advait Ashrama, 1983; original edition London: Sonnenschein, 1900.
[Irishwoman-turned-*sannyasini*, educator, and freedom fighter Sister Nivedita offers her reflections on symbols, Shiva, Ramprasad, Ramakrishna, Dakshineshwar, and Kali the Mother in this collection of brief meditations written originally in 1897.]

659.   Obeyesekere, Gananath. *Medusa's Hair: An Essay on Personal Symbols and Religious Experience.* Chicago: University of Chicago Press, 1981.
[This psychoanalytic study of ecstatic ascetics at the Hindu-Buddhist pilgrimage center of Kataragama in Sri Lanka in-

cludes case studies of three women who undergo posses-
sions.]

660.   ————. *The Cult of the Goddess Pattini*. Chicago: University of Chicago Press, 1984.
[Although this massive study of a Sri Lankan and Tamil
goddess is principally concerned with the goddess herself
and her Sri Lankan setting, its Freudian approach necessi-
tates reflections on men's experience of women in both lo-
cales. Moreover, descriptions of Pattini/Kannaki festivals
incorporate materials on women's roles.]

661.   O'Flaherty, Wendy Doniger. *Women, Androgynes, and Other
Mythical Beasts*. Chicago: University of Chicago Press,
1980.
[This analysis of Indian mythological motifs is less concerned with women per se than with with women (and female beasts) as trope; it nonetheless illumines both constructions of gender and conceptions of sexuality in India.]

662.   O'Hanlon, Rosalind. "Issues of Widowhood: Gender and Resistance in Colonial Western India." *Contesting Power: Resistance and Everyday Social Relations in South Asia*.
Berkeley: University of California Press, 1991.
[Examines perspectives on widow remarriage in nineteenth-
century India, comparing male views with those expressed
in a woman's writing, the *Stree-purusha-tulana* of Tarabai
Shinde.]

663.   Ojha, Catherine. "Feminine Asceticism in Hinduism: Its
Tradition and Present Condition." *Man in India* 61–63
(September 1981), 254–85.
[Surveys historical references to female ascetics in Hinduism and presents the results of the author's inquiry into female ascetics and ascetic communities in the city of Banaras. The latter segment features descriptions of three wom-
en's *ashram*s, two headed by women *guru*s of the Nimbark

tradition (Ganga Ma and Shoba Ma) and a third of the twentieth-century Anandamayi Ma movement. One solitary female ascetic is also described; she is Ram Dulari Das of the Ramanandi Sampradhaya. Concludes that the women described are rebels who nonetheless do not question profoundly the established order and who are dependent on men's institutions for their structure and long-range survival.]

For Ojha, Catherine, see also Clemintin-Ojha, Catherine.

664. Omvedt, Gail. "*Adivasi* Women and Personal Law: A Report from Dhule, Maharashtra." *Manushi* 3, No. 5 (=No. 17; August–September, 1983), 20–22.
[Should the existing Hindu Succession and Marriage Acts be made applicable to tribal women? A tribal women's organization recommends changes in existing practice.]

665. ————. "*Devadasi* Custom and the Fight Against It." *Manushi* 4, No. 1 (=No. 19; November–December 1983), 16–19.
[Charges that Karnataka women are being forcibly abducted, dedicated to Yellama as *devadasi*s, and sold to brothels in Bombay. Challenges the notion that *devadasi*s were independent of the patriarchal system and describes new efforts at *devadasi* rehabilitation.]

666. Orr, Leslie C. *Hindu Temple Women of the Chola Period in South India*. Ph.D. diss., McGill University, 1993.
[No further information was available at the time of publication.]

667. Ortner, Sherri B. *High Religion: A Cultural and Political History of Sherpa Buddhism*. Princeton: Princeton University Press, 1989; Delhi: Motilal Banarsidass, 1992.
[This study of the founding of the first celibate Buddhist monasteries among Nepali Sherpas is included here for its materials on monks and nuns.]

668.   Pande, Rekha. "The *Bhakti* Movement—an Interpretation."
        Proceedings of Indian History Congress. Bambolim: Goa
        University, 1987, pp. 214–21.
        [Attempts to set the *bhakti* movement "in its proper con-
        text" and to determine its perception of women. Suggests
        that the movement arose as an attempt to establish Hindu/
        Muslim harmony; and that women were basically left out of
        reform efforts, despite the existence of women *bhakta*s and
        new opportunities given to women for self-expression.]

669.   ————. "The Bhakti Movement and the Status of Women
        in the Fourteenth and Fifteenth Century." *Aspects of Indian
        History.* Ed. J. P. Mishra. New Delhi: Agam Kala Praka-
        shan, 1991.
        [Asserts that the *bhakti* movement continued and reinforced
        patriarchal values, despite significant contributions by
        women *bhakta*s. Includes a helpful review of early theories
        about *bhakti*.]

670.   Pande, Susmita. *Medieval* Bhakti *Movement, Its History
        and Philosophy.* Meerut: Kusumanjali Prakashan, 1989.
        [Four pages are devoted to Mirabai, amid many descriptions
        of male saints.]

671.   Pandey, Chandra Bhanu. *Risis in Ancient India.* Delhi:
        Sundeep Prakashan, 1987.
        [This ambitious compilation of references to *rishi*s culled
        from Vedic, epic, and Puranic sources is mostly concerned
        with males, but includes some materials on *rishi*s' wives.]

672.   Pandey, Geetanjali. "How Equal? Women in Premchand's
        Writings." *Economic and Political Weekly* 21, No. 50 (De-
        cember 13, 1986), 2183–87.
        [Examines works of a distinguished and influential early
        twentieth-century author who often illustrated women's
        predicaments; holds that Premchand's writings nonetheless
        "cherished the ideal of the traditional Hindu woman."]

673. Pandit, Harshida. *Women of India: An Annotated Bibliography*. New York and London: Garland Publishing, 1985.
[This 1119-entry annotated bibliography was compiled in Bombay libraries. Although it does not treat religion as a separate category, it does cover the status and roles of women in ancient Hindu texts, the legal status and problems of child marriage, infanticide, *sati*, and widowhood, the legal status of marriage, experiences of women in various communities, psychological attitudes towards different communities, and studies of eminent women, including religious teachers of note. Especially rich in older sources, it is an excellent complement to the present collection.]

674. Pandit, Madhav Pundalik, ed. *Champaklal Speaks*. Pondicherry: Sri Aurobindo Press, 1975.
[Records recollections, diary notes, and correspondence of a simple man who became the self-appointed servant and devotee of Sri Aurobindo and "the Mother" of Pondicherry. Champaklal's association with the Mother was to last for fifty years. Repeats much advice from her on a broad range of subjects.]

675. ————. *Memorable Moments with the Mother*. Pondicherry: Dipti Publications, 1975.
[Fourteen disciples of Mirra Alfassa Richard, "The Mother" of the Aurobindo Ashram, describe their most exalted moments in her presence. A forty-two-page book.]

676. ————. *Commentaries on the Mother's Ministry*. Pondicherry: Dipti Publications, 1983.
[Two volumes of anecdotes recount Mother Mirra Alfassa Richard's responses to various hurdles and special occasions in the life of the Pondicherry Aurobindo Ashram. This collection reveals more of Richard's organizational and pragmatic capabilities than most other writings about her.]

677.   ———. *Spiritual Communion: Based upon the Mother's Prayers and Meditations*. Pondicherry: Dipti Publications, 1986.
[Reflects on prayers and meditations of the Aurobindo Ashram's "Mother" Mirra Alfassa Richard.]

678.   Pandit, Vijaya Lakshmi. *The Scope of Happiness: A Personal Memoir*. New York: Crown Publishers, 1979.
[Although this autobiography by the stateswoman-sister of Pandit Nehru is principally devoted to political experiences, it does include snippets on her mother's orthodoxy and father's iconoclasm, religious allegiances of her childhood household's attendants, festivals observed in the childhood household, Vijaya Lakshmi's sojourn at Gandhi's *ashram* and immersion in his movement, her wedding, her father's funeral, and her late-life encounter with Mother Teresa.]

679.   Papanek, Hanna, and Gail Minault, eds. *Separate Worlds: Studies of* Purdah *in South Asia*. Delhi: Chanakya Publications, 1982.
[This collection's eleven articles concentrate primarily on social and political aspects of *purdah*; however, three feature some discussion of the relationship between *purdah* and religious ideology: see Hanna Papanek, "*Purdah*: Separate Worlds and Symbolic Shelter"; Sylvia Vatuk, "*Purdah* Revisited: A Comparison of Hindu and Muslim Interpretations of the Cultural Meaning of *Purdah* in South Asia"; and Mary Higdon Beech, "The Domestic Realm in the Lives of Hindu Women in Calcutta"; note also Fazlur Rahman's more general "The Status of Women in Islam: A Modernist Interpretation." Doranne Jacobson's "*Purdah* and the Hindu Family in Central India" concentrates more specifically on practice.]

For Papanek, Hanna, see also entry 767.

680. Parashar, Archana. *Women and Family Law Reform in India: Uniform Civil Code and Gender Equality.* New Delhi and Newbury Park, Calif.: Sage Publications, 1992.
[Covers personal laws of Hindus, Muslims, and other minorities, Hindu law reform, and issues underlying proposals for a uniform civil code.]

For Parashar, Archana, see also entry 811.

681. Parekh, Ms. Harsha, comp. *Resources on Women: A Pilot Project.* Bombay: Women and Development Studies Information Network, 1988.
[This general bibliography compiled from Network scholars' submissions includes sources both in English and in regional languages.]

682. ————. *Resources on Women, Part II: A Bibliographic Compendium.* Bombay: Women and Development Studies Information Network, 1990.
[Updates the preceding Parekh bibliography.]

683. ————. *Resources on Women: A Bibliographic Compendium, Part III: Religion, Culture, and Politics.* Bombay: Women and Development Studies Information Network, 1991.
[This third update has a more limited focus, reflecting rapid expansion in the literature it covers. It is by no means exhaustive, but very helpful nonetheless, including many sources in Hindi and regional languages.]

684. Parikh, Indira J., and Pulin K. Garg. *Indian Women: An Inner Dialogue.* New Delhi: Sage, 1989.
[This study of socialization and the inculcation of female identity in India explores women's responses to models articulated in Indian myth and folklore.]

685. Parimoo, B. N. "Lalla-Ded, a Mystical Genius." *Samvit* 2 (September 1980), 15–20.

[Recounts spiritual experiences and accomplishments of the fourteenth-century Kashmiri woman saint Lalla-Ded, as gleaned from her poetry; includes several translated citations.]

686.   ————. *Lalleshwari*. New Delhi: National Book Trust, 1987.
[Covers the social context, life, spiritual achievements, miracles, teachings, and role in the *bhakti* movement of the Kashmiri poet-saint Lal Ded; also compares her work with that of the male saint Kabir and analyzes the language of her *vakh*s (poetic sayings). Includes translations of forty-five *vakh*s, with transliterated texts, and twenty selections with translation into both Sanskrit and English. Occasional contortion and archaism in the translations seems intended to lend them a "poetic" cast.]

687.   Pasayat, Chitra Sen. "*Dalkhai*: A Ritual Folk-Dance of Western Orissa: Some Aspects and Significance of the Ceremony." *Folklore* 28 (September 1987), 219–22.
[Describes a dance in honor of Durga/Parvati performed by tribals of the Sambalpur region, formerly performed in the context of a *vrata* for protection of brothers.]

688.   Pasha, Noor Ahmed. *The Muslim Personal Law*. 2nd ed. Bangalore: Noble Publishers, 1986.
[This pamphlet intended for lay information covers marriage, dowry, divorce, a wife's initiative in separation, maintenance for divorced women, polygamy, inheritance, and other topics.]

689.   Patel, Sujata. "Emergence and Proliferation of the Autonomous Women's Organizations in India." Working Paper #14. Bombay: Research Centre for Women's Studies, SNDT Women's University, 1986.
[The duplicated typescript, available through the SNDT Women's University Research Centre for Women's Studies,

offers an overview of the style and scope of independent women's action organizations and the issues they address. Organizations and concerns discussed are largely secular, but some that are named work for *devadasi* reform and for legal rights of Muslim and Christian women.]

690.　———. "The Construction and Reconstruction of Women in Gandhi." New Delhi: Nehru Memorial Museum and Library, 1987.
[This mimeographed paper of fifty-six pages analyzes Gandhi's assumptions about gender differences and their impact on his teachings about women's roles; it moreover tracks the evolution of Gandhi's teachings, locating changes in their historical contexts.]

691.　Patel, Sujata, and Sujata Gothaskar. "The Story of the Bombay Riots: in the Words of Muslim Women." *Manushi* 5, No. 4 (=No. 29; July–August 1985), 41–45.
[Reports women's perceptions of an infamous encounter between Shiv Sena Hindus and a Muslim community, charging harassment, rape, and murder of women both by Shiv Senas and by local police.]

692.　Patel, Sujata, and Krishna Kumar. "Defenders of *Sati*." *Economic and Political Weekly* 23, No. 5 (January 23, 1988), 129–30.
[Argues that writers caught in false dichotomizing between "tradition" and "modernity" tend to rationalize and romanticize the crime of *sati*.]

693.　Patel, Urmila. "Literature and History: Widow Remarriage as Reflected in 'Saras Watichandra'." *Proceedings of the Indian History Congress*. Annamalainagar: Annamalai University, 1984, pp. 737–45.
[The object of this study is a novel in four volumes, published during the late nineteenth century, that contains much discussion of an issue "hot" in Gujarat at the time.

The work's heroine is married to a man whom she does not love. When widowed, she takes *sannyasini* vows rather than marry the man she truly desires.]

694. Patnaik, N. R. *Social History of 19th Century Orissa.* Allahabad: Vohra Publishers, 1989.
[Contains a long chapter (fifty-eight pages) on recorded occurrences of *sati* and the campaign to suppress it.]

695. Patton, Laurie Louise. *The Work of Language and the Vedic Rsi: The Brhaddevata as Canonical Commentary.* Ph.D. diss., University of Chicago, 1991; also forthcoming from DeGruyter Press.
[Sections entitled "Mantra as Cure" and "Selective *Slokas*: Cleaning Up the Vedas" deal with women *rishis* and with issues of sexuality and gender.]

696. Patwa, Subhadra, ed. *Directory of Women's Organizations.* Bombay: Research Centre for Women's Studies, SNDT Women's University, 1990.
[This valuable reference provides names, addresses, years of founding, branches, contact persons, and brief program descriptions for over two hundred women's organizations in Bombay and in India, plus many additional international groups and networks. Revised and enlarged from an earlier directory published in 1985.]

697. Paul, Diana Mary. *The Buddhist Feminine Ideal: Queen Srimala and the Tathagatagarbha.* Missoula, Mont.: Scholars Press, 1980.
[Translates and interprets the Mahayana Buddhist *Srimaladevisutra*, said to be the teaching of the Buddhist queen Srimala.]

698. ———. *Women in Buddhism: Images of the Feminine in Mahayana Tradition.* Berkeley: University of California Press, 1979; 2nd ed. 1985.

[This combination of anthologized passages, with scholarly introduction and commentary, explores roles and images of women throughout the Mahayana textual tradition; however, most of the texts cited had their origins in India. Selections cover "Traditional Views of Women," "Paths for Women Leading to Salvation (i.e., the nuns' path)," "'Good Daughter' and 'Good Friend': Teachers of the Dharma," "The Bodhisattvas with Sexual Transformation," and "Images of the Feminine."]

699.   Payyanad, Raghavan. "Folk Dances of Kerala—an Introduction." *Folklore* 20 (October 1979), 235–42; continues in *Folklore* 20 (November 1979), 257–62.
[Part I of this article offers a general introduction to the concept, origins, types, and functions of folk dance throughout the world; Part II cites types of Keralan dances and the festivals that are their contexts; several are women's dances and festivals.]

700.   Phadke, Y. D. *Women in Maharashtra*. New Delhi: Maharashtra Information Centre, 1989.
[Includes a chapter titled "Social Reformers and Women's Emancipation"; this sketches the widow remarriage movement, the campaign against child marriage, and the birth control movement in Maharashtra.]

701.   Phillimore, Peter. "Unmarried Women of the Dhaula Dhar: Celibacy and Social Control in Northwest India." *Journal of Anthropological Research* 47 (Fall 1991), 331–50.
[Describes women of the Kangra region of Himachal Pradesh who never marry and call themselves *sadhin*—but they continue to live in their natal village, can acquire property, and dress and act like men.]

702.   Phongsai, Arree. "The Eight Chief Rules for *Bhikkunis*." *Tibet Journal* 9, No. 2 (Summer 1984), 35–37.
[This is little more than a listed translation of the rules, with a brief introduction to establish their context.]

703. Pillai, Baskaran. *The Religio-Spiritual Experiences of Manikkavacar.* Ph.D. diss., University of Pittsburgh, 1989. [Although the subject of this study is a male saint of Tamilnadu, the author claims to examine, during a section on ritual, "some of the native fertility rituals practiced by young girls in Tamil Nadu." Described *DAI* 50, No. 6 (December 1989), A-1697.]

704. Poitevin, Guy. "Primary Health Care as a Gender Issue." *Economic and Political Weekly* 23, No. 44 (October 29, 1988), WS65–WS73. [Included here for its discussion of "symbolic strategies" in healing efforts, including ritualistic practices, exorcisms, and the role of the holy person.]

705. Poonacha, Veena. "A Contract in Social Relation: The *Samband Edipa* Ceremony among Coorgs in South India." *Economic and Political Weekly* 23, No. 44 (October 29, 1988), WS50– WS56. [Describes a contractual form of marriage among a non-Brahminized community of southwestern India; shows that this form, while patrilineal and patrilocal, allowed women far more flexibility and freedom than Hindu sacramental marriage.]

706. ———. "Religion and Women's Liberation." Bombay: Research Centre for Women's Studies, SNDT Women's University, 1989. [Duplicated typescript available through SNDT Women's University Research Centre for Women's Studies. Points to both the liberating and restrictive potential of religion, defined broadly to include both ideology and practice; includes a survey of varying Hindu atttitudes towards women.]

707. ———. "Hindutva's Hidden Agenda: Why Women Fear Religious Fundamentalism." *Economic and Political Weekly* 28, No. 11 (March 13, 1993), 438–39.

[Argues that Hindu fundamentalism threatens a revival of role expectations that deprive women of autonomy. It moreover is popularizing a dichotomized view of gender that peripheralizes women's viewpoints and celebrates "macho" traits of domination and aggression.]

708. Poonawalla, Zainab Taher. "Bohra Women, Victims of Persecution." *Illustrated Weekly of India* 105, No. 17 (22 April 1984), 56–57.
[Proclaims the helplessness of a community of conservative Muslim women controlled by the directives of a "religious dictator" called the *Syedna*.]

709. Prabhananda, Swami. "Swami Vivekananda and His 'Only Mother'." *Prabuddha Bharata* 89 (January 1984), 10–19.
[Describes the relationship between Swami Vivekananda and the Ramakrishna Mission's Holy Mother Sarada Devi.]

710. Prabuddhaprana, Pravrajika. "Josephine MacLeod's Mission." *Samvit* 17 (March 1988), 5–12.
[Describes the life and work of a wealthy and fashionable American woman who became an important mentor and donor for Swami Vivekananda. Especially important were her efforts at promoting publication and translations of Vivekananda's books. Josephine MacLeod was one of several Western women who accompanied the swami during his final pilgrimage tour in India.]

711. ———. *Tantine: the Life of Josephine MacLeod, Friend of Swami Vivekananda*. Calcutta: Sri Sarada Math, 1990.
[The title is self-descriptive; Josphine MacLeod is described in entry 710 above.]

712. Pramanick, P. "A Note on the *Brata*s of Bengal." *Folklore* 19 (December 1978), 365–66.
[This simple list of *vrata*s performed by Bengali women includes the anticipated outcome of the twenty deemed most important.]

713.   Prasad, Awadh Kishore. *"Devadasis* in Karnataka." *Proceed-
        ings of the Indian History Congress.* Burdwan: Burdwan
        University, 1983, pp. 149–54.
        [Evidence of *devadasi* dedications is culled from inscrip-
        tions.]

714.   ————. "Function and Gradations of *Devadasis." Proceed-
        ings of the Indian History Congress.* Annamalainagar: An-
        namalai University, 1984, pp. 192–99.
        [Shows the variety of functions among *devadasi*s of South
        Indian temples, as reflected in temple inscriptions.]

715.   Premchand, Munshi. "A Mother of Sons." *Manushi* No.
        42–43 (September–December 1987), 54–61.
        [This short story translated from Hindi portrays the exploi-
        tation of a widowed mother by her sons, as they plot to sep-
        arate her from her *stridhan*, the wealth given to her at
        marriage. One amusing segment portrays the sons' mis-
        handling of a feast while the more knowledgeable mother
        stews.]

716.   *Proceedings of the Third International Symposium on Asian
        Studies, 1981.* Hong Kong: Asian Research Service, 1981.
        [Contains three papers addressing the status, religious
        roles, or images of women in classical literatures of India:
        sources of B. N. Hazarika's "Women in the Brahmanic Lit-
        erature" are the Vedic *samhitas* and *brahmanas*; sources of
        V. L. Sethuraman's "Widow-Remarriage—a View Point" are
        principally *dharmasastra*; sources of Kiran Kumari Singh's
        "Ideals of Womanhood as Reflected in the Works of Bhava-
        bhuti" are the works of a noted eighth-century dramatist.]

717.   *Prostitution with Religious Sanction.* Calcutta: Joint
        Women's Programme, 1989.
        [This issue of the occasional journal *Banhi* reprints three
        special fact-finding reports on girls who are dedicated to
        deities and then used for concubinage and/or prostitution.

The longest, "*Devadasi* System in North Karnataka" (first edition 1981), includes a historical background and description of the practice, its emerging trends, and institutional counter-measures, together with eighteen case histories from Yellamanagudda and Saundatti, plus the full text of the Karnataka *Devadasis* (Prohibition of Dedication) Bill of 1981. Additional reports are "The *Basavi* Cult: Based on Interviews with *Basavi* Women at Adoni, Kurnool District, A.P." (first published 1985) and "*Venkatasani*: Body Sale under Cover of Religion"; this contains additional *Basavi* and *Jogini* materials (first published 1988).]

718.   Puri, Balraj. "Muslim Personal Law: Questions of Reform and Uniformity Be Delinked." *Economic and Political Weekly* 20, No. 23 (June 8, 1985), 987–90.
[Pleads for a debate within the Muslim community on the advantages and costs to women of Muslim personal laws; this should be delinked from defensiveness against the (highly politicized) call for a uniform civil code.]

719.   Qadeer, Imrana, and Zoya Hasan. "Deadly Politics of the State and Its Apologists." *Economic and Political Weekly* 22, No. 46 (November 14, 1987), 1946–49.
[This response to the Roop Kanwar *sati* criticizes the role of the state in deferring to fundamentalists, the attempts by the latter to glorify *sati*, and the role of intellectuals in defining *sati* as a revival of tradition and, hence, in creating a de facto rationalization for the practice. Comes down heavily on Ashis Nandy as an example of the latter problem.]

For Qadeer, Imrana, see also entry 799.

720.   Qureshi, Mohammed A. [OCLC lists as Quershi]. *Marriage and Matrimonial Remedies: A Uniform Civil Code for India*. New Delhi: Concept Publishing Company, 1978.
[Examines India's tangle of communal marriage laws and argues for a uniform civil code.]

721.   Raheja, Gloria Goodwin, and Ann Grodzins Gold. *Listen to the Heron's Words: Reimagining Gender and Kinship in North India*. Berkeley: University of California Press, 1994. [Two anthropologists combine forces to recover the views that rural women of northwestern India hold about themselves. Materials include songs sung during rituals (including wedding insult-songs) and tales of women who achieve miracles as a result of their devotion.]

722.   Raj, Sebasti L., ed. *Quest for Gender Justice: A Critique of the Status of Women in India*. Madras: T. R. Publications for Satya Nilayam Publications, 1991. [A full eight of this volume's seventeen articles bear on women's relationship to either religion or philosophy: Padmini Jesudurai, "Women and the Law"; K. Sundari, "Women in Hinduism"; Clarissa Rodrigues, "Radhakrishnan's Views on Women: An Appraisal"; Abdul Hadi, "Women in Islam"; Tabassum F. Sheikh, "Muslim Women and Social Life"; Cecilia Arocktasamy, "Women in Christianity"; Aruna Gnanadason, "An Eco-Feminist Theology"; and Sebasti L. Raj, S.J., "Women's Liberation: A Philosophical Perspective."]

723.   Raju, Rekhadevi. *Status of Women (a Case Study of Rural and Tribal Women in Karnataka)*. Poona: Dastane Ramchandra and Co., 1988. [This sociological analysis compares the economic, social, and religious status of caste Hindu and tribal Rajgond women in Karnataka; it is based on a survey of four hundred households, with two hundred in each category. Chapter 5 discusses the effect of religion on women, and contrasts their role in religious life with that of men.]

724.   Ram, Mayavanti Rallia. "*Purdah* and Social Stratification of Muslim Society." *Mainstream* (January 19, 1976), 21–22. [Describes variations in interpretation of the reach of *purdah* and of the contexts in which *burqa* should be worn.]

725.   ————. "Modernisation and Muslim Women." *Mainstream*
(July 31, 1976), 22–23.
[Summarizes results of the 1973–74 Jamia Millia Islamia
survey of changing cultural patterns of Muslim women in
northwestern India; this survey explored the extent of
change in attitudes and practice among educated women.
The present article discusses especially survey findings on
uses of *burqa*, expected benefits of education, and attitudes
towards co-education and sex education.]

726.   Ramabai Saraswati, Pandita. *The High Caste Hindu
Woman.* Westport, Conn.: Hyperion Press, 1976; original
edition Philadelphia: J.B. Rogers, 1887.
[A reissue of a classic indictment of sastric teachings about
women, written by a woman *pandit* of the nineteenth century who herself had suffered from their destructive repercussions.]

727.   ————. *The Letters and Correspondence of Pandita
Ramabai.* Comp. by Sister Geraldine. Ed. A. B. Shah. Bombay: Maharashtra State Board for Literature and Culture,
1977.
[Reproduces correspondence by India's first independent
female reformist, along with two brief sketches of Pandita
Ramabai's life and contributions. Includes materials showing Ramabai's conversion to, and struggles with, Christianity.]

728.   ————. *The High Caste Hindu Woman.* Intro. by Uma
Chakravarti. New Delhi: Kali for Women, forthcoming.
[An Indian reissue of the volume listed in entry 726 above
with an introduction by a well-known feminist historian.]

729.   Raman, Sita Anantha. *Female Education and Social Reform
in the Tamil Districts of the Madras Presidency, 1870–1930.*
Ph.D. diss., University of California at Los Angeles, 1992.

[Describes changes in women's status and perceptions initiated by the drive for women's education in Tamilnadu; argues that women's educational reform "was the key . . . to the nationalist's reform agenda." Incorporates some description of the role of missionaries, of women's prior role in maintaining an oral poetic tradition, and of status loss among *devadasis*. Described *DAI* 53, No. 1 (July 1992), A-271.]

730.   Ramanan, Mohan. "Andal's *Tiruppavai*." *Journal of South Asian Literature* 24, No. 2 (Summer–Fall, 1989), 51–64.
[Translates a thirty-verse song of surrender to Krishna by the eighth-century Tamil saint-poetess, Andal.]

For Ramanujan, A. K., see entries 41, 365, and 1002.

731.   Ramath, Suryanath. "Social Reform Movements: Emancipation of Women in Karnataka." *Quarterly Journal of the Mythic Society* 72, No. 2 (April–June 1984), 208–17.
[Includes information on contributions to social reform by Christian missionaries, Brahmo and Arya Samaj members, and the Theosophical movement.]

732.   Ramdas, Lalita, and Jaya Srivastava (interview). "From Day to Day, Envisioning Tomorrow: Working with Victims of Anti-Sikh Riots at Tilak Vihar." *Manushi* 6, No. 6 (No. 36; September–October 1986), 35–40.
[Two workers from a women's center near the West Delhi site of these riots describe the experiences of victims whom they serve. They argue that religion was not the basis for the conflict.]

733.   Ranganathananda, Swami. "Indian Women in the Modern Age." *Samvit* 18 (September 1988), 17–23.
[A distinguished monk of the Ramakrishna Mission stresses the importance of science, a humanistic attitude, and social service for women.]

734.   ————. *Women in the Modern Age*. Bombay: Bharatiya
Vidya Bhavan, 1991.
[This address delivered in 1986 at the Government College
for Women in Srinagar discusses the Western feminist
movement and its disillusionments. The swami argues that
the Indian ideal of God-in-humans and its model of sexual
interdependence holds a superior promise of happiness for
both men and women. He rejects the status quo, however,
condemning violence against women and calling for freedom
of movement.]

735.   Rao, B. Suryanarain, revised by B. V. Raman. *Female
Horoscopy (Strijataka)*. UBSPD, 1992; originally published
Bangalore, B. V. Raman, 1931.
[No further information is available on this volume that
was newly arrived at press time.]

736.   Rao, Prakasa. *Marriage, the Family, and Women in India*.
New Delhi: Heritage, 1982.
[Reports the findings of sociological surveys conducted in
Karnataka; the book's sections cover arranged marriages,
ideal age for marriage, dowry, endogamy versus exogamy,
attitudes towards family, status of women, and employment
of mothers. Includes some breakdowns by religious community.]

737.   Rao, Suguna. "Women and Superstitions." *Andhra Pradesh*
22, No. 8 (June 1978), 36–38.
[Calls upon women to abandon customs that once made
sense but have become meaningless within a modern context.]

738.   Rashsundari Debi. *Amar Jiban (My Life)*. Ed. and with an
introduction by Tanika Sarkar. New Delhi: Kali for Women,
forthcoming.
[A new translation of the first autobiography published by
a Bengali woman (1868). "It was an urge to read a medieval

sacred text dealing with the life of the god Krishna and his devotees that drove Rashsundari Debi into acquiring literacy in secret. . . . The interlocking themes of devotion and writing, of biography and autobiography, constituted her sense of her own self and provided the axis around which the narrative revolves" (from the publisher's description).]

739.   Rasool, G. Javed. "Women in Islamic Ideology." *Social Scientist* 15, No. 2 (February 1987), 62–65.
[Criticizes a book in Urdu on Muslim women by Asghar Ali Engineer; the context is the Shah Bano case, but the author's own position is hard to locate.]

740.   Ratte, Mary Lou. *The Lotus and the Violet: Attitudes Towards Womanhood in Bengal, 1792–1854.* Ph.D. diss., University of Massachusetts, 1977.
[Studies the relationship between British and Bengali attitudes towards women during the time of the first initiatives towards Hindu reform; discusses the *sati* controversy and attitudes towards women's education. Described in *DAI* 38, No. 1 (July 1977), A-415.]

For Ratte, Mary Lou, see also Ratte, Lou, entry 338.

741.   Ray, Ajit Kumar. *Widows Are Not for Burning: Actions and Attitudes of the Christian Missionaries, the Native Hindus, and Lord William Bentinck.* New Delhi: ABC Publishing House, 1985.
[The anti-*sati* movement of Lord Bentinck's era is the subject of this historical study. Eight appendices duplicate valuable *sati*-related documents; a chart shows regional distribution of *sati* immolations.]

742.   Ray, Benoy Bhusan [OCLC lists as Raya, Binaya Bhushana]. *Socioeconomic Impact of Sati in Bengal and the Role of Raja Rammohan Roy.* Calcutta: Naya Prokash, 1987.
[Examines the social class and economic background of

Bengali families with *sati* incidents, also cites evidence of Bengali opposition to *sati* even before Rammohan Roy.]

743.   Ray, Renuka. *My Reminiscences: Social Development during Gandhian Era and After*. New Delhi: Allied, 1982.
[The daughter of a distinguished Brahmo Samaj family recounts her career as a freedom fighter, a worker for women's welfare, and a legislator.]

744.   Ray, Sripati [OCLC lists as Roy, Sripati Charan]. *Customs and Customary Law in British India*. Delhi: Mittal, 1986; originally published Calcutta: Hare Press, 1911.
[Adresses the relationship between custom and law under British colonialism, citing Hindu, Buddhist, and Muslim materials.]

745.   Raza, Musi. "Changing *Purdah* System in Muslim Society." *Islam and the Modern Age* 6, No. 4 (1975), 40–56 and 7, No. 1 (1976), 57–79.
[Presents results of a survey of 103 Muslim women of Patna; this survey sought to determine what percentage of respondents kept *purdah* and what changes were occurring in attitudes toward *purdah*. An introductory section discusses Islamic precedents and sanctions for *purdah*, the subsequent history of *purdah*, and the forms it takes.]

746.   Reddy, Jaganmohan. "Personal Law and Muslim Women's Rights." *Secular Democracy* 19, No. 5 (May 1986), 19–24.
[A retired judge of the Supreme Court of India exposes inconsistencies in the position of those opposing the Supreme Court's verdict in the Shah Bano case.]

747.   Reddy, P. Munirathnam. "Little Traditional Festivals in an Andhra Village: Vemur." *The Eastern Anthropologist* 38, No. 2 (April–June 1985), 169–71.
[Describes *jatra*s for the goddesses Ganga and Vemalamma.]

748.   Reddy, V. Narasa. "Beliefs on Pregnancy and Child Birth among the Pallies and Vada Balijas Fisherfolk of Visakhapatnam District, Andhra Pradesh." *Folklore* 18 (January 1977), 20–24.
        [Covers not only beliefs per se but also taboos observed and procedures followed, including purifications and rites performed after delivery of a child.]

749.   "Relics of Fiery Faith." *The Week* (December 13–19, 1987), 20–21.
        [Reports on *sati* temples in the Delhi area.]

750.   *Religions and the Status of Women*. Special issue, *Religion and Society* 32, No. 2 (June 1985).
        [Articles comprising this issue appear to have been drawn from the Bangalore conference entitled *Authority of the Religions and the Status of Women* (see entry 58, and note also entry 159, drawn from the same conference). Papers reproduced are Jyotsna Chatterji, "Religions and the Status of Women"; Ranjana Kumari, "Femaleness; the Hindu Perspective"; K. V. K. Thampuran, "Hinduism and Its Impact on Women"; Asghar Ali Engineer, "Women under the Authority of Islam"; Muzammil Siddiqui, "Impact of Islam on the Status of Women from the Socio-Cultural Point of View"; Doris Franklin, "Impact of Christianity on the Status of Women from the Socio-Cultural Point of View"; and A. R. Nagaraj and Chandra Keerthi, "Authority of Religion and the Status of Women in the Jain Religion."]

751.   *Report of the 5th National Conference on Religion, Culture and Politics at Jadavpur University, Calcutta from 9–12 February, 1991*. Special issue of *Indian Association for Women's Studies Newsletter*, Nos. 14–15 (December, 1991).
        [Summarizes activities, themes, and emergent findings of the conference; includes a full listing of conference presenters and papers.]

752.   Reymond, Lizelle. *The Dedicated: A Biography of Nivedita*.
         Madras: Samata Books, 1985; 1st ed. 1953.
         [This biography of Swami Vivekananda's most famous
         Western disciple is organized into three divisions: "The
         Questing Soul"; "The Guru"; and "Mother India"—that is to
         say, pre-Vivekananda, with Vivekananda, and post-Vivek-
         ananda.]

753.   Reynell, Josephine. *Honour, Nurture, and Festivity: Aspects
         of Female Religiosity amongst Jain Women in Jaipur*. Ph.D.
         diss., Cambridge University, 1985.
         [No further information is available.]

754.   —————. "Prestige, Honour and the Family: Laywomen's
         Religiosity amongst the Svetambar Murtipujak Jains in
         Jaipur." *Bulletin d'Études Indiennes* 5 (1987), 313–59.
         [Shows how men's and women's religious roles complement
         one another in maintaining family prestige. Furnishes good
         information about marriage practice, fasts undertaken by
         women, and beliefs concerning the relationship between
         spiritual and sexual purity.]

755.   —————. "Women and the Reproduction of the Jain Com-
         munity." *The Assembly of Listeners: Jains in Society*. Ed.
         Michael Carruthers and Caroline Humphrey. Cambridge:
         Cambridge University Press, 1991.
         [Jain women of Jaipur are far more actively engaged in
         overt religious activities than men of their community.
         Reynell describes daily activities, including temple at-
         tendance, periodic fasts, and other activities; she shows how
         all these activities plus women's child-rearing duties help
         to perpetuate and cohere the Jain community. Although she
         pays greatest attention to laywomen's practice, she also
         briefly discusses Jain nuns.]

756.   Reynolds, Holly Baker. *"To Keep the Tali Strong": Women's
         Rituals in Tamilnadu, India*. Ph.D. diss., University of
         Wisconsin at Madison, 1978.

[Explores the actions and meanings of five calendrical rituals called *nonpus*, as these are observed by women of Madurai district, Tamilnadu. Rituals selected are those considered most important by women themselves: Varalaksmi, Savitri, Gauri, Auvaiyar, and Pavai *nonpus*; all are directed towards family protection, in order "to keep the *tali* strong." Includes a chapter on symbolism of the *tali* (marriage necklace) and a long description of the female life-cycle, with its attending ritualization of sexuality.]

757.   Richard, Mirra Alfassa. *Mother's Agenda.* 12 vols. Bombay: Tata Press, 1979–91; Paris: Institut de recherches evolutives, 1979–91.
[Records in exhaustive detail the deeds and words, notes and letters of Mirra Alfassa Richard, "The Mother" of the Pondicherry Aurobindo Ashram.]

758.   ———. *The Sunlit Path: Passages from Conversations and Writings of the Mother.* Pondicherry: Sri Aurobindo Ashram, 1984.
[Compiles short inspirational excerpts from Mirra Alfassa Richard's writings.]

759.   ———. *The Mother: Collected Works.* 16 vols. Pondicherry: Sri Aurobindo Ashram Trust Fund, 1987.
[The title is self-descriptive.]

760.   Richard, Mirra Alfassa, and Sri Aurobindo Ghosh. *The Psychic Ring: Selections from the Works of Sri Aurobindo and the Mother.* Pondicherry: Sri Aurobindo Ashram Trust Fund, 1989.
[Subjects addressed by the teachings assembled in this volume are "Meaning and Nature of the Psychic Being," "The Psychic Being and *Sadhana*," "Afterlife and Rebirth," and "More Lights on the Psychic Being."]

761. Richman, Paula Sue. *Religious Rhetoric in* Manimekalai. Ph.D. diss., University of Chicago, 1983.
[Prototype for *Women, Branch Stories, and Religious Rhetoric in a Tamil Buddhist Text* (see entry 762 below).]

762. ————. *Women, Branch Stories, and Religious Rhetoric in a Tamil Buddhist Text*. Syracuse: Maxwell School of Citizenship and Public Affairs, Syracuse University, 1988.
[The text in question is Cattanar's *Manimekalai*, whose courtesan-heroine becomes a Buddhist nun. Two chapters are significant for this listing: Chapter 2 examines the epic's main theme of female renunciation, and Chapter 6 explores relationships between laypeople and renouncers.]

For Richman, Paula Sue, see also entries 127 and 128.

763. Richman, Paula Sue, and Michael Fisher. "Sources and Strategies for the Study of Women in India." *Journal of Ethnic Studies* 8, No. 3 (Fall 1980), 123–41.
[This methodological essay classifies resources available for the study of Indian women and reviews approaches that have arisen from these, ranging from indigenous precolonial *dharmasastra* and mythology to recent works. Cautioning that most existing materials reflect male and/or colonial constructions of women, it recommends an attempt to uncover women's actual experiences.]

764. Robinson, Betty Sue. *The Ramakrishna Sarada Math: A Study of a Women's Movement in Bengal*. Ph.D. diss., Columbia University, 1978.
[Studies the origins, ideals, organization, and services of a distinguished organization for women renouncers (*sannyasini*s) derived initially from Bengal's Ramakrishna Math and Mission. Described in *DAI* 39, No. 4 (October 1978), A-2468–69.]

765. Roche, Paul. "The Marriage Ceremonies of the Malayalis of the Pachamalais." *Asian Folklore Studies* 39, No. 2 (1980), 123–36.
[Provides a straightforward description of a typical ceremony; pays no special attention to the bride.]

766. Rohner, Ronald P., and Manjusri Chaki-Sircar. *Women and Children in a Bengali Village.* Hanover, N.H.: University Press of New England, for the University of Connecticut, 1988.
[A chapter entitled "Religious Beliefs: Festivals and Rituals" covers domestic rites, where women lead, and women's role in public rituals, where males are paramount.]

767. Rokeya, Begum. *Sultana's Dream and Selections from The Secluded Ones.* Ed. and trans. Roushan Jahan. New York: Feminist Press, 1988.
[The short story "Sultana's Dream," first published in 1910, portrays a feminist utopia in which men are confined in *purdah.* This small volume includes also a selection of the most dramatic accounts from the Bengali Muslim author's *purdah* exposé, *Avarodhbasini,* as well as a brief biography of the author and an essay on *purdah* by anthropologist Hanna Papanek.]

For Rokeya, Begum, see also entry 399.

768. Rose, H. A., et al. *Quintessence of Islamic Culture and History.* Delhi: Amar Prakashan, 1986.
[Two articles of this collection link women with religious precept or practice: S. A. Ali's "Islamic Culture in India" includes subsections on the status of women and on ladies' bazaars; Mazhar-ul-Haq Khan's "*Purdah* System: Bane of Muslim Society" includes sections on *purdah* and the family, and on constructions of sex difference.]

769. Roy, Dilip Kumar. *Chaitanya and Mira: Two Plays*. Pondicherry: Sri Aurobindo Ashram, 1979.
[In the second of the plays published in this volume, playwright Roy dramatizes experiences of the woman *bhakta* Mirabai. According to its preface, a saint named Indira Devi saw these experiences occurring at Brindavan while in a state of mystic trance. Mirabai came to her daily with these and other communications.]

770. Roy, Manisha. *Bengali Women*. Chicago: University of Chicago Press, 1975 and 1992.
[Studies the roles and relationships of upper-class Bengali women whom the author interviewed between 1964 and 1968. Largely concerns the dilemmas of marriage and complex-family living, but also offers insight into the relationship between middle-aged women and gurus.]

771. Roy, Shibani. *Status of Muslim Women in North India*. Delhi: B. R. Publishing Corporation, 1979.
[Covers *purdah*, the effects of education, marriage and married life, women's place in the family economy, and "religion and its effects."]

772. Roy, Shreela. "Life and Teachings of Holy Mother Sarada Devi: Their Relevance for the Modern Indian Woman." *Bulletin of the Ramakrishna Mission Institute of Culture* 35, No. 12 (December 1984), 272–77.
[The title of this brief piece is self-explanatory.]

773. Rozario, M. Rita, Sister. *Trafficking in Women and Children in India (Sexual Exploitation and Sale)*. New Delhi: Uppal Publishing House, 1988.
[This sociological study sponsored by the Joint Women's Programme of the William Carey Study and Research Centre is based on nationwide surveys conducted in red-light districts—often at considerable risk to researchers. Of principal interest for the present listing are a chapter en-

titled "The Impact of Religion on the Status of Women," covering Hinduism, Islam, and Christianity, and a profile that identifies the religious communities of respondents.]

774. Rozario, Santi. "Marginality and the Case of Unmarried Christian Women in a Bangladeshi Village." *Contributions to Indian Sociology* N.S. 20, No. 2 (July–December 1986), 261–78.
[Shows how change has affected women's access to the public marketplace among three religious communities in a Bangladeshi village. Although Christian women have the greatest freedom of movement, this freedom breeds anxiety and backlash. Meanwhile the number of unmarried women, less controlled by males, increases.]

775. ———. *Purity and Communal Boundaries.* London: Zed Books, 1992.
[Patterns of domination by class and religious community reinforce gender domination in a Bangladeshi village with Muslim, Hindu, and Christian inhabitants. The author describes constraints imposed on women of the Christian community by the political maneuvering of Christian and Muslim males and by values that all villagers share relating to purity, honor, *jati*, and community.]

776. Ruhi, Nusrat Bano. "Islam and Women's Rights." *Mainstream* (July 20, 1985), 28–32.
[This article was one of a 1985 *Mainstream* series that debated the Supreme Court decision in the Shah Bano case (on the right to maintenance of Muslim women divorcees). For others of the series, see Tara Ali Baig (May 18), Asghar Ali Engineer (May 25 and August 3), Vasudha Dhagamwar (July 6), Syed Shahabuddin (June 1 and July 13), and Sakina Hyder (August 24). Note also Rumki Basu's two-part article "Divorce in India" published on March 2 and 9 of the same year.]

777. Sabiruddin. *A Muslim Husband and Wife: Rights and Duties*. New Delhi: Kitab Bhavan, 1990.
      [This guidebook for Muslim spouses in India is based on the Qur'an and *sunnah*.]

778. Safaya, Raghunath. "Swami Vivekananda on Women." *The Educational Review* 81, No. 12 (December 1975), 221–23.
      [Summarizes the position of India's most influential swami of the turn of the century: women are not inferior to men in any way, but the Sita ideal is still the best one, and the sex life of the Western woman is to be stringently avoided.]

779. Sahai, Shrinath. *Women in Changing Society: A Bibliograpic Study*. Delhi: Mittal Publications, 1985.
      [This general bibliography covering a wide variety of topics includes no special category for women and religion. It does, however, treat "Women and Marriage," "Women and Their Status," "Women and Their Problems" (which include the subheadings *"Devadasi"* and *"Sati"*), and "Women and Their Liberation" (including "Abolition of Sati"); it moreover has special listings for Annie Besant, Kasturba Gandhi, and Pandita Rama Bai.]

780. Saharay, H. K. *Laws of Marriage and Divorce*. 2nd ed. Calcutta: Eastern Law House, 1984; 1st ed. 1980.
      [Covers the institution of marriage, ancient Hindu laws of marriage and divorce, the Hindu Marriage Act of 1955 and 1976, the Special Marriage and Divorce Law of 1954, the Indian Christian Marriage Act of 1872, the Foreign Marriage Act of 1969, Muslim marriage and divorce law, the Dissolution of Muslim Marriages Act of 1939, the Parsee Marriage and Divorce Act of 1936, and the Dowry Prohibition Act of 1961. Includes detailed descriptions of all Acts currently in force, plus summaries of important High Court rulings and other rulings on registration of marriage. Clearly intended as a reference work for legal professionals.]

For Saiyed, A. R., see entries 10, 38, and 57.

781.   Sakala, Carol. *Women of South Asia: A Guide to Resources.*
Millwood, N.Y.: Kraus International Publications, 1980.
[The 4,629 entries of this ambitious undertaking include
numerous entries pertaining to India's religious ideologies
and practices. See, for example, the section entitled "The
Spiritual Life and Religious Observances" under Category
I ("Perspectives Unbounded by Time and Space"); note also
subheadings on *sati* and *devadasis* in the preceding section.
Under Category II ("Perspectives on South Asian Women in
Temporal and Spatial Contexts"), see sections entitled
"Roots of the Hindu Tradition," "Heterodox Challenges to
Brahmanism," "Seventh Century to 1820 C.E.: Development
of the *Sakta* Tradition, Coming of Islam, Regional States,
and More"; under Category IV ("South Asian Women in the
Modern Period"), see subheadings "On Hindu Women," "On
Muslim Women," "Three Intertwined Movements" (espe-
cially segments on the social reform movement and on
Christian missions), also, under "Continuity and Change in
Contemporary South Asia," see segment "Women of the
Subcontinent's Major Religious Traditions." See also subheadings on: missionaries; marriage; puberty, marriage,
and domestic rites; and biographical entries in sections on
individual cultural regions. Part II of Sakala's bibliography
contains a helpful series of essays on "Libraries, Archives,
and Other Local Resources" in India, Pakistan, Bangladesh,
and the United Kingdom.]

782.   Sakya, Jamyang, and Julie Emery. *Princess in the Land of
Snows: The Life of Jamyang Sakya in Tibet.* Boston:
Shambala, 1990.
[The Tibetan author of this autobiography was born in
western China among the Cham Tibetan peoples. She describes her early life in a prosperous family with two distinguished monk-uncles and an aunt who was a nun, her education in a monastic school, her pilgrimage to holy sites of

western Tibet with her family during her teens, her meeting and subsequent marriage with the heir apparent of the Sakya monastic lineage, ensuing political intrigues and travels to the East by his side, attempts by the Chinese to win their allegiance, and their family's eventual flight to India and subsequent transfer to the United States.]

783.   Salgado, Kshanike Minoli. *Towards a Definition of Indian Literary Feminism: An Analysis of the Novels of Kamala Markandaya, Nayantara Sahgal and Anita Desai*. Ph.D. diss., University of Warwick (U.K.), 1991.
[One of the four stated "focal areas" of this dissertation explores "the intersection between Hindu ideology and ideals of passivity and suffering," while another treats "specific forms of female suffering and oppression," such as *sati*. Cited from author's description in *DAI* 53, No. 3 (September 1992), A-813.]

784.   Sandhu, J. K. "Role of Sikh Women in History." *Sikh Review* 35 (May 1987), 8–15.
[Cites contributions of women who aided the rise of the Sikh community. Most of the women described are either wives, mothers, or daughters of the Sikh gurus, although one was a warrior who fought for the faith.]

785.   Sandhu, R. S. "Rites de Passage of Some Scheduled Castes: Pregnancy and Birth Rites." *Eastern Anthropologist* 33, No. 1 (1980), 63–70.
[Describes rites of the Chuhra and Chamar castes in rural Punjab. Data are based on interviews with twelve respondents, most of whom were women.]

786.   Sangari, Kumkum. "Mirabai and the Spiritual Economy of *Bhakti*." New Delhi: Nehru Memorial Museum and Library, 1990. (Occasional Papers on History and Society, 2nd Series, No. 28).
[Also published as a two-part article in *Economic and Polit-*

ical Weekly 35, No. 27 (July 7, 1990), 1464–75, and 35, No. 28 (July 14, 1990), 1537–52. This nearly book-length study of songs of the sixteenth-century Rajasthani poet-saint Mirabai locates them in the contexts of Rajput patriarchy and brahmanic precepts for women. It moreover compares the songs' female "voice" with songs of contemporary male *bhakta*s; this latter portion of the work is especially original and important.]

787. ———. "Relating Histories: Literacy, Literature and Gender in Early 19th Century England and Calcutta." New Delhi: Center for Contemporary Studies, Nehru Memorial Museum and Library, n.d. (Occasional Papers on History and Society, 2nd Series, No. 65).
[Discusses the language and constructs of colonialism, as reflected in ideologies about women and about Sanskrit literature; again a nearly book-length article.]

For Sangari, Kumkum, see also entries 35, 629, 799, and 959.

788. Sangari, Kumkum, and Sudesh Vaid. "*Sati* in Modern India: A Report." *Economic and Political Weekly* 16, No. 31 (August 1, 1981), 5–7.
[Reports on the incidence and ideological climate of *sati* in Rajasthan, citing two examples of *sati*, stories of *sati* miracles, idealizations of the practice, benefits brought by *sati*s to their in-laws' villages, and lack of official opposition to *sati* incidents. Published six years before the much-publicized Roop Kanwar *sati*, this study shows that Roop Kanwar's death was neither singular nor unpredictable.]

789. ———, eds. *Women and Culture*. Bombay: Research Centre for Women's Studies, SNDT Women's University, 1985.
[A volume in typescript, available through SNDT Women's University Research Centre for Women's Studies and in microfiche at the U.S. Library of Congress. This collection

of eighteen papers from a 1981 seminar features nine studies focussed on aspects of Indian classical literature, and seven concentrated on contemporary materials; the remaining two are introductory. Most have some relevance for research on religion; see especially: Ramashraya Sharma, "The Ramakatha from Valmiki to Tulsidasa"; Uma Chakravarti, "The Development of the Sita Myth"; Alka Habib Agera, "The Position of Women as Depicted in the Buddhist Therigatha and Jataka Tales"; Neera Desai, "Women and the *Bhakti* Movement"; Sisirkumar Das, "The Radha Theme"; Jamuna Krishnan, "Shringara: Ashtanayikas"; Sumir Sarkar, "The 'Women's Question' in Nineteenth Century Bengal"; Veena Das, "The Mythological Film and Its Framework of Meaning: Analysis of Jai Santoshi Ma"; and Kumkum Sangari and Sudesh Vaid, "*Sati* in Modern India: A Report."]

790. ————, eds. *Recasting Women: Essays in Colonial History.* New Delhi: Kali for Women, 1989; New Brunswick, N.J.: Rutgers University Press, 1990 [as *Recasting Women: Essays in Indian Colonial History*].
[Containing several fine essays on the impact of the colonial experience on India's image of the past and its paradigms for women, this volume is methodologically important to anyone reconstructing religious history in India or studying the impact of feminine models. Most noteworthy essays for these purposes are: Uma Chakravarti, "Whatever Happened to the Vedic *Dasi*? Orientalism, Nationalism, and a Script for the Past"; Lata Mani, "Contentious Traditions: The Debate on *Sati* in Colonial India"; Partha Chatterjee, "The Nationalist Resolution of the Women's Question"; and Susie Tharu, "Tracing Savitri's Pedigree: Victorian Racism and the Image of Women in Indo-Anglian Literature." Sumanta Banerjee's "Marginalization of Women's Popular Culture in Nineteenth Century Bengal," moreover, offers rich material on women's roles in popular religious practice; other articles also refer at times to religious values or customs.]

Bibliography

See also Vaid, Sudesh, and Kumkum Sangari, entry 959.

791. Sangave, Vilas Adinath. *Jaina Community: A Social Survey.* Bombay: Popular Prakashan, 1980; original edition Popular Book Depot, 1959.
[Includes a section on marriage and the position of women in Jainism,; also describes problems of Jaina widows.]

792. Sanjanwala, Jyotsna, compiler. *Women's Studies in Indian Universities 1984–89: A Directory of UGC Supported Centres/Cells.* Bombay: Research Centre for Women's Studies, SNDT Women's University, 1990.
[This reference work describes the endeavors of thirty-one women's studies centers or cells associated with Indian universities. Some descriptions list current and published research of faculty members and/or group projects undertaken; some list courses taught and/or required reading for syllabi. Reveals a small but growing interest in the study of religion.]

793. Saradeshananda, Swami. *The Mother as I Saw Her: Being Reminiscences of the Holy Mother Sri Sarada Devi.* Trans. J. N. Dey. Madras: Sri Ramakrishna Math, 1982.
[Originally written in Bengali, this volume records personal reminiscences of Sri Sarada Devi by a Ramakrishna monk who was very close to her. Especially important is its record of incidents that occurred during visits to her natal village, as well as during her later life, following the death of Sri Ramakrishna.]

794. Saraswati, Baidyanath. "The Kashivasi Widows." *Man in India* 65, No. 2 (June 1985), 107–20.
[On widows who live in Banaras and observe religious discipline, in hopes of attaining *moksha* (liberation) after death.]

795. Sarkar, Lotika. "Women and the Law." *Annual Survey of Indian Law* 21 (1985), 493–500.

[Decries the negative nature of laws imposed on women in the name of freedom of religion.]

For Sarkar, Lotika, see also entries 527 and 635.

796. Sarkar, Tanika. "Nationalist Iconography: Image of Women in 19th Century Bengali Literature." *Economic and Political Weekly* 22, No. 47 (November 21, 1987), 2011–15.
[Shows how nationalists reshaped the Bengali imagery of womanhood, in accordance with their "new sacred principles of nationalism."]

797. ———. "The Woman as Communal Subject: Rashtra-sevika Samiti and Ram Janmabhoomi Movement." *Economic and Political Weekly* 26, No. 35 (August 31, 1991), 2057–62.
[Describes and explains the emerging prominence of women in militantly communalist Hindu movements. Argues that participation of women in right-wing movements has helped women to claim public spaces: to acquire a public identity, an intellectual life, and even roles of leadership. But their public identity is grim and regimented, while their intellectual exchange has immersed them in a hate campaign that threatens to wreck democratic politics.]

798. Sarker, Profulla C. "'Vaishnavization' and Widow Remarriage among the Hindus in Rural Bangladesh." *International Journal of Asian Studies* 3, No. 1 (1983), 34–44.
[Conversion to Vaishnavism is enabling remarriage of widows in the region studied; includes descriptions of both the rites of conversion and the circumstances and rites of remarriage.]

799. *Sati: A Symposium on Widow Immolation and its Social Context.* Special Issue of *Seminar*, vol. 342 (February 1988).
[Contents of this special issue that followed the Roop Kanwar *sati* are: Kamla Bhasin, "The Problem"; Romila Thapar,

"In History"; Sudesh Vaid, "Politics of Widow Immolation"; Kumkum Sangari, "Perpetuating the Myth"; Imrana Qadeer, "Roop Kanwar and Shah Bano"; Vasudha Dhagamwar, "Saint, Victim, or Criminal?"; and Kavita et al., "Rural Women Speak."]

800. "*Sati*: Extending the Debate." *Manushi* No. 45 (March–April 1988), 40–41.
[Reports on a meeting on women's rights in Haryana, sponsored by the Arya Samaj and Bandhua Mukti Morcha and led by Arya Samaj Swami Agnivesh. Tells of Agnivesh's attempt to debate the Shankaracarya of Jagannathpuri on *sati* and subsequent police action to prevent the debate from materializing.]

801. Satprem. *Mother, a Trilogy: The Divine Materialism; The New Species; The Mutation of Death.* New York: Institute for Evolutionary Research, 1980, 1982, 1987, respectively.
[Offers three important writings by Mirra Alfassa Richard, "the Mother" of Pondicherry's Aurobindo Ashram.]

802. Sattar, Abdus. "Place of Menstruating Women in Tribal World." *Folklore* 20 (May and June, 1979), 111–18.
[Cites stories about the origins of menstruation, quarantine practices, euphemisms referring to menstrual periods, and festivals staged to acknowledge a menstruating earth. One group described celebrates in public when a girl achieves her first menstruation. Cites both Indian and cross-cultural examples.]

803. Savvas, Carol Diane. *A Study of the Profound Path of gCod: The Mahayana Buddhist Meditation Tradition of Tibet's Great Women Saint Machig Labdron.* Ph.D. diss., University of Wisconsin, 1990.
[Based on textual analysis, this dissertation is divided in three parts: the first describes the gCod path in general: its history, teachings, and techniques of meditation; the second

introduces Machig Labdron and translates her texts; the third describes gCod lineages and translates a gCod commentary and four newer recitation texts. Described *DAI* 51, No. 11 (May 1991), A-3789.]

804. Sax, William S. "Village Daughter, Village Goddess: Residence, Gender, and Politics in a Himalayan Pilgrimage." *American Ethnologist* 17, No. 3 (August 1990), 491–512.
[Although the cult of the goddess Nandadevi of Uttar Pradesh is "thoroughly gynocentric," nonetheless its most spectacular and grueling pilgrimage prohibits women from completing its final stage; this article shows how the pilgrimage partly remedies, but also perpetuates, women's marital problems.]

805. ————. *Mountain Goddess: Gender and Politics in a Himalayan Pilgrimage.* New York: Oxford University Press, 1991.
[The goddess is Nandadevi, the locale the Uttarakhand region of Uttar Pradesh. The author describes and contextualizes socially both local and region-wide "royal" pilgrimages that escort Nandadevi from her "natal" villages below to the high mountain home of her ascetic husband Shiva. The roles of gender and politics in the pilgrimages are discrete motifs; concerning gender, Sax shows how the pilgrimage both affirms village daughters' importance and sustains a marriage system oppressive to women.]

806. Saxena, Rajendra Kumar. *Social Reforms: Infanticide and Sati.* New Delhi: Trimurti Publications, 1975.
[Describes efforts during the period of British rule to put an end to infanticide and *sati* in the state of Maharashtra. Shows little sympathy for "the priestly class," which is blamed for influencing "ignorant masses" to resist reform efforts.]

807. Saxena, T. P. *Women in Indian History: A Biographical Dictionary*. Ludhiana and New Delhi: Kalyani Publishers, 1979.
[An alphabetized listing of noted women, from celebrated dancing girls to poets and saints. Short descriptive blurbs identify each figure.]

808. Schmidt, Hanns-Peter. *Some Women's Rites and Rights in the Veda*. Pune: Bhandarkar Oriental Research Institute, 1987.
[Originally delivered as the Professor P. D. Gune Memorial Lectures at the Bhandarkar Institute in March, 1984. The three lectures published are "The Affliction of Apala," "The Predicament of the Brotherless Maiden and the Childless Wife," and "To Choose or Not to Choose: How Many Forms of *Svayamvara?*"]

809. Schouten, Johan Peter [OCLC lists as Jan Peter]. *Revolution of the Mystics: On the Social Aspects of Virashaivism*. Kampen, Netherlands: Kok Pharos Publishing House, 1991.
[Reconstructs positions of Virashaiva reformers on the subjects of caste, labor and property, status of women, and education. Although the Virashaiva movement at first advocated equality of men and women, the movement later "adjusted . . . to the traditional Hindu culture."]

810. Scindia, Vijayaraje, with Manohar Malgonkor. *Princess: The Autobiography of the Dowager Maharani of Gwalior*. London: Century, 1985; Albany: State University of New York Press, 1987 [as *The Last Maharani of Gwalior: An Autobiography*].
[Includes a sparse account of the Maharani's childhood religiosity and her grandmother's impact as a religious model.]

811. *Second National Conference on Women's Studies*. Trivandrum: Kerala University, April 9–12, 1984. Available at the Institute for Social Studies Trust, New Delhi.

[Several papers on religious law appear in an extensive section entitled "Politics and the Law." See especially the following: Rajkumari Agrawala, "Women and the Family Law"; Sulabha Bapat, "Manu's Law Relating to Women"; Archana Parashar, "Conflict Situations in Marriage" (includes conversion as a conflict situation); Indu Malhur, "Marriage Law: Awareness, Opinions, and Behavior"; Smriti Karas, "Moral Codes Prescribed for a Woman in *Niyoga*"; Sheela Shukla, "Bigamy among Hindus—Legal Loopholes and their Remedies"; and Asghar Ali Engineer, "Muslim Family Law." Note, in addition, Sarojini Shinti, "Women and the Virashaiva Movement"; Neera Desai, "Women and the *Bhakti* Movement"; Ramala M. Baxamusa, "A Historic Perspective on Muslim Personal Law in India"; Leela Mullati, "Economic Life and Gender Justice among Virasaivis"; and Mariamma Joseph, "Need for Reform on Inheritance Legislation Regarding Syrian Christian Communities in Kerala."]

812. *Select Bibliography on Indian Women.* Hyderabad: Indian Council of Social Science Research, Southern Regional Centre, Osmania University Library, 1982.
[Treats books and articles in separate sections; each includes a subtopic covering "Women and Family, Marriage, Customs, Religion, Folklore." Although this bibliography lists many sources not seen elsewhere, its usefulness is limited by frequent typographic errors and by omission of page references for journal articles.]

813. Selvi, Y., and Ruth Manorama. "Theological Reflections on Our Experiences in the Struggles of Women in the Oppressed Section of Society." *Religion and Society* 27, No. 4 (December 1980), 59–63.
[Compares the authors' understanding of Biblical teachings on women with the treatment of women in rural and slum areas where they work. Concludes: "We feel that the women's liberation movement is a spiritual movement because

198

it aims at the humanisation of women and therefore of the whole species as well."]

814. Sen, Boshi. "Sister Christine." *Samvit* 18 (September 1988), 10–16.
[Describes the life and work of a German-American woman disciple of Swami Vivekananda; she traveled to India and worked with Nivedita to found the school now known as the Nivedita Girls' School.]

815. Sen, S. P., ed. *Social Contexts of Indian Religious Reform Movements*. Calcutta: Institute of Historical Studies, 1978.
[The thirty-three essays of this volume span the whole of Indian religious history, from Buddhism to the present day. Discussions of the nineteenth-century movements treat the campaign for women's emancipation. Even where women are not specifically discussed, this volume's contextual materials will be helpful in research.]

816. Sen Gupta, Sankar. "Social Significance of Durga Puja in Bengal." *Folklore* 28 (September 1987), 231–34.
[Principally a very general description of the Durga Puja story and celebration, but includes a one-paragraph description of a rite special to women performed prior to immersion.]

817. Sengupta, Mrs. Gita. "Henna: Symbol of Domestic Felicity and Good Fortune." *Folklore* 32, Nos. 11–12 (November–December 1991), 209–10, 208.
[Describes preparation and uses of the *mehndi* dye applied to women's hands in auspicious designs for weddings and other important ritual occasions.]

818. Serrou, Robert. *Teresa of Calcutta: A Pictorial Biography*. New York: McGraw-Hill, 1980.
[This picture book in popular style was compiled by a journalist and photographic team with minimal knowledge of

India. Many anecdotes, and even several photographs, are drawn from Desmond Doig's *Mother Teresa: Her People and Her Work* (see entry 244). The text describes Teresa's youth, her early years in India, her mission, world response, and awards bestowed upon her. Appended is the full text of her Nobel acceptance speech.]

819. Sethi, V. K., ed. and trans. *Mira: The Divine Lover*. Punjab: Radha Soami Satsang Beas, 1979; 2nd ed., 1988 [rev. and enl.].
[Fifty-two pages on the life and message of the sixteenth-century Rajasthani poet-saint Mirabai are followed by a translation of ninety-six of her poems. Texts of the poems are not included; translations are somewhat tortured by the translator's attempts to rhyme them.]

820. Settar, S., and Gunther D. Sontheimer, eds. *Memorial Stones: A Study of Their Origin, Significance, and Variety*. Dharwad: Institute of Indian Art History, Karnataka University and Heidelberg: South Asia Institute, University of Heidelberg, 1982.
[Many of the memorial stones described in essays of this volume commemorate *sati*s; the volume's index aids in locating them. Typical examples are S. B. Deo, "A *Sati* Memorial from Markandi," and Gunther D. Sontheimer, "Hero and *Sati*-stones of Maharashtra."]

821. Shah, Amritlal B. *Religion and Society in India*. Bombay: Somaiya Publications, 1981.
This collection of the author's essays pays little attention overall to gender issues but contains one essay on "Pandita Ramabai, a Rebel in Religion."]

For Shah, A. B., see also entries 545 and 727.

822. Shah, Kalpana. *Women's Liberation and Voluntary Action*. Delhi: Ajanta, 1984.

[Includes a description of nineteenth-century reform movements and their efforts towards women's liberation.]

823. Shahabuddin, Syed. "Law of Maintenance of Divorcee in Islam." *Mainstream* (June 1, 1985), 9, 35.
[This article and the one that follows were part of a 1985 *Mainstream* series that debated the Supreme Court decision in the Shah Bano case (on the right to maintenance of Muslim women divorcees). For others of the series, see Tara Ali Baig (May 18), Asghar Ali Engineer (May 25 and August 3), Vasudha Dhagamwar (July 6), Nusrat Bano Ruhi (July 20), and Sakina Hyder (August 24). Note also Rumki Basu's two-part article "Divorce in India" published on March 2 and 9 of the same year.]

824. ————. "Muslim Personal Law." *Mainstream* (July 13, 1985), 28.
[See note in entry 823 above.]

825. Shahabuddin, Syed, and Gargi Chakravartty. "Muslim Female Education." *Mainstream* (February 9, 1985), 31–32.
[An exchange between the two authors responds to a note published by Chakravartty on the subject.]

826. *The Shah Bano Case: Nation Speaks Out.* Bangalore: Jagarana Prakasha, n.d.
[Assembles newspaper editorials on the Shah Bano case concerning Muslim women's right to maintenance.]

827. Shakir, Moin. "Status of Women: Islamic View." *Social Scientist* 4, No. 7 (February 1976), 70–75.
[Rights that Muhammad conferred on women initially raised their status; however, society has changed so much that Muslim laws based on conditions in the Prophet's times no longer make sense. Elevating women's status will require "a concerted attack upon poverty and on social and religious restrictions which presuppose male superiority."]

828.   Shams, Shamsuddin, ed. *Women, Law, and Social Change.*
New Delhi: Ashish Publishing House, 1991.
[A collection of twenty-one articles addresses family law,
property law, criminal law, labor law, constitutional law,
and social change. Most relevant for religionists are the
editor's "Socio-Legal Rights and Privileges of Women in
Islam"; Ranbir Singh's "Women and Compulsory Registration of Hindu Marriages: Need for Uniform Registration";
and Danial Latifi's "Women, Family Law, and Social
Change."]

829.   Shankar, Jogan. *Devadasi Cult: A Sociological Analysis.*
New Delhi: Ashish Publishing House, 1990.
[This study of Yellamma devotees in Belgaum District at
the Maharashtra/Karnataka border offers a historical background, a sociological profile, brief case studies of individual
*devadasi*s, and an analysis of the *devadasi* reform movement's impact.]

830.   Sharma, A. N. (Major-General). *Modern Saints and Mystics.*
3rd ed. Sivanandanagar: Divine Life Society, 1982; 1st ed.
1969.
[This series of short reports on the author's encounters with
spiritual teachers includes information about eight who are
women.]

831.   Sharma, Arvind. "Suttee: A Study in Western Reactions."
Journal of Indian History 54, No. 3 (December 1976),
589–612.
[Cites records of Western comments regarding *sati* from
Greeks of the fourth century B.C. until the early twentieth
century.]

832.   ————. "How and Why Did the Women in Ancient India
Become Buddhist Nuns?" *Sociological Analysis* 38, No. 3
(1977), 239–51.

[Sharma's source is the Pali *Therigatha* and its commentary; he asks to what extent women authors of *gatha*s were "magically drawn to Buddhism" and to what extent their commitment was "circumstantially launched." He argues that forty-two of the seventy-two authors seem motivated by sheer spiritual attraction, thus contradicting relative deprivation theory.]

833.   ————. "Gandhi as a Feminist Emancipator and Kasturba as a Martyr." *Gandhi Marg* 3, No. 4 (July 1981), 214–20.
[Although Mahatma Gandhi was indeed an emancipator, he could assume this role only by forcing his wife, Kasturba, to uphold his social ideals.]

834.   ————. "Hindu Religious Reformers as Feminists: Paradox or Hypocrisy?" *Asian Profile* 11, No. 2 (April 1983), 195–99.
[The private lifestyles of five noted Hindu reformers are shown to be inconsistent with their public pronouncements. Subjects are Raja Rammohun Roy, Keshab Chunder Sen, Swami Dayananda Saraswati, Swami Ramakrishna Paramahamsa, and Mahatma Gandhi.]

835.   ————, ed. *Spokes of the Wheel: Studies in Buddha's Dhamma*. New Delhi: Books and Books, 1985.
[Two of this volume's studies, both written by its editor, address aspects of women's status in the one collection of Pali Buddhist texts attributed to women's authorship. Titles are "The Position of Women in Theravada Buddhism in the Light of the *Therigatha*," and "How and Why did the Psalmists of the *Therigatha* become *Bhikkunis*?"]

836.   ————, ed. *Women in World Religions*. Albany: State University of New York Press, 1987.
[This introductory survey of the roles and status of women in seven of the world's major religious traditions includes two entries with materials pertinent to India: Katherine K.

Young, "Women in Hinduism"; and Nancy Schuster Barnes, "Buddhism." The former covers all major developments from the *Rig-Veda* to the present. The latter, although not restricted to Indian materials, has sections on early Indian Buddhism, early Mahayana, and on the Vajrayana in India and Tibet.]

837. ————, ed. *Sati: Historical and Phenomenological Essays.* Delhi: Motilal Banarsidass, 1988.
[Assorted brief essays by Sharma himself, Ajit Ray, Alaka Hejib, and Katherine Young examine Western reactions to *sati*, indigenous protests, Brahmin widows' relationship to *sati*, scriptural sanctions for the practice, roles of Indian reformers, Ram Mohan Roy's use of the *Bhagavad-Gita* in challenging *sati*, and ascetic ideals for widows.]

838. ————, ed. *Religion and Women.* Albany: State University of New York Press, 1994.
[This collection of introductory articles on seven lesser-known religious traditions is intended as a supplement to Sharma's *Women in World Religions.* Three of its articles are addressed either entirely or partially to Indian traditions: Nalini Balbir, "Women in Jainism"; Rajkumari Shanker, "Women in Sikhism"; and Ketayun H. Gould, "Outside the Discipline, Inside the Experience: Women in Zoroastrianism" (roughly half of this work is devoted to the Indian Parsee community).]

For Sharma, Arvind, see also entries 228, 322, and 348.

839. Sharma, Hira Lal. *Ahilyabai.* 2nd ed. New Delhi: National Book Trust, 1983; originally published 1969.
[This simple and highly adulatory biography portrays a pious Hindu woman who became a queen and highly competent ruler. Describes Ahilyabai's religious tolerance, daily practice, and donations.]

840. Sharma, Preeti. *Hindu Women's Right to Maintenance*. New Delhi: Deep and Deep, 1990.

[Tracks seven aspects of the right to maintenance throughout the history of Hindu law, from *dharmasutra*s to the present, with ample commentary on cases. Aspects considered are the concept of property itself, the concept of maintenance, married women's right to maintenance, married women's right to live separately and claim maintenance, maintenance in matrimonial proceedings (divorce) and after divorce has been granted, claim to maintenance of mothers, daughters, and daughters-in-law, rights against joint family property, and amount of maintenance.]

841. Sharma, Radha Krishna. *Nationalism, Social Reform and Indian Women: A Study of the Interaction between Our National Movement and the Movement of Social Reform among Indian Women, 1921–1937*. Patna: Janaki Prakashan, 1981.

[The title is self-descriptive; subjects covered include the age of consent issue and intercaste marrying.]

842. Sharma, Ram Sharan. *Perspectives in Social and Economic History of Early India*. New Delhi: Munshiram Manoharlal, 1983.

[Includes one chapter on references to women and property in the epics and *purana*s, and another on women and *sudra*s in the early literature; a subsection of the latter discusses the shastric *sudra*-woman equivalence.]

843. Sharma, Satish. "Social Welfare of Women: A Note on the Early Status of Women in India." *Proceedings of the Third International Symposium on Asian Studies, 1981*. Hong Kong: Asian Research Service, 1981.

[This very brief and impressionistic survey of women's status in early sacred texts of India reiterates a familiar position: men and women were nearly equal in early Vedic times; Brahmanic priests corrupted this condition; Upanishaddic teachers, Buddhists, and Jains sought to correct this fall from grace, but failed. Texts cited extend from the Vedas through the Puranas.]

844.   ————. *Gandhi, Women and Social Development: In Search of Peaceful Development Planning in the Indian and Global Contexts*. Hong Kong: Asian Research Service, 1982. [This small book briefly surveys women's status in the Vedas, Brahmanas, Upanishads, and Puranas, then presents Gandhi's views on women and social development, his vision of an ideal social order, and the philosophy, planning, and strategy of the Sarvodaya movement, an experiment working towards such an order.]

845.   Sharma, Tripat. *Women in Ancient India, from 320 A.D. to c. 1200 A.D.* New Delhi: Ess Ess Publications, 1987. [Compiles information on women's status, roles, and activities in Vedic, epic, Buddhist, Jain, and classical Sanskrit texts.]

846.   Shastri, A. Mahadevi. *The Vedic Law of Marriage or the Emancipation of Women*. New Delhi: Asian Educational Services, 1988; originally published 1908. [Reprints documents of the author's controversy with Dewan Bahadur R. Ragoonath Rao over appropriate ages for marriage, including the original article that provoked the controversy (first presented in 1907).]

847.   Shastri, Madhu. *Status of Hindu Women: A Study of Legislative Trends and Judicial Behavior*. Jaipur: RBSA Publishers, 1990. [Covers women's Vedic, post-Vedic, and Constitutional status, including discussions of family law, matrimonial wrongs, and property rights.]

848.   Shattan [OCLC lists as Chattanar]. *Manimekhalai: The Dancer with the Magic Bowl*. Trans. Alain Danielou. New York: New Directions Books, 1989.

[This recent publication offers the first complete English translation of Tamil Nadu's second most famous epic; the heroine, a courtesan's daughter, becomes a Buddhist nun and goes on pilgrimage in search of knowledge.]

849. Shaukat Ali, Zeenat. *Marriage and Divorce in Islam, an Appraisal*. Delhi: Jaico Publishing Company, 1987.
[A woman justice examines in detail both Muslim sources for marriage and divorce law and contemporary test cases.]

850. Shaw, Miranda Eberle. *Passionate Enlightenment: Women in Tantric Buddhism in India*. Ph.D. diss., Harvard University, 1992.
["This work presents historical and textual data . . . gathered in India and Nepal about the lives, practices, and accomplishments of women in early Tantric Buddhism. A major source of documentation is biographies and writings of the women themselves." Cited from the author's description, *DAI* 53, No. 6 (December 1992), A-1966.]

851. ————. *Passionate Enlightenment: Women in Tantric Buddhism*. Princeton: Princeton University Press, 1994.
[A published version of the author's dissertation. See above, entry 850.]

For Shaw, Miranda Eberle, see also entries 997 and 998.

852. Shekhawat, Prahlad Singh. "The Culture of *Sati* in Rajasthan." *Manushi* No. 42–43 (September–December 1987), 30–33.
[Examines *sati* cults and temples in contemporary Rajasthan, thus establishing the context for the Roop Kanwar *sati*.]

For Shekhawat, Prahlad Singh, see also entry 200.

853.   Shepherd, Kevin. *A Sufi Matriarch: Hazrat Babajan*. Cambridge: Anthropographia Publications, 1985.
[Recounts the little that is known of the long life and remarkable deeds of a Sufi holy woman who began her life sometime during the early 1800s and completed it in 1931. Born the daughter of an Afghani Pathan chief, Hazrat Babajan spent most of her recorded days receiving devotees under a neem tree in the Poona cantonment.]

854.   Shervani, Nusrat, and Ahmad Rashid Shervani. "Education of Muslim Girls in Uttar Pradesh." *Mainstream* (November 18, 1978), 5–8.
[Surveys nineteen Muslim girls' high schools and fifteen intercolleges to determine levels of achievement; compares this with achievement of non-Muslims.]

855.   Shikhare, Dilip. "*Talaq Mukti Morcha* in Maharashtra." *Manushi* 6, No. 2 (=No. 32; January–February 1986), 23.
[Reports on a women's demonstration against Muslim divorce laws.]

856.   Shourie, Arun. "*Shariat*." *Illustrated Weekly of India* (January 5, 1986), 6–17.
[A well-known journalist's contribution to the Shah Bano controversy calls for a change in Personal Laws.]

857.   ———. *Religion in Politics*. New Delhi: Roli Books International, 1987.
[This collection of writings compiled from columns by a renowned political journalist includes two essays on legal issues affecting women. "'Your Wives Are Your Field'," especially addresses Muslim personal law; "The Muslim Women's Bill" analyzes politics of the Shah Bano issue.]

858.   Shraddhaprana, Pravrajika. "Sudhira Devi." *Samvit* 10 (September 1984), 20–26.

[Describes the life and work of a distinguished teacher and first Indian principal of the Sister Nivedita Girls' School in Calcutta.]

859. Shukla, Sonal. "A Women's Festival Taken Over: The Gujarati *Navratri.*" *Manushi* 7, No. 2 (=No. 38; January–February, 1987), 10–13.
[Young men infiltrating dances once performed solely by women have turned a formerly modest festival into a public spectacle.]

860. ————. "Govardhanram's Women." *Economic and Political Weekly* 22, No. 44 (October 31, 1987), WS63–WS69.
[Examines the ideal of woman as "domestic angel" shaped by Gujarati reformist and writer Govardhanram Tripathi— and shows how this ideal destroyed Govardhanram's wife and daughter.]

For Shukla, Sonal, see also entry 1002.

861. Siddiqi, Mohammad Mazheruddin. *Women in Islam.* New Delhi: Adam Publishers, 1980.
[Covers equality between the sexes, women in marriage, divorce, social restrictions on women, polygamy, and birth control, reflecting a conservative position.]

862. Siddiqi, Muhammad Iqbal. *Islam Forbids Free Mixing of Men and Women.* Lahore, Pakistan: Kazi Publications, 1983; Delhi: Adam Publishers, 1986.
[Responds to liberal challenges to *purdah.*]

863. ————. *The Family Laws of Islam.* Lahore, Pakistan: Kazi Publications, 1984; New Delhi: International Islamic Publishers, 1986.
[Covers the importance and benefits of marriage, equality between the sexes, dowry, marriage ceremonies and feasts, conjugal sex roles, duties of a wife, maintenance, *purdah,*

intermarriage with other "people of the Book," polygamy, divorce, children, and other marriage customs. For non-specialists.]

864. Siddiqui, H. Y. *Muslim Women in Transition: A Social Profile*. New Delhi: Harnam Publications, 1987.
[This report sponsored by the Government of India Department of Social Welfare furnishes economic, educational, and social profiles, as well as information on religious orthodoxy, *purdah*, marriage, divorce, and related practices. The sample is from Delhi area and western Uttar Pradesh; Jamia Millia Islamia University conducted the research.]

For Siddiqui, H. Y., see also entry 38.

865. Simha, S. L. N. *Tiruppavai of Goda: Our Lady Saint Andal's Garland of Krishna Poem*. Bombay: Anathacharya Indological Research Institute, 1982.
[Consists of a stanza-by-stanza English translation and commentary on the most famous work by the Tamil woman saint Andal. Includes an eight-page introduction and outline of the poem.]

866. Singh, A. K. *Devadasi System in Ancient India (A Case Study of Temple Dancing Girls of South India*. Delhi: H.K. Publishers, 1990.
[Traces the origins and history of *devadasi*s, shows their distribution by region, describes their functions and activities, and examines the role of paramour among them. The book's final chapter looks "Towards Prevention." Based extensively on epigraphic evidence.]

867. Singh, Alka. *Women in Muslim Personal Laws*. Jaipur: Rawat Publications, 1992.
[No further information was available at time of publication.]

868. Singh, Amar Kumar. "Women: The Most-Disliked Group—Ranking of Prejudices." *Social Change* (September–December, 1980), 3–9.
[A survey of prejudices conducted among school students of various religious communities makes the shocking finding that males of each community dislike their own women even more than they dislike members of other groups.]

869. Singh, Ardaman. "A Model Wedding Sermon: Bhayee Saheb of Bagrian." *Sikh Review* 31 (April 1983), 76–81.
[Bhayee Saheb was the author of this sermon, which the article cites at length. It includes a description of the Sikh marriage ceremony, an affirmation of the value of life in the world, an interpretation of marriage as sacrament, and a description of stages in the life of union.]

870. Singh, Chandramani, and Ronald Amend. *Marriage Songs from Bhojpuri Region*. Jaipur: Kitab Mahal, 1979.
[Provides a Hindi text and translation of songs sung by women during marriages in the Bhojpuri region of northeast India. Includes seventy-two songs, plus an introduction describing the marriage rituals themselves.]

871. Singh, Gulcharan S. "A Sikh Heroine of the Ghadar Party: Gular Kaur." *Journal of Sikh Studies* 4, No. 2 (1977), 93–98. Also published in *Sikh Review* 31 (September 1983), 58–63.
[Tells the tale of a woman activist in a group of Sikh emigrees who returned to India at the start of World War I to incite rebellion against the British. Eluding round-up and arrest on arrival, Gular Kaur went on to become the movement's principal communications contact at Lahore.]

872. ————. "Women Lib in Sikh Scriptures and Ideology." *Sikh Review* (March 1988), 38–43.
[Argues that the Sikh gurus were champions on behalf of women's uplift, and cites exemplary women who have distinguished themselves by their courage and creativity.]

873. Singh, Harchand. "A Lady Saint of Lahore." *Sikh Review* 28 (December 1980), 46–49.
[A Muslim girl aspiring to be a mystic is condemned by her community and granted protection and aid by Sikhs.]

874. Singh, Harnam. "Bibi Harsaran Kaur." *Sikh Review* 30 (November 1982), 57–60.
[A wicked Khan kidnaps a young Hindu bride-to-be; her family appeals, successfully, to Sikhs to save her. She later converts.]

875. Singh, Indu Prakash. *Women, Law, and Social Change in India*. New Delhi: Radiant Publishers, 1989.
[Treats the Hindu Code, *sati*, *stridhana*, and Muslim women's maintenance in divorce, among other issues.]

876. —————. *Indian Women: The Captured Beings*. New Delhi: Intellectual Publishing House, 1990.
[Includes sections on Indian patriarchy, "the women's question," Muslim women, capitalism, dowry, *sati*, and police brutality.]

For Singh, Indu Prakash, see also entries 38 and 200.

877. Singh, Khushwant. "Mother Valikamma." *Sunday* 8 (December 14, 1991), 7.
[A short piece from Singh's column "Gossip Sweet and Sour" describes Singh's meeting with the thirty-six year old Keralan *sadhvi* known as Mata Amritanandamayi; she is known for the warmth that exudes from her body.]

878. Singh, Maheep. "The Status of Women in Hindu and Sikh Societies." *Studies in Sikhism and Comparative Religion* 9 (1990), 133–39.
[Most of this essay concerns the wrongs done to women by Hinduism. Among Sikhs, the author claims complete equality of women, but points to a distinction that Guru Nanak

drew between "accomplished" and "non-accomplished" women. The former, approved, version "surrenders herself to her husband and always abides by his sweet will."]

879. Singh, Nikky-Guninder Kaur. *The Feminine Principle in the Sikh Vision of the Transcendent*. Ph.D. diss., Temple University, 1987.
["The purpose of this essay is to disclose the prominence of the feminine in Sikh literature which could lessen the disparity between men and women in contemporary Punjabi culture while presenting a rich picture of the female to contemporary western culture." Cited from the author's description, *DAI* 48, No. 2 (August 1987), A-415.]

880. ————. "The Sikh Bridal Symbol: An Epiphany of Interconnections." *Journal of Feminist Studies in Religion* 8, No. 2 (Fall 1992), 41–64.
[A Sikh woman reflects on a central symbol of her own tradition, arguing that it reconciles dualistic polarities found to be problematic by Western feminist theologians.]

881. ————. *The Feminine Principle in the Sikh Vision of the Transcendent*. Cambridge and New York: Cambridge University Press, 1993.
[A Sikh feminist explores portrayals of the feminine from the literature of her own heritage, extending from feminine metaphors of the Infinite to treatments of the Hindu goddess Durga to portrayals of women as ideal devotees, moral models, and mystic aspirants. Appears to be a published version of the author's dissertation; see entry 879.]

882. Singh, Ramindar. "Sati Debate: Polemics Postponed." *India Today* (April 30, 1988), 71.
[The arrest of the Arya Samaj's Swami Agnivesh, controversial *sati* opponent, forestalls his scheduled debate with its leading orthodox supporter.]

883.   Singh, Renuka. *The Womb of Mind: A Sociological Explora-
         tion of the Status-Experience of Women in Delhi*. New Delhi:
         Vikas Publishing House, 1990.
         [Reporting a survey of two hundred women of varying reli-
         gious and caste backgrounds in the Delhi area, this volume
         includes not only tables but also extensive citations from in-
         terviews. A thirty-eight-page chapter titled "Chains of Reli-
         gious Consciousness?" explores perceptions of the Sita
         myth—the ideal of devotion to husband—as well as caste-
         consciousness, religious consciousness, religious activities,
         and the phenomenon of endurance in abusive relationships.]

For Singh, Renuka, see also entries 200 and 894.

884.   Singh, Surjit. "How Raji Found Her Husband." *Sikh Review*
         24 (May 1976), 49–50.
         [A Protestant Christian girl finds a viable match after a
         Sikh friend teaches her to recite *Waheguru*.]

885.   Sinha, B. B. *Society in Tribal India*. New Delhi: B. R. Pub-
         lishing Corporation, 1982.
         [This study of peoples of the Chotanagpur plateau includes
         a section on the social status of Muslim, Hindu, and tribal
         women.]

886.   Sinha, Pradip. "Folk Songs of Bengal: An Aspect of Social
         History." *Bengal: Past and Present* 106 (January–December
         1987), 213–17.
         [Included principally for its one-paragraph description of
         the role of the *bostomi*, a female Vaishnava singer.]

887.   Sivananda, Swami. "Ideal Womanhood." *Hindutva* 10, No.
         2 (May 1979), 1–12.
         [Reiterates excerpts from the volume cited in entry 888
         below.]

888.   ————. *Sthree Dharma*. 2nd ed. Durban: Sivananda
        Press, 1981.
        [A famous Hindu *yogi* and teacher of *yogi*s states his posi-
        tion on the capabilities, roles, and duties of women.]

889.   Sivananda Radha, Swami (Sylvia Hellman). *Radha: Diary
        of a Woman's Search*. Palo Alto: Timeless Books, 1981.
        [The "Radha" of this diary is a woman of German birth and
        Canadian citizenship who went to seek salvation at the feet
        of Swami Sivananda. Contains a spellbinding account of life
        inside the Sivananda Ashram while its founder was still
        alive.]

890.   Sivaramayya, B. "Women's Studies in Law in India."
        Teaching Politics 14, No. 3 (1990), 21–29.
        [The journal is published by the University of Delhi's Politi-
        cal Science Department. Surveys discussions of the relation-
        ship between women and law since the nineteenth century,
        incorporating valuable citations from the literature. Con-
        cludes by describing curriculum proposals for universities
        relating to the area of Gender Justice.]

For Sivaramayya, B., see also entry 545.

891.   Skjonsberg, Else. *A Special Caste? Tamil Women of Sri
        Lanka*. London: Zed Press, 1982.
        [Analyzes the interplay of sex and caste in a small village
        of Sri Lanka. A chapter on "Rites of Passage" summarizes
        rites of childhood, puberty, and marriage, plus rights and
        duties of the life-stages which they initiate.]

892.   Sondhu, Madhuri. "A Vedantic Strategy for Women's Liber-
        ation." *Hinduism with a Human Face*. Ed. M. L. Sondhu
        and Madhuri Sondhu. New Delhi: Raaj Prakashan, 1990.
        [The subject is the Ramakrishna movement, with a special
        discussion of female leader Gayatri Devi. This widowed
        niece of Swami Paramananda followed him to the United
        States, where she became a noted teacher.]

893.   Soni, Lok Nath. "Marriage among the Rauts of Chhattis-
        garh." *Folklore* 16 (January 1975), 16–33.
        [Chhattisgarh is in Madhya Pradesh; the Rauts are patri-
        lineal, patriarchal cattleherders. The article describes in de-
        tail rites of the formal priestly ritual from betrothal to the
        couple's arrival at the bridegroom's village, with variations
        among community subdivisions; it summarizes more briefly
        eight alternative forms of marriage, and compensations
        paid for eloping with a married woman.]

894.   Sood, Sushma. *Violence against Women*. Jaipur: Arihant
        Publications, 1990.
        [Includes a subsection on *sati* and widowhood; its two *sati*
        articles are Kamala Kumar, "*Sati*: A Crime against Wom-
        en"; and Indu Prakash Singh and Renuka Singh, "*Sati*: The
        Patri Politics."]

895.   Southard, Barbara. "Bengal Women's Education League:
        Pressure Group and Professional Association." *Modern
        Asian Studies* 18, No. 1 (1984), 55–88.
        [This league was secular in orientation and included women
        of all religious communities, but its top leadership was
        dominated by women of the Brahmo Samaj.]

896.   Srinivas, M. N. "The Changing Position of Indian Women."
        Man 12, No. 2 (August 1977), 221–38; also published as
        Changing Position of Indian Women. Delhi: Oxford Univer-
        sity Press, 1978.
        [Reproduces the T. H. Huxley Memorial Lecture, delivered
        by the celebrated social scientist who first described and
        named the phenomenon of "Sanskritization." The lecture de-
        scribes the impact of the Sanskritization process on the
        lives of Indian women.]

897.   Srinivasin, Amrit. *Temple "Prostitution" and Community
        Reform: An Example of the Ethnographic, Historical and*

Textual Context of the Devadasi of Tamil Nadu. Ph.D. diss., Cambridge University, 1984.
[No descriptive information is available save the title.]

898. —————. "Reform and Revival: The *Devadasi* and Her Dance." *Economic and Political Weekly* 20, No. 44 (November 2, 1985), 1869–76.
[A long and thorough article that describes the *devadasi* system of Tamil Nadu prior to the 1947 ban on *devadasi* dedication, and political and economic factors influencing the ban itself; shows connections between the *devadasi* ban and the Theosophical Society's drive for "revival" of Indian classical dance.]

899. —————. "The Hindu Temple-Dancer: Prostitute or Nun?" *Cambridge Anthropology, Art and Society* 8, No. 1, 73–79.
[Recounts how polite society stole the dance from the *devadasi*s, describing the anti-nautch controversy and its connections to the Theosophical Society's revival of Indian dance.]

900. —————. "Women and Reform of Indian Tradition: Gandhian Alternative to Liberalism." *Economic and Political Weekly* 22, No. 51 (December 19, 1987), 2225–28.
[Contrasts the Gandhian affirmation of indigenous traditions and its "feminized" methods of protest with the monolithic liberal program for modernizing India; cites *devadasi* reforms and attacks on Nayar marriage customs as destructive examples of the latter.]

901. —————. "Reform or Conformity: Temple Prostitution and the Community in the Madras Presidency." *Structures of Patriarchy: State, Community and Household in Modernizing Asia*. Ed. Bina Agarwal. New Delhi: Kali for Women, 1988.
[The first half of this chapter describes the *devadasi* system prior to 1947 reform legislation, the second analyzes politi-

cal aspects of the reforms and their dubious benefit for *devadasi*s.]

902.   *Sri Sarada Devi: A Biography in Pictures*. Calcutta: Advaita Ashram, 1988.
[Features photographs of the Ramakrishna Mission's Holy Mother, the people she knew, and the places where she stayed. The reproductions are, unfortunately, poor.]

903.   Srivastava, I. "Women as Portrayed in Women's Folk Songs of Northern India." *Asian Folklore Studies* 50, No. 2 (1991), 270–82.
[Songs cited concern female deities, birth and wedding ceremonies, festivals, seasons, and daily chores. The author concludes: "The portrait of women is often at variance with the conventional stereotypes of an obedient, acquiescent, and conformist woman."]

904.   Srivastava, T. N. *Women and the Law*. New Delhi: Intellectual Publishing House, 1985.
[Discusses laws relevant to women on marriage, divorce, succession, adoption, and employment.]

905.   Staelin, Charlotte Dennett. *The Influence of Missions on Women's Education in India: The American Marathi Mission in Ahmadnagar, 1830–1930*. Ph.D. diss., University of Michigan, 1977.
["Describes the inauguration and history of six institutions founded by [American Marathi] Mission for Indian women: the Farrar schools for Hindu girls, the Ahmadnagar Girls' Boarding School, the Alice House Orphanage, the Chapin Home for Women. the Bible Women's Training School, and the Ahmadnagar Hospital for Women and Children. . . . Postulates that American Women had a unique and ambiguous position in Mission organization: on the one hand they were indispensable, on the other, they were only 'helpmates.' Their position resulted in a confused and somewhat

contradictory message being transmitted to the Indian women trained by the Mission as to what the proper role of women in modern society should be." Cited from author's description, *DAI* 38, No. 3 (September 1977), A-1582.]

906. Stein, Dorothy. "Burning Widows, Burning Brides: The Perils of Daughterhood in India." *Pacific Affairs* 61 (Fall 1988), 465–85.
[The origins of *sati*, its rationale, the drive for abolition, its reemergence, and dowry murder are surveyed here. The author argues that widow-burning and bride-burning are by-products of the Indian insistence on marriage itself; they will not disappear "until single women are accepted in Indian society."]

907. Stevenson, Joseph McClendon. "Mother Teresa's First Love: The Nirmal Hriday Home in Calcutta Thirty Years Later." *Coevolution Quarterly* No. 39 (Fall 1983), 68–78.
[The Nirmal Hriday Home is the home for dying destitutes. The journalist who visits the home reports that there is more curing and less dying going on these days. Describes the daily life, a few of the patients, the sisters, staffers, and the home's fading link with Mother Teresa herself.]

908. Subbamma, Malladi. *Personal Laws and Women.* New Delhi: All India Women's Conference, 1987.
[Describes the status of women under Hindu, Muslim, Christian and Parsee personal laws and specifies women's rights in relation to marriage, divorce, maintenance, and custody.]

909. ————. "Radical Humanism and Women's Movement." *The Radical Humanist* 51, No. 3 (June 1987), 19–21.
[The President of the Andhra Pradesh Radical Humanist Association proposes that Humanist Feminism should guide the women's movement. Its program would include teaching women to "question the basis of social customs, religious rites, traditional practices, and even political doctrines."]

910. —————. *Islam and Women*. Trans. M. V. Ramamurty.
New Delhi: Sterling Publishers, 1988.
[A woman of humanist conviction surveys Muslim restrictions on women. The first chapter, entitled "The Background," reveals the author's critical stance.]

911. "Sued for Condemning Sati." *Manushi* No. 54–55 (September–December 1989), 31.
[The heat of the *sati* controversy is reflected in this brief notice about a lawsuit filed against Prabhu Dixit for publishing an article against *sati* in *Chauthi Dixit* weekly.]

912. Suleri, Sara. *Meatless Days*. Chicago: University of Chicago Press, 1989. This autobiography of the daughter of a well-known Pakistani journalist is principally concerned with the politics of partition and with the author's own process of maturation; it does, however, include some scant information about Ramazan fasting and religious practices of older women in the author's family.

913. —————. *The Rhetoric of English India*. Chicago: University of Chicago Press, 1992.
[Concerns the problem of colonial discourse, as reflected largely in writings of British males; a lone chapter entitled "The Feminine Picturesque" examines British women's accounts of their own perceptions and experiences. They respond to gods and goddesses, *zenana*s, dancing girls, maternity, death, mutiny, veils, and much else.]

914. Sultana, Tajwara. "Status of Women in Muslim Society."
Prasara 4, No. 1 (April 1976), 20–32.
[Covers the Quranic view of marriage and the family, and the reciprocal responsibilities of husbands and wives. The viewpoint is conservative; the author argues that woman has a very high status in Islam and that biology accounts for differences in responsibilities assigned to the sexes.]

915.   Sutherland, Gail Hinrich. *"Bija* (seed) and *ksetra* (field): male surrogacy or *niyoga* in the Mahabharata." *Contributions to Indian Sociology* (n.s.) 24, No. 1 (1990), 77–103. [Analyzes passages in India's longest epic concerning the practice of acquiring children from a wife by appointing a surrogate husband. Although allowed in ancient codes of religious law—and undertaken several times in the Mahabharata—this practice, according to the author, is sufficiently questioned in epic dialogues to be viewed as a source of moral quandary.]

916.   Sutherland, Sally (J. M.). "Sita and Draupadi: Aggressive Behavior and Female Role Models in the Sanskrit Epics." *Journal of the American Oriental Society* 109, No. 1 (January–March 1989), 63–80. [Asks why the more masochistic Sita is singled out by Indians as their ideal woman, after comparing her with the forceful Draupadi.]

917.   —————, ed. *Bridging Worlds: Studies on Women in South Asia*. Berkeley: University of California at Berkeley Center for South Asia Studies, 1991. [Although no paper in this volume addresses religion as its focal concern, the following touch peripherally on religiously transmitted themes or values: Sally J. M. Sutherland, "The Bad Seed: Senior Wives and Elder Sons"; Gautam Vajracharya, "She is Bad: A Study of Change and Continuity in the Lifestyle of Women in Ancient Nepal due to Sanskritization"; Frances W. Pritchett, "Women, Death, and Fate: Sexual Politics in the *Dastan-e Amir Hamzah*"; Usha Nilsson, "Women in Contemporary Indian Literature: Revised Scripts and Changed Roles"; Roshni Rustomji-Kerns, "The Reconstruction of Tradition: Women in Anita Desai's Novels"; and Amita Sinha, "Women's Local Space: Home and Neighborhood.]

918.   ————. "Seduction, Counter Seduction, and Sexual Role Models: Bedroom Politics and the Indian Epics." *Journal of Indian Philosophy* 20, No. 2 (June 1992), 243–51.
[Reconstructs the image of the *Ramayana* villainess Kaikeyi, who sent prince Rama into his wilderness exile. Kaikeyi was trying to right an injustice; poet Valmiki's negative portrayal of her deed reflects a prevailing Hindu attitude of "fear and hatred for women."]

919.   Swaminathan, Padmini. "State and Subordination of Women." *Economic and Political Weekly* 22, No. 44 (October 31, 1987), WS34–WS39.
[Shows how the Indian state contributes to women's subordination. One segment assesses surviving inequities in the Hindu law of inheritance.]

920.   Swarup, Hem Lata, and Sarojini Bisaria, eds. *Women Politics and Religion*. Etawah: A.C. Brothers, 1991.
[Twelve of these essays from a seminar sponsored by the International Sociological Association relate to India, covering Hindu, Muslim, or tribal communities. See Hem Lata Swarup, "Women, Religion and Politics in India"; Leela and Saurabh Dube, "Women, in India: Religion, and the Category of Politics"; Sarojini Bisaria, "Women and Festivals of India"; Kiran Saxena, "Legitimising Subjugation of Women: Role of Religion in India"; Niroj Sinha, "Reinforcing Second Class Status of Women in India: A Study of the Impact of Religion through Education on Women's Status"; Minoti Bhattacharyya, "Hindu Religion and Women's Rights"; Najima Chowdhury, "Women in Politics: Impact of Religion on Women's Participation—the Case of Bangladesh"; Zarina Bhatty, "Islamic Fundamentalism and Muslim Women in India"; Kunja Medhi, "The Tribal Society of Assam and the North-east Region: A Study of the Status of Women in the Context of Their Religion and Personal Life"; Anima Bose, "Women—in the Ethos of Gandhian Perspective"; Rahnuma Ahmed, "Religious Ideology and the Women's Movement in

Bangladesh"; and Devaki Jain, "Women, Religion and Social Change."]

921. Tagore, Prossono Coomar. *Vivada Chintamani: A Succinct Commentary on the Hindoo Law Prevalent in Mithila, from the Original Sanskrit of Vachaspati Misra.* 2nd ed. Delhi: Vishwa-Kala Prakashan, 1986; original edition Madras: J. Higgerbotham, 1865.
[Translates a law treatise originally published in 1865. This contains a short section titled "Women and Other Matters," plus provisions on women's property rights and the inheritance of women's property.]

922. Tak, Raghubir Singh. "Ritual in Sikh Society of the Seventeenth Century." *Folklore* 22 (March 1981), 122–27.
[The wedding ritual and its preparations attract this article's principal attention, but rites at birth and death also receive some coverage.]

923. Talwar, K. S. "The Anand Marriage Act." *Sikh Review* 31 (February 1983), 33–41.
[Traces the origins of the Sikh marriage ceremony and the history of the Bill that acknowledges its validity. Argues that Anand marriage is an original feature of the Sikh community, not an innovation of reformers.]

924. Tapasyananda, Swami. *Sri Sarada Devi: The Holy Mother.* 5th ed. Madras: Sri Ramakrishna Math, 1977; original edition 1940.
[A swami of the Ramakrishna Mission offers a biography of the Mission's Holy Mother.]

925. —————, ed. and trans. *Stotranjalih: Hymn Offerings to Sri Ramakrshna and the Holy Mother, by Several Great Disciples and Devotees.* Madras: Sri Ramakrishna Math, 1988.
[Three *stotras* (praise songs) by great disciples addressed to Sri Sarada Devi are included in this small collection.]

926. Tapper, Bruce Elliot. "Widows and Goddesses: Female Roles in Deity Symbolism in a South Indian Village." *Contributions to Indian Sociology* N.S. 13, No. 1 (January–June, 1979), 1–31.
[Analyzes implications of a goddess festival of Telegu-speaking Andhra Pradesh for the ideology of female roles that the festival reflects. Features portrayals of women in skits and women's own festal activities.]

927. Tarachand, K. C. *Devadasi Custom: Rural Social Structure and Flesh Markets*. New Delhi: Reliance, 1991.
[Despite a negative attitude towards *devadasis*, this volume contains good information on the history and practice of Karnataka's Yellama shrine, and on the rites and economic bases for *devadasi* dedication.]

928. Teays, Wanda. "The Burning Bride: The Dowry Problem in India." *Journal of Feminist Studies in Religion* 7, No. 2 (Fall 1991), 29–54.
[Considers the contemporary problem of dowry murder in India, its roots in custom and religion, its links to *sati*, its current legal status, predicaments of anti-dowry enforcement, and the relationship between dowry and education. Asks what Western feminists can do about this problem.]

929. Tellis-Nayak, Jessie B. *Indian Womanhood Then and Now: Situation, Efforts, Profiles*. Indore: Satprakashan Sanchar Kendra, 1983.
[Includes materials on Pandita Ramabai and Kasturba Gandhi; also on *purdah*, dowry, widowhood, and Muslim women.]

930. ————. "Impact of the Women's Movement on the Church in India." *Samya Shakti: A Journal of Women's Studies* 2, No. 2 (1986), 13–25.
[Surveys the roles of women and women's groups in both Catholic and Protestant churches of India, citing recent evi-

dences of "awakening." Helpful especially for its information on Christian women's organizations.]

931.   ————. "Efforts at Women's Development: A Professional and Personal Perspective." *Journal of Feminist Studies
in Religion* 7 (Fall 1991), 139–48.
[A pioneer in the area of women's development describes
her own work, first with the Jesuit-sponsored Indian Social
Institute and its Program for Women's Development, and
later with WINA (Women's Institute for New Awakening)
India; the latter is still Christian in inspiration, although
secular in approach and independent of any church. Cites
WINA's efforts to evolve an indigenous feminist theology.]

For Tellis-Nayak, Jessie B., see also entry 1014.

932.   Tewari, Laxmi G. "The Folk Festival of *Jhonjhi-Tesu.*"
Asian Folklore Studies 41, No. 2 (1982), 217–30.
[Describes mythological origins, present-day practice, song
texts and types, and social importance of a festival of Uttar
Pradesh that prepares girls for leaving their homes after
marriage.]

933.   ————. "Women's Fasts and Festivals from Uttar
Pradesh: Their Art, Rituals, and Stories." *South Asia* (Ned-
lands, Western Australia) 5, No. 1 (June 1982), 42–50.
[This general introduction to the author's fieldwork describes the sociological import, art, stories, and origins of
the *vrata*s she studied, as well as changes they are currently undergoing.]

934.   ————. *The Splendour of Worship: Women's Fasts,
Rituals, Stories and Art.* New Delhi: Manohar, 1991.
[This study based on the author's fieldwork features stories
told in connection with fourteen women's *vrata*s observed by
Kanyakubja Brahmins of Kanpur district, Uttar Pradesh.
The *vrata*s themselves are described very briefly; illustra-
tions depict ephemeral art produced for the celebrations.]

935.   Thakur, M. L. "Arya Samaj and the Emancipation of Wom-
en." *Maharishi Dayanand University Research Journal
(Arts)* 3, No. 2 (October 1988), 179–86.
[Lauds the role of the Arya Samaj in promoting "emancipation of women," especially with reference to child marriage,
widow marriage, *purdah*, dowry, polygamy, and education.]

936.   Thambiah, Pushpawathy. *Important Ceremonies during the
Life of a Hindu Girl.* Ph.D. diss., University of Sri Lanka
Kathabedu Campus, 1976.
[Describes ceremonies of birth, girlhood, puberty, marriage,
pregnancy, and widowhood.]

937.   Thapar, Romila, with Madhu Kishwar and Ruth Vanita.
"Traditions versus Misconceptions." *Manushi* Nos. 42–43
(September–December 1987), 2–14.
[An interview with India's most celebrated woman historian
elicits comments on Shakuntala, Sita, *sati*, goddesses, the
husband as a god, Islam's impact on women, dowry, and
other topics.]

For Thapar, Romila, see also entries 35, 401, and 799.

938.   Tharu, Susie, and K. Lalita, eds. *Women Writing in India:
600 B.C. to the Present.* Volume I: *600 B.C. to the Early
20th Century*; Volume II, *The Twentieth Century.* Delhi:
Oxford University Press, 1991–93; also New York: Feminist
Press at the City University of New York, 1991–93.
[This remarkable achievement of cooperative scholarship
assembles materials ranging from songs of Buddhist nuns
and medieval saints to letters, stories, and autobiographical
accounts by women experiencing religious and social
changes of the nineteenth and twentieth centuries. Most
items selected for the anthology are translated from regional languages, many for the first time; several were rescued
from near-loss via super-sleuthing by the volume's contributors.]

For Tharu, Susie, see also entries 790 and 1003.

939. Theempalangatti, Joseph. *Role of Missionaries in the Emancipation of Women in India, 1813–1857.* Ph.D. diss., Jamia Millia Islamia University, 1991.
[Located at Jamia Millia Islamia University library; no description is available.]

940. *Third National Conference on Women's Studies.* Chandigarh, 1986.
[The general theme of the conference was Rural and Tribal Women; subtheme 8 was "Religion, Secularism, and Women's Rights." See especially the following papers: Jiwan Jat, "Religion, Secularism, and Women's Rights" (largely on Sikh materials); Mira Chatterjee, "Religion, Secularism and Organizing Women Workers: Some Reflections"; and Ammu Krishnaswamy, "Shah Bano and After."]

941. Thiruchandran, Selvi. "Women in Hinduism." *Logos* 21, No. 4 (November 1982), 48–73.
[Surveys the status of women in Hinduism, beginning with a brief account of the decay in women's status between Vedic days and the classical period. Cites the importance of chastity in women, the concept of *shakti*, the significance of female saints, the role of women in preserving Hindu culture, *sati*, restrictions on widows and on upper-class women, women's roles in rites, the dowry system, and changes made by nineteenth-century reformers.]

942. Thompson, Catherine Susannah. *Ritual States in the Lifecycles of Hindu Women in a Village of Central India.* Ph.D. diss., University of London, 1984.
[No further information is available.]

943. ————. "The Power to Pollute and the Power to Preserve: Perceptions of Female Power in a Hindu Village." *Social Science and Medicine* 21, No. 6 (1985), 701–11.

[Analysis of beliefs about women's ability to pollute and preserve shows that female sexuality acquires negative and polluting connotations only when women are estranged from men. When women identify their own interests with those of men, they are considered to have positive powers such as the ability to preserve life.]

944. Thuravackai, Jose. "The Male-Female Symbolism in Religious Literature." *Journal of Dharma* 16, No. 2 (April–June 1991), 115–24.
[Compares imagery found in Hindu texts (Vedic gods and goddesses, Shiva-Shakti, *purusha-prakriti*) with imagery of the Christian and Rabbinic traditions; concludes that the Hindu imagery demonstrates the essential complementarity of men and women.]

945. Tikoo, Prithvi Nath. *Indian Women (A Brief Socio-Cultural Survey)*. Delhi: B. R. Publishing Corporation, 1985.
[Some information on the status of women in texts is cited; however, this book's most interesting feature is two first-person accounts by women, one older and uneducated, and one a young physician. The older woman was married as a child and suffered greatly from in-laws' harshness, but found peace from an encounter with a famous saint visiting a local *gurudwara*.]

946. Tiwana, Dalip Kaur. *A Journey on Bare Feet*. Trans. Jai Ratan. New Delhi: Orient Longman, 1990.
[This autobiographical novel by the niece of a well-known Punjabi zamindar describes her family's rites to produce a male child, religious practices of the heroine's grandmother, and the heroine's own never-consummated marriage, as well as crises produced by the family's loss of status following her uncle's death.]

947. Tope, T. K. *Hindu Family Law and Social Change*. Bombay: University of Bombay, 1982.

[The Dr. P. B. Gajendragadkar lecture series for 1978. Argues that Hindu law is quite adaptable to social change; cites changes in family, concepts of women's property, marriage, and includes a segment on problems yet to be faced. Quotes extensively from *dharmasastra*.]

948.   *Towards Equality: Report of the Committee on the Status of Women in India*. New Delhi: Government of India, Ministry of Education and Social Welfare, 1975.
[This report shocked Indian leadership by showing how many Indian women remained unaffected by the constitutional rights granted to them following independence. The volume includes an extensive section on images of women in religious traditions, including "Hinduism," the *bhakti* movement, Veerasaivism, Islam, Christianity, Jainism, Buddhism, Sikhism, Zoroastrianism, tribal religions, and the reform movements Brahmo Samaj, Prarthana Samaj, Arya Samaj, and the Muslim reform movement. A long chapter on Women and the Law covers the Hindu Marriage Act and many provisions of Hindu, Muslim, Christian, Parsee, and Jewish law.]

949.   Trivedi, G. M. "Women in the Folklore of Awadh." *Sangeet Natak* 37 (July–September 1975), 29–41.
[This analysis of folk song lyrics primarily reveals attitudes towards and practice connected with marriage and widowhood; songs show continued centering on home and conventional morality.]

950.   Trivedi, Harshad R. *Scheduled Caste Women: Studies in Exploitation with Reference to Superstition, Ignorance, and Poverty*. New Delhi: Concept Publishing Company, 1977.
[Includes a chapter on "Sacred Exploitation" in the Bijapur region—i.e., *devadasi* prostitution.]

951.   Tsomo, Karma Lekshe, ed. *Sakyadhita: Daughters of the Buddha*. Ithaca, N.Y.: Snow Lion Publications, 1988.

[These proceedings of the first international conference on nuns in Buddhism consist principally of reports on the status, ideals, aspirations, and problems of nuns in the Buddhist world of today. However, three papers from its section entitled "The *Bhiksuni* Issue" address historical origins of the nuns' order in India and the interruptions suffered during external transmissions of its lineage: Chatsumarn Kabilsingh, "The Role of Women in Buddhism; Bhiksuni Karma Lekshe Tsomo, "Prospects for an International *Bhikshini Samgha*"; Kusuma Devendra, "Establishment of the Order of Buddhist Nuns and Its Development in Sri Lanka"; and "An Interview with His Holiness the Dalai Lama."]

For Tsomo, Karma Lekshe, see also entries 997 and 998.

952.   Uberoi, Patricia. "Feminine Identity and National Ethos in Indian Calendar Art." *Economic and Political Weekly* 25, No. 17 (April 28, 1990), WS41–WS48.
[Examines representations of women—including goddesses—in a genre of Indian popular art; argues that these show both a "commoditisation" of women—an assimilation with "status symbol consumer products"—and a "tropizing"—a metaphoric use to represent the tension between unity and variety in Indian culture and religion.]

953.   ———. "Reciprocity in Social Science: Gender Issues." *The Indian Journal of Social Science* 6, No. 3 (1993), 243–58.
[Examines a number of issues relating to the construction of knowledge about women's lives in India, from fallacious assumptions affecting older literature, to overreliance on Western theory, to pitfalls in emerging attempts to indigenize theory, several of which take religion as a point of departure. Excellent both for the methodological issues it raises and for the overview it offers of current work.]

954. Uchida, Norihiko. "Folksongs and the Observance of Puberty Ceremony in Tamil Nadu." *Folklore* 20 (May–June 1979), 119–22.
[Description of a ceremony formerly performed at first menstruation by women of the Saurashtra weavers of Tamil Nadu. Note its connection with consummation of marriage.]

955. Ullrich, Helen E. "Caste Differences between Brahmin and Non-Brahmin Women in a South Indian Village." *Sexual Stratification: A Cross-Cultural View*. Ed. Alice Schlegel. New York: Columbia University Press, 1977.
[Roles and behavior of the Havik Brahmin women of this study are largely consistent with *dharmasastra* strictures; the Haviks are more constricted and subordinate than their non-Brahmin counterparts. Includes a section on ritual status, including observance of menstrual taboos.]

956. *Uniform Civil Law: The Great Debate*. Special issue of *Manthan* (July 1986).
[The journal of an ultraconservative Hindu group argues the case for a uniform civil code. Contains the following articles (authors are not always named): "Editorial: Uniform Civil Law: The Great Debate"; "Shri Guruji on the Issue of Uniform Civil Law"; "Shahbano Case Judgement: The Full Text"; "A Case for the Muslim Woman" (by Danial Latifi); "Hindus Are Guilty of Ignoring the Sufferings of Muslim Women" (by C. Achutha Menon); and "The Shahbano Showdown" (by V. R. Krishna Iyer).]

957. Upreti, H. C., and Nandini Upreti. *The Myth of Sati: Some Dimensions of Widow Burning*. Bombay: Himalaya Publishing House, 1991.
[An extensive analysis of the Roop Kanwar *sati* treats the event itself, the responses to it, and its socio-historical context.]

958. Urquhart, Margaret M. *Women of Bengal*. Delhi: Cultural Publishing House, 1983; Gian Publishing House, 1987; originally published 1925.
[This product of a Western woman's twenty-five year sojourn in Calcutta includes a full chapter on "The Bengali Woman's Religion." This describes family shrines and daily worship, use of *mantras*, husband worship, popular beliefs, reciters of epics, gurus, "depraved" (i.e., Tantric) forms of worship, religious literature known, dominant ideas, the worship of Kali, and human saviors.]

959. Vaid, Sudesh, and Kumkum Sangari. "Institutions, Beliefs, Ideologies: Widow Immolation in Contemporary Rajasthan." *Economic and Political Weekly* 26, No. 17 (April 27, 1991), WS2–WS18.
[This complex analysis centers on a widow immolation in the Shekhawati region of Rajasthan. Part 1 compares this *sati* with others in the area; Part 2 explores the interaction of local beliefs, ideologies, and institutions which provided the act's context; Part 3 "discusses the overlaps and distinctions between regional and metropolitan ideologic formations, and concludes with an analysis of the interrelated issues of popular belief and the question of consent."]

For Vaid, Sudesh, see also entries 35, 629, 788, 789, 790, and 799.

960. Vajapeyi, Dhirendra K., ed. *Boeings and Bullock-Carts: Studies in Change and Continuity in Indian Civilization (Essays in Honor of K. Ishwaran)*, Vol. 2: *Indian Civilization in Its Local, Regional, and National Aspects*. Delhi: Chanakya Publications, 1990.
[Although devoted to the study of changing India as a whole, this volume contains two articles addressed to the juncture of women and religion. Bina Gupta's "Women's Roles and Religious Consciousness: India—Ancient and Modern," treats sastric, Upanishaddic, and Gandhian constructions of women's roles; Katherine Young and Lily

Miller's "Sacred Biography and the Restructuring of Society: A Study of Anandamai Ma, Lady-Saint of Modern Hinduism" is principally concerned with this modern saint's hagiography and its accounts of her links to political figures such as Gandhi, Kamala Nehru, and the latter's daughter Indira Gandhi.]

961. Vandana, Sister. *Gurus, Ashrams and Christians*. London: Darton, Longmann and Todd, 1978.
[A portrayal of *ashram* life in India. The author dwells at greatest length on the Sivananda Ashram, but includes a few pages of descriptive material on each of twenty others that she has visited. Three house women's communities: Brahma Vidya Mandir, Kanya Kumari Sthan, and Sri Sarada Math.]

962. Van der Veen, Klaas W [OCLC lists as Veen, Klaas van der]. *I Give Thee My Daughter: A Study of Marriage and Hierarchy among the Anavil Brahmans of South Gujarat*. Trans. Nanette Jockin. Assen: Van Gorcum and Company, 1972. Dutch version published 1969.
[Most of this volume treats the marriage system per se; however, it contains one chapter on "Brahman Ideology and Anavil Brahman Practice," and offers comments on Arya Samaj influence in the chapter that precedes this.]

963. Vanita, Ruth. "The Special Marriage Act: Not Special Enough." *Manushi* No. 58 (May–June 1990), 14–23.
[Describes additional amendments needed to improve the modern version of an 1872 Act providing for a civil, non-religious, form of marriage.]

For Vanita, Ruth, see also entries 493, 494, 495, 937, and 1002.

964. Varma, Mahadevi. *A Pilgrimage to the Himalayas and Other Silhouettes from Memory*. Trans. Radhika Prasad Srivastava and Lillian Srivastava. London: Peter Owen, 1975; Hindi edition, 1942.

[This series of vignettes about poor Indians known to the author occasionally touches upon religion and its impact; see especially "Munnu's Mother," the story of a poor brahmin woman, and "Grandpa Thakuri," which contains a description of a *kirtan* in which women are prominent.]

965.   Vashista, B. K., ed. *Encyclopedia of Women in India*. New Delhi: Praveen Encyclopedia Publishers, 1976.
[This volume is less an encyclopedia, as claimed, than a collection of twenty essays that attempts to cover broad facets of women's lives in India. Includes one chapter on "Religious Systems and Systems of Descent" and another on "Manu and His Psychology of Womanhood."]

966.   Vatsa, Rajendra Singh. "The Remarriage and Rehabilitation of the Hindu Widows in India 1856–1914." *Journal of Indian History* 54, No. 3 (December 1976), 713–30.
[Surveys movements and institutions that worked for widow marriage and education. Shows the role of the Brahmo Samaj and Pandita Ramabai.]

967.   Venkatraman, R. "Role of Women in the Religious Practices of the Yoga *Siddha*s of Tamilnadu." *Proceedings of the Indian History Congress*, Vol. 1. Hyderabad: Osmania University, 1978.
[Examines references to functions of "live" women in a tantric group of the Shakta tradition. The references are sparse and the roles seem passive; the women are mostly called "virgins."]

968.   Verghese, Jamila. *Her Gold and Her Body*. New Delhi: Vikas Publishing House, 1980.
[This major work addresses dowry customs and abuses.]

969.   Verma, B. R. *Islamic Law—Personal: Being Commentaries on Mohammedan Law in India, Pakistan and Bangladesh*. 6th ed. Allahabad: Law Publishers, 1986.

[This large and technical reference work on cases and precedents covers marriage, dissolution of marriage, parentage, maintenance, inheritance, and other topics.]

970. —————. *Muslim Marriage, Dissolution and Maintenance.* 2nd ed. Allahabad: Law Book Company, 1988; first ed. 1971, under the title *Muslim Marriage and Dissolution.*
[This technical work for legal professionals covers the definition of marriage, criteria for valid marriage, marriage prohibitions, inter-religious marriage, divorce, *iddat*, rights and duties in marriage, dissolution of marriage and its implications, guardianship, inheritance, missing husbands, and impotency.]

971. Verma, H. N., and Amrit Verma. *Eminent Indian Women.* New Delhi: Great Indian, 1976.
[Thumbnail biographies of famous women, both legendary and historical, include a number of *bhakti* saints. Chapter headings are a mite confusing: e.g., the chapter headed "Islamic" includes the Hindu *bhakta*s Mirabai and Muktabai.]

972. Verma, Jyoti. "Life Patterns and Thinking of Three Generations of Middle Class Bihari Women." *Social Change* 15, No. 2 (June 1985), 25–28.
[Reports the findings of interviews with thirty women of three generations; one question asked was about the role of religion and ritual in their lives.]

973. Vetschera, Traude. "The Potaraja and Their Goddess." *Asian Folklore Studies* 37, No. 2 (1978), 105–53.
[The Potaraja live in Ahmednagar District, Maharashtra; the goddess is called Mari or Lakshmi and is both benevolent and terrible.]

974. "Victim of Family Conspiracy: The Abduction of Farah." *Manushi* No. 56 (January–February 1990), 11–13.
[On a family's kidnapping, sequestering, and eventual murder of a girl who married a boy of another religion.]

975.   Vidyasagar, Ishwara Chandra. *Marriage of Hindu Widow*.
        Calcutta: K.P. Bagchi, 1976; original edition Calcutta:
        Sanskit Press, 1856.
        [Reissues in English translation a classic nineteenth-cen-
        tury argument in favor of permitting Hindu widows to re-
        marry; Vidyasagar was the first and most famous propo-
        nent of this cause.]

976.   Vijaysree, M. "Contributions of Women to Sanskrit Litera-
        ture." *Triveni* 54, No. 1 (April–June 1985), 74–78. [This
        swift overview principally lists women authors and their
        products—and much of the literature described is secular.
        However, it does include one author of a long work on
        smritis, as well as several with works relating to Krishna
        or to *Ramayana*. Shows that some women learned Sanskrit
        well enough to compose with it even at times when Sanskrit
        learning was supposedly forbidden to women.]

977.   Vinoba. *Women's Power*. Varanasi: Sarva Seva Sangh
        Prakashan, 1975.
        [A famous former politician and religious leader recounts
        his convictions concerning women; Vinoba was founder of
        the Brahma Vidya Mandir, which houses an order of
        brahmacarinis.]

978.   Vireshwarananda, Swami. "Genesis of the Women's Math."
        Samvit 19 (March 1989), 8–10.
        [A reprint of a 1968 address by the Ramakrishna Mission
        President at the laying of the foundation stone of the New
        Delhi Sarada Mission describes the founding and services
        of the Sarada Math and Mission.]

979.   Visvanathan, Susan. "Marriage, Birth and Death: Property
        Rights and Domestic Relationships of the Orthodox Jacobite
        Syrian Christians of Kerala." *Economic and Political Weekly*
        24, No. 24 (June 17, 1989), 1341–46.

[The title is self-descriptive; this article covers *stridhanam*, domestic relationships in marriage, rites and gifts at child-birth, changing patterns of relationships as children are born and households split, and the problem of inheritance. Contains much information throughout about the roles of women in a religious community thus far only rarely described.]

980. Vyas, Anju, and Sunita Asija. *Women and the Law: An Annotated Bibliography*. New Delhi: Centre for Women's Development Studies, 1988.
[Covers not only personal laws, marriage, divorce, and inheritance, but also criminal laws, employment and prostitution.]

981. Vyas, Anju, and Meena Usmani. *Women, An Annotated Bibliography of Bibliographies: An Update*. New Delhi: Centre for Women's Development Studies, 1989.
[Bibliographies are grouped according to the following categories: General, Agricultural, Conferences, Crimes, Education, Employment, Female Child, Femicide, Fertility, History, Law, Nutrition, Prostitution, Rural, and Tribal. Despite the lack of a separate listing for religion, this work is potentially helpful for gathering background information.]

982. Vyas, Anju, and Meenu Chachra. *Women: An Annotated Bibliography of Directories and Statistical Resources*. New Delhi: Center for Women's Development Studies, 1989.
[Includes citations on directories for women's voluntary organizations, social service agencies, and women's studies centers and researchers.]

983. Wadia, A. R. *The Ethics of Feminism: A Study of the Revolt of Women*. New Delhi: Asian Books, 1977; original editions London: G. Allen and Unwin, and New York: George H. Doran Company, 1923.

[This decidedly anti-feminist book does review the status of women among Hindus, Parsees, and Muslims.]

984. Wadley, Susan Snow. *Shakti: Power in the Conceptual Structure of Karimpur Religion.* University of Chicago Studies in Anthropology, Series in Social, Cultural, and Linguistic Anthropology 2. Chicago: University of Chicago, 1975.
[Concerns transactions between gods and humans in a village of Madhya Pradesh; contains extensive materials on women's songs and song-sessions and on women's roles in the calendrical rituals known as *vrats*.]

985. ————. "Women and the Hindu Tradition." *Signs* 3, No. 1 (Autumn 1977), 113–25.
[This convenient overview describes Hindu ideology concerning women, Hindu role models for women, women's roles in religious practice, and evidences of change; the section on ideology covers the concepts of *shakti*, *prakriti*, and women's simultaneous danger and benevolence.]

986. ————, ed. *The Powers of Tamil Women.* South Asia Series No. 6. Syracuse: Maxwell School of Citizenship and Public Affairs, Syracuse University, 1980 and 1991.
[This much-cited collaborative volume is the outcome of a panel at the March 1978 meeting of the the Association for Asian Studies. Papers included are: Margaret Egnor: "On the Meaning of *Sakti* to Women in Tamil Nadu"; Holly Baker Reynolds, "The Auspicious Married Women"; Sheryl B. Daniel, "Marriage in Tamil Culture: The Problem of Conflicting 'Models'"; Kenneth David, "Hidden Powers: Cultural and Socio-economic Accounts of Jaffna Women"; James Lindholm, "A Note on the Nobility of Women in Popular Tamil Fiction"; and Susan S. Wadley, "The Paradoxical Powers of Tamil Women."]

987.   ————. "*Vrat*s: Transformers of Destiny." *Karma: An Anthropological Inquiry.* Ed. Charles F. Keyes and E. Valentine Daniel. Berkeley: University of California Press, 1983.
[The rituals known as *vrat*s, commonly practiced by Hindu women, have the power to transform past *karma* and, hence, to alter destiny. Sources are popular *vrat* manuals; extensive translations are included.]

For Wadley, Susan Snow, see also entries 270, 301, and 396.

988.   Wanasundera, Leelangi. *Women of Sri Lanka: An Annotated Bibliography.* Colombo: Centre for Women's Research, 1986.
[Most entries in this listing are on secular subjects; however section 11, titled "Socio-cultural," includes two pages subtitled "Religion"; see also subtitles "Anthropology," "Customs, Ceremony and Dress," and "Family" for treatments of rites, popular practice, and marriage customs. Rich in materials from the nineteenth and early twentieth centuries.]

989.   Webster, Ellen Purdy. "Some Aspects of the Religiosity of Punjabi Christian Girls: A Sociological Study." *Bulletin of the Christian Institute of Sikh Studies* 5 (July 1976), 2–23.
[Thirty-three Christian girls of the Punjab were interviewed in this study to determine what Christianity meant to them and whether it has produced significant changes in their lives.]

For Webster, Ellen, see also entry 156.

990.   Webster, John C. B., and Ellen Low Webster, eds. *The Church and Women in the Third World.* Philadelphia: Westminster Press, 1985.
[Two of this collection's nine articles address Indian women. John C. B. Webster's "Assumptions about the Indian Women Underlying Protestant Church Policies and Programs, 1947–1982" argues that Christians have not differed signifi-

cantly from other Indians in their basic attitudes and actions towards women. Stella Faria's "Catholic Women of India" surveys Catholic women's activities and organizations. One essay of the volume offers a cross-cultural, annotated bibliography on the third-world church and women; however, few Indian materials are included.]

991.   Wessinger, Catherine Lowman. *Annie Besant and Progressive Messianism (1847–1933)*. Lewiston, N.Y.: Edwin Mellen Press, 1988.
[Traces the evolution of a focal theme in the thought of Theosophical Society leader and freedom fighter Annie Besant.]

992.   White, James Daniel. *Secularization and Krsna Bhakti among Urban Indians*. Ph.D. diss., University of Pennsylvania, 1982.
[Studies the influence of secularization among male and female upper class urban *bhakta*s. Discovers that *bhajana*s remain important communal gatherings for many women, providing an opening for verbal, emotional, sexual, artistic, and charitable expression. Described *DAI* 43, No. 11 (May 1983), A-3626.]

993.   "Who's Afraid of the Supreme Court?" *Manushi* No. 42–43 (September–December 1987), 45–46.
[Reports two Christian women's challenges to the Travancore Christian Succession Act, which denies women equal rights to inheritance.]

994.   *Who's Who in Women's Studies in India*. Bombay: SNDT Women's University Research Unit on Women's Studies, 1984.
[This list identifies the location, activities, publications, and current research of persons engaging in Women's Studies in India. Listees are classified as researchers, activists, and activists *cum* researchers. Although by now quite outdated, this list remains a helpful resource for locating researchers.]

995. "A Wife's Right to Maintenance: The Subanu Case."
      Manushi 7, 5 (No. 41; July–August 1987), 37–38.
      ["Subanu" is the "Shah Bano" mentioned throughout the
      bibliography; this article was *Manushi*'s early response to
      the case.]

996. Williams, Raymond Brady. *A New Face of Hinduism: The
      Swaminarayan Religion.* Cambridge: Cambridge University
      Press, 1984.
      [This lone study of a religious group strong in Gujarat in-
      cludes a brief section on roles of women in the movement.
      They conduct their own affairs, and have their own temples,
      meeting-halls, rituals, meetings, and religious specialists.
      Nonetheless, men have the higher status and the greater
      institutional power.]

997. Willis, Janice D., ed. *Feminine Ground: Essays on Women
      and Tibet.* Ithaca, N.Y.: Snow Lion Publications, 1989.
      [Six essays from a special issue of *Tibet Journal* on women
      in Tibet are reproduced in this volume: Rita M. Gross,
      "Yeshe Tsogyel: Enlightened Consort, Great Teacher, Fe-
      male Role Model"; Janet Gyatso, "Down with the Demoness:
      Reflections on a Feminine Ground in Tibet"; Miranda Shaw,
      "An Ecstatic Song by Lakshminkara"; Janice D. Willis, "*Da-
      kini*: Some Comments on Its Nature and Meaning"; Barbara
      Nimri Aziz, "Moving Towards a Sociology of Tibet"; and
      Karma Leshe Tsomo, "Tibetan Nuns and Nunneries." Editor
      Willis has also added a new article of her own: "Tibetan
      Ani-s: The Nun's Life in Tibet."]

998. —————, ed. *Women and Tibet.* Special Issue, *Tibet
      Journal* 12, no. 4 (1987).
      [Features the six essays cited in entry 997 above, an intro-
      duction by editor Willis, and two additional pieces: Anne
      Carolyn Klein, "The Birthless Birthgiver: Reflections on the
      liturgy of Yeshe Tsogyel, the Great Bliss Queen"; and Geshe
      Wangyal, "The Jewelled Staircase."]

For Willis, Janice D., see also entry 338.

999.   Winslow, Deborah. "Rituals of First Menstruation in Sri Lanka." *Man* 14, No. 4 (December 1980), 603–25.
[Shows how variations in a ritual common to different religious communities reflect different understandings of womanhood within these communities.]

1000.   *Women and Buddhism*. Special issue, *Spring Wind—Buddhist Cultural Forum* 6, No. 1–3 (1986).
[Much of this issue concerns issues of contemporary Buddhism in Southeast and East Asia and the West; however, see Audrey McK. Fernandez, "Women in Buddhism: For 2500 Years, a Persisting Force," pp. 35–57; James Hughes, "Buddhist Feminism," pp. 58–79; "Women in Sri Lankan Buddhism," pp. 163–65 (no author cited); also "A Bibliography on Women and Buddhism," pp. 271–86.]

1001.   *Women and Religion: Proceedings of a Seminar Held on 26–27 March, 1990*. Varanasi: Banaras Hindu University, 1990; available at Women's Studies and Development Centre, University of Delhi.
[Records papers plus discussion summaries from a two day conference intended "to focus on the role which religion plays in determining the rights, defining the claims, and assigning the position of women in society." Eleven papers covered women in India and China, the status of women in Buddhism, Muslim women, Hindu *dharma*, discrimination by sex, changes in religious outlook, the impact of religion on women's education, and the Western writer Simone Weil. Presenters were Govind Kelka, N. H. Samtaur, Muniza R. Khan, Kavita Srivastava, Nomita Acharya, Devendra K. Mishra, Kusum Giri, Vijai Shivapuri, Chitra Sahasrabudhey. The level is exploratory; two papers are in Hindi.]

1002.   *Women Bhakta Poets*. Special issue of *Manushi*, Nos. 50–51–52 (January–June 1989).

[Features articles on woman *bhakta*s from South India, Maharashtra, and Gujarat, as well as three on Mirabai and her impact, with excellent samples of their poetry. Contributors are Madhu Kishwar, A. K. Ramanujan, Uma Chakravarty, Renuka Vishwanathan, K. Meenakshi, Vijaya Dube and Robert Zydenbos, Ruth Vanita, Sonal Shukla, and Parita Mukta.]

1003. *Women in the Struggle for a New Humanism.* Special issue, *Religion and Society* 23, No. 1 (March 1976).
[Papers in this issue especially relevant for researchers on women and Indian religion are Monica E. David, "The Legal Status of Women in India" (pp. 33–41), Susie Tharu, "Three Meditations on the Fall: Problems Women have with the Church" (pp. 42–50), Geetha Muliyil, "Women's Liberation: A Purely Human Problem" (pp. 53–63), and T. M. Philip, "The Biblical and Theological Understanding of Sex and Man-Women Relations in Society" (pp. 64–75).]

For Wulff, Donna, see entries 338 and 365.

1004. Yang, Anand. "The Many Faces of *Sati* in the Early Nineteenth Century." *Manushi* No. 42–43 (September–December 1987), 26–29.
[Offers a social profile of women in nineteenth-century Bengal who undertook *sati* after their husbands died.]

1005. ————. "Whose *Sati*? Widow-Burning in Early Nineteenth-Century India." *Journal of Women's History* 1, No. 2 (Fall 1989), 8–33.
["Attempts to identify the faces of *sati* victims by highlighting their social and economic conditions and circumstances." This is a longer version of the article cited in entry 1004 above.]

1006. Yaqin, Anwarul. *Protection of Women under the Law: An Annotated Bibliography.* New Delhi: Deep and Deep Publications, 1982.

[Covers general literature, judicial decisions, and government instructions pertaining to Hindu, Muslim, Parsee, Christian, and general civil, criminal, and procedural laws; literature covered dates from 1950–July 1981. Sources cited are periodicals, books, newspaper articles, and case reports; the periodicals range from specialized journals in law and sociology to general scholarly magazines such as *Seminar* and *Mainstream*. A few seminar papers are included as well.]

1007. Yashpal. "The Girl Who Was a Devotee." Trans. Karine Schomer. *Journal of South Asian Literature* 16, No. 1 (Winter–Spring 1981), 197–204.
[A young Brahmin widow of a poor family protects herself from vicious neighbors by making a show of religious devotion, but finally runs away, in this modern Hindi short story.]

1008. Young, Katherine (K). "Why Are Hindu Women Traditionally Oriented to Rebirth Rather than Liberation (*moksha*)?" *Proceedings of the Third International Symposium on Asian Studies, 1981.* Hong Kong: Asian Research Service, 1981, 937–45.
[Argues that lack of access to scripture and its interpretation is responsible for the low spiritual status and aspirations of women in orthodox Brahmanism.]

1009. —————. "From Hindu *Stridharma* to Universal Feminism: A Study of the Women of the Nehru Family." *Traditions in Contact and Change.* Ed. Peter Slater and Donald Wiebe. Waterloo, Ontario, Canada: Wilfrid Laurier University Press, 1983.
[Examines changing roles for women of three Nehru family generations to demonstrate shifts in their perceptions of the feminine ideal; Includes comments on the attractions of Gandhi's *satyagraha* for women and the influence of life in Gandhi's *ashram* on Swarup Rani Vijaya Lakshmi, Kamala Nehru, and Indira Gandhi.]

1010. ————. "Srivaisnava Feminism: Intent or Effect?" *Studies in Religion / Sciences religieuses* 12, No. 2 (Spring 1983), 183–90.
[Although apparently not intending to take a specifically feminist stance, Tamil Srivaisnava philosophy is "radically supportive of women." Examining a number of potential explanations, the author concludes that this is the simple effect of a Tamil tradition that had "always enjoyed and respected femininity."]

1011. ————. "Women in Hinduism." *Today's Woman in World Religions.* Albany: State University of New York Press, 1994.
[This article is an update of Young's more historical study in the earlier Sharma/Young collection, *Women in World Religions.* Based on work done by Young in the Bombay area in 1991, it attempts to give an overview both of contemporary issues confronting Hindu women and the range of potential responses to these issues. An especially valuable feature of the article is three small "case studies" of activist women of Hindu background: dramatist and rural worker Jyoti Mhapasekara, whose work is infused with a Marxist critique of religion; journalist/editor Madhu Kishwar, whose inclinations are likewise secularist, but who has a solid appreciation for the role of religion in women's history; and Parliament member and *sannyasini* Uma Bharati (now Uma Shri Bharati), who has worked with right-wing Hindus seeking to overthrow India's secular democracy and institute a Hindu state. A few materials on Muslim women in India are also included.]

For Young, Katherine K., see also entries 228, 348, 836, 837, and 960.

1012. Yuichi, Kajiyama. "Women in Buddhism." *The Eastern Buddhist* 15, No. 2 (1982), 53–70.

[This article identifies five historical stages in the development of Buddhist attitudes concerning women's capacity for
enlightenment, using as focus the dictum that a woman
cannot be a Buddha. Based on analysis of Pali, Chinese
Agama, and Mahayana materials.]

1013. Yuthok, Dorje Yudon. *House of the Turquoise Roof*. Ed.
Michael Harlin. Ithaca, N.Y.: Snow Lion Publications, 1990.
[A woman born into the Tibetan nobility tells the story of
her life until the Chinese invasion and her own escape with
her family. Meetings with nuns, monks, and gurus, as well
as pilgrimages, festivals, and her own devotions figure
prominently.]

1014. Zeitler, Engelbert, Lucy Misquita, and Jessie Tellis-Nayak,
eds. *Women in India and in the Church*. Indore: Divine
Word Publishers, for Ishvani Kendra Pune, 1978.
[A full half of the essays in this collection address only the
social status of women; others are concerned with the
church outside of India. However, see M. Amaldoss, "The
Role of Women in the Churches of India"; E. Zeitler, "The
Dawn of a New Age for Women in the Indian Church"; and
Jessie Tellis-Nayak, "Christian Women in India."]

For Zelliot, Eleanor, see also entry 128.

1015. Zelliot, Eleanor, and Maxine Berntsen, eds. *The Experience
of Hinduism: Essays on Religion in Maharashtra*. Albany:
State University of New York Press, 1988.
[Three selections from this anthology translated from writings by Irawati Karve reflect her own religious experiences
and/or reflections: "Boy-Friend?: An Essay" speaks of her relationship to the popular Maharashtrian deity Vithoba; "A
Town without a Temple: An Essay" reflects on spaces oriented to the sacred; and "On the Road: A Maharashtrian
Pilgrimage" is her famous account of pilgrimage to Vithoba.

A fourth short but significant piece is Carolyn Slocum's
"*Shakti*: Women's Inner Strength," a page-long citation from
an anonymous Indian woman's interpretation of the term
shakti; the latter is found in the volume's chapter entitled
"The Experience of Ritual."]

Libraries and Booksellers Consulted

Libraries in India

Centre for Women's Development Studies, New Delhi
Indian International Centre Library, New Delhi
Institute for Social Studies Trust, New Delhi
Jamia Millia Islamia University Library, New Delhi
Nehru Memorial Library, New Delhi
Research Centre for Women's Studies, SNDT Women's University,
    Bombay
School of Economics Library, University of Delhi, Delhi
Women's Studies and Development Centre, University of Delhi,
    Delhi

Booksellers and Publishers in India

Amrit Book Company, New Delhi
Bahri Sons, New Delhi
D.K. Publishers Distributors, New Delhi
Divine Life Society, Sivananda Publication League, Shiv-
    anandanagar, Dt. Tehri-Garwhal, U.P.
Kali for Women, New Delhi
Manohar Publishers and Distributors, New Delhi
Manushi headquarters, New Delhi
Motilal Banarsidass Indological Publishers and Distributors,
    Delhi
Oxford Book and Stationery Co., New Delhi
Oxford University Press, New Delhi
Picadilly Book Stall, New Delhi
Ramakrishna Vedanta Math Publication Department, Calcutta
Sage Publications, India Private Limited, New Delhi
'Samvit' Publication and Circulation Office, New Delhi

249

Sri Aurobindo Ashram Bookstore, New Delhi
Sri Sathya Sai Books and Publications Trust, Prasanthi Nilay-
    am, Anantapur District, Andhra Pradesh

Libraries in the U.S.

Michigan State University Library, East Lansing, MI
Regenstein Library, University of Chicago, Chicago, IL
University of Michigan Graduate Library, Ann Arbor, MI
Western Michigan University Library, Kalamazoo, MI
(plus many more through the U.S. Interlibrary Loan system)

Booksellers in the U.S.

Nataraj Books, Springfield, Virginia
Seminary Cooperative Bookstore, Chicago
South Asia Books, Columbia, Missouri

Index

Index

Index

Index

Conflicting Values, 265

Consciousness, Religious, 962

Conservative: chief justice, 181; communities, 87; family, 582; Hindus (male) 956; Muslims, 163, 708, (males) 861–63, 914; views on gender, 599. *See also* Orthodox women

Conspiracy, 974

Constitution, Indian, on women, 68, 181, 847

Constitutional rights to equality, 1, 181, 948

Construction and Reconstruction of Women in Gandhi, 690

Contemporary, 233, 294, 330, 457, 789, 852, 879, 928; Buddhism, 128, 359, 1000; Family Laws, 49; India, 83, 227; Literature, 917; Maharashtrian Conversion Movement, 128; *Muslim Societies*, 286; *Narratives*, 353; Panjabi Hinduism, 262; Rajasthan, 959; South Asia, 781; *Women's Movement*, 294. *See also* Modern period

Contentious Traditions, 558, 790

Contributions: to religion, 28; to Sanskrit literature, 976

Conversion, 75, 230, 427, 474, 798, 811; to Sikhism, 874

Coorgs, 705

Courage, 422

Courtesan, 32, 139, 406, 511, 526, 602, 761–62, 848

Courtyard, 97

Cowasjee, Dosebai, 450

Cowgirl. *See Gopi*

Cry, Anguished, 478

Cult: *Devadasi*, 829; Goddess, 189, 261–63, 804–05; *of Draupadi*, 371; *of Kumari*, 21; of Sufi saints, 427, 549; *of the Goddess Pattini*, 213, 577, 660; of Virabhadra, 36; of Yellama, 123; Possession, 188–89; *Sati*, 46, 852. *See also* Festival; Goddess, cult of; Rites; Ritual; Worship

Culture/s, 356; *and Reality*, 475; *-Change*, 43; Hindu, 541, 563; Indian Culture and Womanhood, 543; in Indian, 272; Indian Public, 336; *Islamic*, 392, 768; *Non-Western*, 270; of *sati*, 852; *Politics and*, 637; Popular, 347; *purdah*, 143; *Religion, Culture, and Politics*, 683, 751; Religious, 284; *Society and*, 618; *Tamil*, 204, 252, 986; *Women and*, 789; Women, Culture, and Politics, 614; Women's Language and Culture, 591

Curse, 3

Customary law, 744

Customary Succession, 7

Dai, 171

Dakini, 997–98

Dalit, 117. See also *Harijan*;, Scheduled castes; Untouchable

Dalkhai festival, 278, 687

Dance, 278, 630, 646; folk, 687, 699; of *devadasi*s, 467–68,

Possession, 36, 188–89, 261–63, 374, 444, 654, 659

Potaraja, 973

Poverty, 326; responses to, in the Women's Movement, 405. *See also* Poor women

Power, 41, 654, 984; lost to men, 463; *of Ideology*, 238; sexual, 516, 576; to Pollute and to Preserve, 943; women's, 19, 252, 392, 577, 614

Powerful, 53

Powers of Tamil Women, 986

Pox, 95

Praise and Struggle, 157

Prakriti, 985; *purusha-*, 944

Pramalai Kallar, 312

Prarthana Samaj, 85, 948

Prayers, 677

Pregnancy: Beliefs on, 748; longings, 111; rites of, 785, 936. *See also* Childbirth, Childbirth rites

Prejudices, rankings of, 868

Premchand, 672

Pre-puberty rites, 21, 23, 445

Presbyterian Women, 193

Preserve, The Power to, 943

Press: in India, 604; on *sati*, 638; on Shah Bano, 604

Priestess, 598

Princess, 810, 782

Principles, 464

Problem of Choice, 533

Proceedings, 1001

Profile/s, 235; *in Female Poverty*, 326; Political, of Muslim Women, 163

Progressive Messianism, 991

Property, Control of, 506

Property rights, 504; Christian women's, 504; Hindu women's, 133, 309, 504, 561, 636, 640, 840, 847, 921, 947; Muslim women's, 118, 259, 343, 504, 506

Prostitute/s, 68; or Nun? 899; *Profane*, 428; Rights as Citizens, 549; survey of, 773

Prostitution, 32, 50, 308, 665, 950, 980–81; Child, 284; *in Calcutta*, 424; in Jain sources, 316; Temple, 897, 901; *with Religious Sanction*, 717

Protest: demonstration, 410, 855, 900; Violence and, 637

Protestant, 990. *See also* Christian/Christianity; Presbyterian; Reformed Church in America; Missionaries

Proverbs, 183

Pro-Women or Anti-Muslim? 258

Psychic Ring, 760

Psychological approaches, 36, 296, 444, 637, 659–60; critique of, 498

Psychology, 637

Puberty, 312; rites, 115, 326, 379, 445, 781, 891, 954. *See also* Menstruation, rites of first; Pre-puberty rites

Public life, Parsee women in, 633

Puja, 60, 344, 568, 816; role of "prostitutes" in, 424. *See also* Durga Puja; Lakshmi, *Puja*

Index

Rizong monastery, 320

Role/s, 375, 917, 926; a
Sarvodaya View, 517;
according to Gandhi, 690;
among Syrian Christians,
979; and Religious Con-
sciousness, 960; Changing,
122, 395, 412; determinants
of, 590; *for Hindu Women*,
532; in Buddhism, 323, 698;
in festivals, 72; in Krishna
Consciousness, 484; in
Rural India, 395; in the
Churches, 1014; *Sex*, 556;
Muslim, 524; Perceptions of,
411

Roop Kanwar, 35, 64–66, 69,
197, 200, 221, 410, 421, 494,
559, 639, 642, 719, 788, 799,
852, 957

Roots, 433

Roy, Ram Mohan (also written
Rammohan Roy and
Rammohun Roy), 23, 35,
195, 216, 332, 637, 742, 834,
837

*Rules and Remedies in
Classical Hindu Law*, 533

Rural, 286–87, 395, 451, 723,
785, 798, 813, 940, 981; *and
Tribal*, 723, 940;
Bangladesh, 508; Kerala,
654; Muslim, 649; of
Pakistan, 536; *Social
Structure*, 927. *See also*
Village

Sacrament, 42, 448

Sacred Spell, 252

Sacrifice, 64, 279; ideology of,
455; roles in, 27; to Kali,
318

Sadgati, 458

Sadhin, 701

Sadhvi, 435, 877. *See also*
Nuns, Jain

Sage/s, 112, 465

Sahadharmini, 67; *See also
Pativrata*

Sahgal, Nayantara, 783

Sai Baba. *See* Sathya Sai Baba

Saint/s, 274, 361, 365, 573–74,
941; Buddhist, 620;
Christian, 603; *East and
West*, 302; Kashmiri, 112,
460; Lady, of Lahore, 873;
Madness of the, 574; male,
woman's account of, 627,
945; medieval, 225, 264,
274, 302, 349, 434, 481–82,
485, 509, 522, 588, 634,
685–86, 769, 786, 819, 971,
1002; middle-class, 345;
modern, 102, 162, 184,
302–03, 331, 337, 381, 425,
430, 537, 567, 830, 960; *sati*
as, 799; Shaiva, 29, 196,
219–20, 302, 460, 588;
Songs of the, 364; Sufi, 427,
549, 853; Tamil, 219–20,
302; Tibetan, 803;
Vaishnava, 26, 127, 219,
302, 360, 364, 588, 819. *See
also Bhakti*; Guru (female)

Saiva. *See* Shaiva

Sakta. See Shakta

Sakti. See Shakti

Sakuntala. *See* Shakuntala

Sakyadhita, 951

Salvation, 532; *Gender and*,
414; *Prison*, 104

Samband Edipa, 705

284